ONE OF BUTCH'S BOYS

First published in 2004 by

WOODFIELD PUBLISHING
Bognor Regis, West Sussex, England
www.woodfieldpublishing.com

ISBN 1-903953-73-1

One of Butch's Boys

The Wartime Exploits of Allen Clifford, a Bomber Command Navigator

PHILIP TURNER

Woodfield

This book is dedicated to the crew of Lancaster PD 374 HA-C 'Charlie', shot down over Homberg on the morning of November 8th. 1944.

Les – Flying Officer L M Hough RAAF
Jack – Warrant Officer J H Tales
Allen – Flight Sergeant J A Clifford
John – Flying Officer J H Barron
Harry – Sergeant H C Burnside
Geordie – Sergeant J Lawson
Stan – Sergeant S K Lee

The troubles of our proud and angry dust
Are from eternity, and shall not fail.
Bear them we can, and if we can we must.
Shoulder the sky, my lad, and drink your ale.

A.E. Houseman – *Last Poems*

Contents

Allen as an aircrew cadet at Initial Training Wing, Babbacombe, spring 1942

Introduction

From the foundation of the Royal Air Force in 1918 an influential group of senior officers was convinced that their service had the potential ability to win future wars virtually unaided. They believed that long-range strategic bomber aircraft could seek out enemy munitions factories, could destroy lines of communication and batter armies into submission by intimidating the civil population and destroying the industrial base that supported them. In the years after the Armistice they argued that they could avoid the bloody and exhausting land battles that had characterized the First World War by carrying the war direct to the enemy homeland.

The generation of officers that held high command in Hitler's war had been rankers and regimental officers in the Kaiser's war. They believed themselves to be survivors of a lost generation, a generation so savagely thinned by the bloodbath of the Western Front that the post-war world was starved of talent. It is ironic that the pursuit of this theory was to lead to a selective cull that killed off a large proportion of the best-educated men in Britain and the old Dominions. It is equally ironic that the most senior advocates of strategic bombing were to prove as reluctant as the Great War generals to modify their ideas in the light of experience.

By 1939 military aircraft were becoming highly complex machines. Conflict between them involved lethal competition between advanced technologies and the products of advanced technologies. These in turn demanded highly trained and intelligent men to operate them. Air war therefore, was to involve not the indiscriminate slaughter of the trenches but a highly discriminating attrition of many of the brightest young men that a nation could select.

Within weeks of the beginning of war it became obvious, even to Bomber Command zealots, that unescorted daylight bombers could not survive in the face of opposition from contemporary fighter aircraft. The British Air Marshals responded by switching the offensive largely to night bombing and the subsequent campaign was to claim the lives of nearly 56,000 young men from Britain and the Dominions in north-west Europe alone.

In the beginning, after the fall of France, it can be argued that if they were to do **something**, night bombing was almost the only offensive measure open to the British and Commonwealth armed forces. It is hard to criticize the war cabinet for resorting to such a policy; what is surprising is that it persisted with it long after it had lost its purpose. As a means of waging war it took a long time to become even partially effective. For the first three years of the war crews could rarely find the factories, airfields, airfields, warships, or railway marshalling yards that were their targets and as the defences improved their casualties grew. At times the German defences were inflicting more casualties on the aircrews attacking them than the bombers were randomly inflicting on the inhabitants of Germany.

When their objectives were changed to vast "area" targets, the weight of high explosive required to devastate urban areas demanded even more aircraft and an increasing stream of expensively trained crews. It is probable that the demands of the bomber offensive consumed about a third of Britain's entire industrial capacity and the lion's share of the scarce scientific and engineering talent available. It is perhaps not surprising that the British armoured forces were constantly handicapped by the inferiority of their tanks and that British infantry weapons were a generation behind those available to the Wehrmacht.

Even more extraordinary, in early 1943, when the loss of torpedoed merchant ships in the battle of the Atlantic came close to completely defeating the Anglo-American alliance, Coastal Command of the RAF could only deploy one squadron of their highly effective long- range anti-submarine aircraft against the U-Boats. This was at a time when Bomber Command could accept the loss of more machines than that on every night of routine operations.

The area bombing policy was to exact a very high price and Air Marshal Arthur Harris, the leader of Bomber Command, was its most powerful advocate. He was single-minded, forceful and determined and managed to keep the attention of the air staff firmly committed to his vision. It is however almost unbelievable, that when his crews developed the ability to find and hit genuinely strategic objectives, he refused to be diverted into attacking what he called "panacea" targets but insisted in continuing with the area bombing of cities.

Harris's ruthless determination was well understood by his command. To the general public in Britain he became known as "Bomber Harris". His young aircrews however called him "Butch" or "Butcher" and given his complete dominance of the senior commanders that surrounded him, they were in a very real sense, the Butcher's boys.

All aircrew were volunteers and as less than half of those that flew on operations with Bomber Command were destined to survive unharmed one wonders why they were prepared to run such risks.

It is reasonably certain that few of them had any illusions about the nature of war. Only twenty-one years after the First World War the experience of the Somme was no further away in time than the Falklands campaign or the Miner's strike is from us. The images of the plodding ranks of the Pals Battalions being scythed down by machine gun fire, or the charnel house that Passchendaele became, were still very fresh in the collective memory.

For some, a few, the war was a crusade against Fascism. For others, air war seemed likely to be a more comfortable way of fighting than serving in the infantry. For many, perhaps most, the principal objective was the desire to fly. For many of them the reality was to be stringent selection, a long period of highly demanding and frequently dangerous training (over 8,000 aircrew died in training accidents) and a brief operational life before they were shot down and killed.

With the benefit of hindsight it is arguable that they were badly led by their high command; what is indisputable is the courage and fortitude of the crews, those little groups of mainly very young men, who flew their aircraft in the cold dark skies of occupied Europe.

This book is the story of one of the survivors.

About the Author

Phil Turner was born in 1937 and has been fascinated by history for most of his life. He has had a career in education; as a teacher, education officer and schools inspector. His last venture in retirement was joining his wife as the co-proprietor of a children's bookshop.

His fascination with history resulted in his writing a number of biographies. His love affair with flying made him an enthusiastic pilot. This book has been over twenty five years in the making and has combined both interests.

1. Overture

Flight Sergeant Allen Clifford was sprawled on his back, falling through the cold winter air eighteen or so thousand feet above the German countryside and watching the black bursts of exploding flak shells just above him. He looked up at the fiercely burning Lancaster bomber that he had just abandoned and saw the moment when the blazing high octane petrol from the wing tanks finally torched through the main spar and severed the port wing. He could see two other parachutes drifting down some way away and wondered anxiously where the others might be.

Allen reached across his body, grabbed the D-ring and pulled hard. The parachute pack clipped to his chest opened, the pilot chute was ejected by its spring and he was conscious of a mass of fabric and rigging lines being pulled past his face before the canopy deployed and he was abruptly slowed down. It was a bright November morning, the air temperature at his height was around twenty degrees below zero Fahrenheit and as he drifted slowly down towards a town that Bomber Command had been trying to devastate for years he wondered quite how the Hell he had got there?

Allen Clifford was destined to be among the lucky ones, he was among the twelve per-cent of Bomber Command aircrew who were shot down and taken prisoner, most of whom survived to be liberated at the end of the war. Sixty percent of those that volunteered to become aircrew and served in Bomber Command did not survive at all. Over fifty five thousand were killed in action, a casualty rate higher than that suffered by infantry officers in the First World War. All of these men were volunteers. They were above average in intelligence and hence most of them started with, or soon acquired, a fairly shrewd idea of the danger that they were going to face. Armed with this all-too-certain knowledge of mortality they still however, continued to volunteer.

In the Air Force at least, a series of interviews suggests that the desire to fight Hitler might have got them into the forces but it was very much a secondary reason for such a hazardous vocation. Motives undoubtedly differed but most aircrew recruits seemed to have been fascinated by the idea of flight. It was a fascination that was not confined to children of the machine age. It wasn't just the passion of the sublimated mechanic for faster and noisier machinery. It seems to have been rooted in something almost approaching romanticism.

Certainly that is the impression given by Allen, who seems to be, and probably was, something of a romantic. He is highly intelligent, well read and, although he might be embarrassed to be described as such, sensitive. His answer to the question of how he got into such a hideously dangerous occupation was surprisingly simple. Basically, he just wanted to fly.

He was born in Darlington on the 7th April 1923, just twenty years after the Wright Brothers first flew at Kittyhawk and grew up in a period when aviation was brand new and wildly exciting. Most bright young lads of the time were, to use the cliché of the time "air minded", and Allen was a very bright young lad indeed. He had followed the achievements of the professional record breakers; Bert Hinkler; Sir Alan Cobham, Amy Johnson and a host of others. He read all he could on the subject from Flight and The Aeroplane to American pulp magazines about combat flying in The Great War. Whenever possible he had stood on the perimeter of the nearby RAF station at Catterick and watched the aircraft in the circuit, the majority of them biplanes, Yellow painted Avro Tutor trainers, silver finished Hawker Hart light bombers and more latterly the new monoplane bombers of the early re-armament programme; Blenheims, Whitleys and Hampdens.

Allen was fascinated by the idea of flying and the exciting notion of being able to cut free from the ground and become a part of the whole absorbing, exciting, sub-culture of aviation. It was however an apparently unattainable ambition, as the Cliffords, even by the unexacting standards of the time, were poor. Private flying was expensive and the pre-war Air Force largely recruited aircrew from middle class families. When war came; and his adolescence was one long prelude to war despite Mr Chamberlain's optimistic promise of "peace in our time", it seemed like an unbelievable chance to do something otherwise quite unattainable. He would become a flyer; an airman in the language of the period.

With the 20\20 vision imparted by hindsight it may seem an improbable reason for following the road which led to Hiroshima via Warsaw, Rotterdam and Dresden and the appalling civilian casualties suffered in these cities. It may seem even more unlikely given the actuarial certainty of death for six out of ten of the young men who flew the aircraft that inflicted these casualties.

These things were, however, all in the future and despite the gloomy prognostications of such unlikely fellows as Stanley Baldwin and H.G. Wells, most sixteen year old boys could hardly be expected to anticipate them.

The first step of the journey that was to lead him through the front hatch of his burning Lancaster was, paradoxically enough, taken by his parents with their willingness to keep him at school. Without a School Certificate (a predecessor to the GCSE), Allen could never have commenced aircrew training in the elite PNB (Pilot, Navigator, Bomb-Aimer) group. In order to gain a School Certificate in the state educational system of the nineteen thirties it was necessary to attend a Grammar school. Attending a Grammar school involved a parental commitment to keep a child at school until the age of sixteen. With a minimum school leaving age of fourteen there were few working class families that were willing to forego the earning capacity of any member and very many poor children who "passed the scholarship", the eleven plus examination, were not allowed to go beyond the Elementary school..

Allen's parents were not just hard-up, they were by any standards grindingly poor. His father, a Gloucestershire gardener, had come north to work on one of the big estates. He later married a local girl and then disastrously contracted chronic heart disease shortly before the birth of their first child. In 1923, chronic meant chronic. Even for those sufficiently well-off to afford it there was little heart surgery and not much by way of palliative treatment. They were a respectable working-class couple but people like that had little by way of reserve capital. Private medical treatment was out of the question and his life expectancy was given as a few months. In the event he was destined to survive the war and see his son safe home but he was never fit enough to do a full days work and in the economic climate of the time was virtually unemployable. The family therefore lived on Public Assistance, a grudgingly doled out pittance which was calculated to just about enable bare survival.

The Cliffords somehow or other beat the system. Houses were hard to sell in the north east in the Twenties and Thirties and the family that Allen's mother had worked for before her marriage offered them tenancy of a large Victorian villa on condition that they looked after it. It had an enormous garden and heart disease didn't prevent Dad from raising enough produce in it to make them damned near self-supporting in the Summer as well as maintaining a cricket pitch sized lawn in bowling green condition. Home grown food supplemented the dole and Mum was such a superb manager that Allen's wife in later years did not think of the family as poor. Young as he was, Allen noticed that his mother was never "skint" unlike the parents of a number of friends who were in regular work and hence had more than twice their family income coming into the house. What is more, when he passed the scholarship he was encouraged to go on to Darlington Grammar School and the Public Assistance Board, who would normally have insisted that he go out to work as soon as possible, were somehow outwitted.

Darlington Grammar School, untypically for its day, was longer on scholarship than snobbery. The uniform demanded was not exacting, a school cap and tie was all that was required, and the teaching was excellent. Before Allen left school at the age of sixteen he had passed the School Certificate examination. This qualification was usually seen as the passport to a safe job, and a safe job in the parlance of the time usually meant a nice secure white collar post; a bank clerk at best but a respectable clerical job of some kind in any case. God knows how the jovial, intelligent, extrovert that he was to become would have responded to such a future but as he left school in the Summer of 1939, it seemed unlikely that boredom would be among his major problems.

Curiously enough, although Allen left school at the end of July, it was nearly six months before he got a job. He wasn't unusual in that. None of the others that left Darlington Grammar School that July found a job any faster and he had to write a lot of letters applying for work before he got an interview. Despite the outbreak of war, announced by Mr Chamberlain's singularly uninspiring address of September the third, many were still unemployed. Indeed, during the summer of the Battle of Britain nearly a year later there were still a million men on the dole, this at a time when the men of Fighter Command were struggling to fight and service aircraft at the same time as they filled in bomb craters on their own airfields.

After the outbreak of war Allen found something to occupy him when he enrolled as a voluntary ARP messenger, but paid work was much harder to come by. After a good deal of trying Allen eventually found himself a job as a junior clerk with the London and North Eastern Railway Company but it wasn't an easy process. Like a lot of working class kids he was a bit gauche and the interview with an intimidating panel of men in suits proved a bit of an ordeal. They started off by asking him where the London and North Eastern Railway ran to and were not content with the answer "from London to the North East". Nor would "London to Scotland" do, one of the inquisitors asked precisely where in Scotland the terminus was to be found. Allen made a guess at Aberdeen, only to be answered with a shake of the head and a helpful clue that Ramsay Macdonald spent his fishing holidays there. Allen knew who Ramsay Macdonald was but knew nothing and cared less about his social life. He admitted rather unhappily that he didn't know (it was Lossiemouth actually), but he got the job anyway.

In the November of 1939 he became a clerk working for the Passenger Department of the London and North Eastern Railway

Company and was despatched to work in the booking office at Catterick Bridge in Yorkshire. The life that he described sounds like something directly out of the script of Oh Mr Porter with Catterick substituting for Buggleskelly and the Station Master a straight stand-in for the late Will Hay. He became one of the staff of some half a dozen who ran the station, where he seems to have become a kind of Lord High Everything Else. Among his duties were: entering up the ticket sales in a great old fashioned leather-bound ledger; emptying the coin boxes from the vending machines on the station platform and replenishing their depleted stocks with penny bars of chocolate; making the tea; stoking the waiting room fires, collecting tickets and generally making himself useful in his abundant spare time.

The office was Dickensian with a great high desk at which the duty clerk would stand to work and an enormous manuscript ledger in which the fares to every station on the national railway network were recorded in copper plate handwriting. The first journey that Allen ever booked was to Ballykelly in Northern Ireland and he clearly remembers searching through the pages, looking up the fare and issuing the hand-written ticket. Even the stationery was antique, as every document, pen, pencil and rubber stamp still bore the logo of the old North Eastern Railway Company and hence they dated back to before the 1921 reorganisation of the railways. In the event reality was a good deal less intimidating than appearance. The station staff were very kind to their new junior clerk. The station-master was an amiable man and the women in the office proved a friendly lot who tended to mother their rather diffident junior. It was to be one of the many ironies of a war that saw Allen survive against all the odds in the most hazardous of all services, that most of them were destined to be killed in 1943 when an ammunition train blew up in the station freight yard.

Catterick Camp, with its complex of Army and Air Force installations, was just a little way away from the station and the travelling habits of servicemen were soon to become a sore trial to him. Hard-up rankers had little money to spend on rail fares and in any case they regarded any authority as fair game. Allen was to learn this the hard way one day when he went out to collect the tickets from passengers on an incoming train. The engine drew to a halt at the platform and stood there hissing and exuding steam and sulphurous smoke while he collected a handful of tickets at the barrier. He didn't seem to have collected very many and was a little puzzled because the train had seemed fairly full when it arrived. He didn't take a great deal of notice until, as the train pulled out again, he realised that there were very few figures at the carriage windows. As the train cleared his line of vision he saw why. The field on the other side of the track was thick with uniformed figures who had baled out of the train on the blind side, scrambled over the fence and were making off towards the distant Catterick camp at their best speed. Horrified at his own failure he was very nearly in tears and yelled after them to stop, but not surprisingly they took absolutely no notice. He went back to the Station Master, seething with indignation and fearing instant dismissal, and told him how most of the passengers on the train had simply disappeared over the far side of the track without paying. The Station Master seemed fairly unmoved by this revelation as he sucked at his pipe, nodded gravely and said "Aye, they do that".

At first going to work was something of an adventure, so much so that the distant war in Europe was rather overshadowed by the immediate novelty of having a job. Indeed the war news in that first winter was uniformly dull. Poland had been defeated and occupied during the late summer and autumn without any effective interference from Britain or France.

The British Expeditionary Force crossed the Channel and dug-in, in preparation for a re-run of the trench warfare of the Great War. The French army occupied the Maginot Line and pursued an unexciting policy of live and let live. RAF Bomber Command after a number of disastrous daylight bombing raids on the German fleet, resorted to making leaflet raids by night. German air activity over Britain was minimal so Fighter Command had little to do and even the Air Component of the BEF rarely made contact with the Luftwaffe.

There might not have been much military activity, but for ordinary people like the Cliffords the winter was not without incident. With the outbreak of war, blackout regulations were introduced and with all street lighting extinguished, windows shrouded with dark material and car and cycle headlights masked nearly to extinction, movement after dark became hazardous in the extreme. The civilian population suffered more road accident casualties in the first six months of the war than were inflicted by the Germans on the armed forces.

Then to compound the gloom, the winter of 1939\1940 was dreadful. Roads and railways were blocked by snowdrifts, plumbing froze up, and the unemployed, debilitated by years of poverty, froze as well as starved. Allen got to work somehow. He was a conscientious boy, well aware of the sacrifices that his parents had made to put him through school and the difference that his small salary would make to the household budget.

Each working morning of that appalling winter he left the house in the dark and made his way through the blacked out streets to Darlington station. He would reach the gritty and fume-laden security of the "up" platform in time to board the early train to Catterick where he would thaw out over the smoky open fire in the booking office. Cold, fog, smoke and darkness were very much a feature of that first winter of the war and the spring was destined to bring little in the way of good news.

The beginning of the good weather was to mark the end of the "Phoney War"!

In April the Germans invaded Denmark and Norway and in a swift and competent campaign bustled the Anglo-French forces out of Scandinavia. In May the Germans struck in the west. By early June the BEF was evacuated over the beaches at Dunkirk, abandoning all its heavy equipment en-route. Paris fell to the Wehrmacht on the 14th.of June and on the 22nd.the French signed an armistice.

Suddenly the situation had changed again and the remote fantasy of German armoured columns rolling up the Great North Road and through Catterick no longer seemed so fantastic.

For Allen, like millions of his fellow countrymen, the World suddenly became a very busy place as he was caught up in a whirl of preparations to repel the expected attack. It is hard for us to imagine quite how real and immediate the threat of invasion seemed in that summer of 1940. At the time, the collapse of the Western Front and the fall of our only major ally made us the obvious next target.

The result was a surge of populist militarism which put hundreds of thousands of civilians into a range of volunteer services. Allen's contribution was not untypical and by the end of the year he was serving in three different units. With conscription for National Service looming up once he reached his eighteenth birthday, he tried to maximise his chances of getting into the RAF by joining the Air Defence Cadet Corps (renamed the Air Training Corps in February 1941). As a member of this organisation he was learning the rudiments of weapons training and some elementary signalling and navigation and as time went on he was promoted to the rank of cadet sergeant and was to lead parties on air experience flights in Ansons and Whitleys from RAF Dishforth.

He had also abandoned the ARP and joined the Royal Observer Corps as a spotter. The ROC were a surprisingly important part of the air defence system in an age before efficient inland radar cover and their main job was the visual sighting and reporting of aircraft which had penetrated the Chain Home radar defences. His rare ability to actually recognise individual types of aircraft made him a much valued member of the ROC despite his youth. This incidentally is no piece of author's license. The vast majority of the Englishmen of the time, or for that matter the vast majority of Germans, couldn't tell a Spitfire from a Junkers 87 without asking it to land and making polite enquiries of the pilot. The ability to identify aircraft in the air is a rare one and throughout the war aircraft on both sides were often hacked down by their own anti-aircraft guns or, rather less frequently, by their own fighters or air-gunners. Allen had the knack, born of years of interested study, of recognising a type almost instantly, noticing perhaps the way it sat in the sky, or its distinctive configuration.

Then, superimposed on his passion for the air was a more mundane role as an infantryman. He joined the one and a half million men who placed themselves under arms by the end of 1940 and became a member of the Home Guard. He eventually managed to become simultaneously a sergeant in the Air Training Corps, an ROC observer and a lance-corporal in the Durham Light Infantry (LNER Home Guard), as well as maintaining the day job at Catterick station.

None of these things was a sinecure either. As an Observer Corps spotter he was expected to take post during air raid alerts and pass information back to the local Fighter Command filter room. As a lance-corporal in the DLI he did one full night's guard duty each week and as an ATC sergeant he did another two nights of reasonably serious training in drill, signalling and basic airmanship. He also somehow managed to attend the local church youth club serve as secretary of the Darlington Model Aircraft Club and take out his current girl-friend!

Apart from two separate uniforms his wardrobe contained a surprising collection of lethal hardware. They very rapidly took away his Remington 0.300 rifle when they decided that the Home Guard lacked fire-power and he was equipped with a Browning automatic-rifle, a bipod mounted light machine gun. Contrast the atmosphere of the times with my own not untypical reluctance to let a teenager own an air-rifle. My contemporary abhorrence of firearms seems a little extreme when I contemplate the loaded arsenal that the seventeen year old Allen kept propped beside his best suit.

The Christmas of 1940 was anything but happy. It was hard to imagine an Allied victory and indeed the Allies were essentially the British and Commonwealth forces, supplemented by a determined but tiny handful of refugees-in-arms from occupied Europe. What little attempt that was made to strike directly at Germany was being made by the RAF and in the year that followed the Spitfire Summer of the Battle of Britain, their prestige was high.

Not surprisingly, as soon as he reached the minimum age of seventeen and a quarter, Allen had volunteered, in the words of the advertisement "for flying duties with the Royal Air Force". He didn't know that pilot-officer Roy Marchand, photographed in flying kit for the poster that invited him to apply, had been killed the previous summer, before the picture had time to reach the hoardings.

His was not the only letter of application to come from Darlington. Every one of his contemporaries at the Grammar School volunteered, although Allen was destined to be one of the only three that survived the war. After a long wait the first response from authority was a letter importantly franked "On His Majesty's Service". The content was something of a let-down given the apparent urgency of the recruiting posters. They acknowledged his interest and undertook to write again with further information in due course.

In the event it was to be another sixteen months before he heard a word and then, out of the blue, came a letter inviting him to attend for interview the following month. He was to report to the Aircrew Selection Centre, at St John's Wood in London. The letter enclosed a third class railway warrant and armed with this, he set off on his first journey to the Capital in November 1941.

The experience, like much of his subsequent life in the Royal Air Force, was a fairly chaotic one. After a tedious journey, during which the train stopped incomprehensibly at stations from which the name-boards had been removed during the invasion scare, the train eventually reached London. The main line terminus at Kings Cross had been badly battered by bombing and the familiar eggy station smell was overlaid by a curious compound of wet plaster, soot and the acrid after-taste of explosives, the characteristic smell of the Blitz.

The Underground journey to St.John's Wood gave the startled Allen a quick introduction to the mole-like existence pursued by some Londoners who camped nightly in the "tubes". The station platforms were divided by two white lines, behind the second of which bedding rolls were stacked ready for the night. Every time the doors opened the carriage was filled with yet another reminder of the nightly invasion of shelterers, the odour of unwashed humanity, urine and chemical lavatories. London during that period of night bombing was clearly not a pleasant place for its citizens to live in.

Emerging from the Underground he made his way to the address given on the letter, only to find himself entering the administrative building at Lord's Cricket Ground where he was to spend the next three days performing a variety of tests. Before the process started he was first taken to an apparently new and partially completed nearby house, where he was invited to dump his case in a room furnished only with mattresses. These were piled neatly along the walls, each mound of bedding surmounted by a stack of unappetising looking grey Air Force blankets. The windows were criss-crossed with brown sticky tape, designed to prevent splintering in the event of bomb blast, and apart from the ubiquitous blackout curtains the house was otherwise innocent of furniture. The mess-hall was located in the Lord's pavilion, so eating, as well as the selection process was to involve a short walk through the sporadically bombed and largely abandoned mansions of St John's Wood.

The selection procedure proved to be a mixture of conventional intelligence testing, such proofs of manual dexterity as turning parti-coloured black and white pegs through ninety degrees and a series of interviews in which he was asked about his family background, his education, what he had been doing since he left school and his reasons for volunteering.

Allen didn't find the tests difficult but the interviews were pretty intimidating for a working-class boy from Darlington. The panel were dressed in civilian suits and may well have been civil servants but their manner was unfriendly and they seemed singularly unimpressed by his social background. Nor were they influenced by his obvious wish to pull his weight. The fact that he had accepted the heavy commitment of joining the Home Guard cut no ice at all. They merely asked him why, if he was so keen to fly, he had joined the Army. It was at this stage that he told them of his parallel role with the ATC and after a hasty look at his documents the penny dropped. A good report from his squadron commanding-officer tipped the balance and he was once more back in contention. However, while all this was going on the candidates were given a series of medical examinations before preliminary results were given and it was at this stage that the blow fell. The medical seemed to show an imbalance in Allen's eyesight that might cause difficulty in judging distances. It was quite simple, He was not deemed medically fit to train as a pilot.

Almost before the disappointment had time to register, the interviewing officer went on. Allen was still, he said, "eligible for flying duties". The Air Force needed Air-Observers and his minor vision problem would not bar him from that role. The interviewer went on sonorously extol the virtues of the Observer. " He was responsible (at that time) for navigation, bomb-aiming and signalling and was a vital member of the crew of bombing, strike and reconnaissance aircraft". "Modern multi-engined aircraft were flown by a team". His pitch was entirely unnecessary. Allen didn't need any persuading. He wanted to fly and if he couldn't fly as a pilot then an observer it would have to be. He accepted the offer before they had a chance to change their minds and with that simple action took another step towards the exit door, the parachute and the POW camp.

The next stage proved anti-climactic. He was given a small silver lapel badge with RAFVR.(for Royal Air Force Volunteer Reserve) inscribed on it and sent home to await call-up. The return journey, ominously enough on 13th November, was as dreary as the outward one but this time he was warmed by the thought that he had made it. He was going to realise an ambition that he had nurtured ever since he was old enough to look up and recognise an aeroplane. He was going to be an airman. It seemed something of an achievement for an ordinary lad from Darlington and he was entitled to be proud of it.

Most young men at the time would have shared Allen's feeling of elation on that homeward journey, for the prestige of the RAF was high. There hadn't been a lot to celebrate since the costly daylight victories of the Battle of Britain, and the face of Pilot Officer Keith Gillman, smiling from the front cover of the popular Hulton photo-journal *Picture Post* was still fresh in the public mind. Once again Allen, like most of his fellow countrymen, didn't know that Gillman was dead. He had been shot down and killed on 15th August 1940, less than a week after the publication of his picture.

The prospect of action was still a long way away and before that loomed the mundane prospect of the booking office at Catterick. Life went on. Sometimes he occupied an office stool, sometimes he put on one of his various uniforms for a spell as a cadet or a temporary infantryman. He applied for promotion with the railway and was transferred to the District Engineers Department. He even found time for some private life from time to time going dancing, to the cinema, and generally doing the best he could to make the best of a fairly bleak war time existence.

He began to wonder if the RAF had forgotten him as 1941 faded into 1942. Christmas came and went until, in April 1942, just over two months before his nineteenth birthday, either somebody found his file or the log-jam in the Observers training units cleared and he received his calling-up papers, joining instructions and a railway warrant. He was ordered to report back to St John's Wood to be documented, kitted out and fed into the training machine.

Once again to traversed the slow journey from Darlington to London and reported to the Aircrew Reception Centre at Lord's. The new recruits were billeted in a recently built mansion block near the London Zoo and part of the business of enrolment and the issue of identity discs was carried out at Lord's Cricket Ground while the rest of it and the acquisition of a mountain of kit took place in the unlikely surroundings of the zoo. Allen and his fellow cadets were shuttled between improvised rooms and offices in the complex while endless forms were completed and medical orderlies with blunt needles in their syringes jabbed their arms and arses and filled their veins with a variety of inoculations and injections. It was an almost surreal experience and although he can't remember seeing any animals he has a clear recollection of strolling past the empty Mappin Terraces while waiting for the next part of the process to continue. A corporal shepherded them into the zoo restaurant, now devoid of food and the walls lined with shelves, in which they were given a kit-bag which was rapidly filled with clothing and equipment as they filed past the counters. Blue-grey trousers without turn-ups, rather old-fashioned tunics, a great-coat, shirts, detachable collars, ties, forage caps, pyjamas, cellular underwear, button sticks, boots, shoes, PT kit, gas masks, packs, webbing belts, an apparent mountain of impedimenta which was to grow as they progressed through the service.

Once the process actually started it didn't take long and less than a fortnight later Allen was told he was to be trained as an Observer WT (a role that combined the duties of Observer and wireless operator) and would have to undergo a complete wireless operators course before he would be allowed anywhere near an air navigation school. On 2nd May 1942 he was posted to the Royal Air Force Initial Training Wing at Babbacombe in Devon to begin the long process of becoming an operational flyer.

Mr. Clifford of the London and North Eastern Railway and the Royal Observer Corps, Sergeant Clifford of the Air Training Corps and Lance Corporal Clifford of the Durham Light Infantry (London North-Eastern Railway Home Guard) were no more. Allen was now Aircraftsman Second Class, or more familiarly AC2 Clifford, Royal Air Force. His training was at last about to begin. What is more, his newly issued uniform forage cap bore the white flash of an aircrew cadet.

2. Beginners

Babbacombe was a small rather genteel seaside resort just to the east of Torquay sandwiched between the Atlantic cliffs and beaches and the red-soiled farmlands that rose to the edge of Dartmoor a dozen or so miles to the north. Devon in May was windy, frequently wet, and by the standards of a lad raised in County Durham, warm. Spring comes early in those parts, and as the weeks wore on the sun was more and more in evidence Allen decided that in many ways it was quite a pleasant place. Initial Training Wing was not, as one might expect, a forbidding military installation but like most things in the wartime Air Force a makeshift and in this case a rather homely one. Billets, mess halls and lecture rooms were scattered around in the small hotels that lined the sea front and instructional films were shown in the little theatre that in peace-time had been the home of repertory companies and concert parties.

By now, after nearly three years in the ATC, Allen was familiar with RAF camps and he slipped into the routine with surprising assurance. He was a rather diffident young man, very conscious of his Durham accent and a little in awe of people who he tended to see as more sophisticated southerners. For the first time in his life he found himself more at ease with his surroundings and more confident than most of his fellows. What is more, he was considerably more knowledgeable. For a start of course, he had actually flown in a number of service aircraft as a cadet NCO when he had been in charge of air-experience trips, something that was unusual in 1942 even among aircrew cadets.

The training was a fairly mixed process. Some of it seemed highly relevant to the business of flying and fighting in military aeroplanes. They learned about elementary navigation, had an introduction to a variety of machine guns, had ship and aircraft recognition lectures and film shows and did some signalling and Morse code. They also spent a great deal of time on one of the great military pursuits, foot drill or, as it was universally known in the services, square bashing. This reached an unprecedented peak when, towards the end of the course, King George the Sixth and the Prime Minister, Winston Churchill made a formal inspection visit to the unit. This resulted in a positive frenzy of drilling, with training suspended for a week and all time that was not spent on the square devoted to cleaning, polishing and painting. The effect was slightly spoiled by the fact that ITW didn't actually possess a square. Drill was usually conducted on any hard surfaces that happened to be available; playgrounds, roads and tennis courts and none of those was big enough for a wing parade. In the event they had to rehearse and parade on mown turf where the crunch and crash of nailed boots was reduced to a muffled pounding. Presumably both the King and Mr Churchill had a nice day out and once it was all over life went back to normal.

As well as learning these new martial arts the cadets were lectured on military law and also on the consequences of indulging in those equally traditional martial pastimes that led to the contraction of venereal disease. The film that accompanied that lecture was graphic, nauseating and made even more incongruous by the incidental music played on the gramophone as they filed into the theatre. It was in fact apparently the only record that they possessed and was entitled *You are my Sunshine.*

His long stint with the Home Guard and the ATC paid off for Allen at Babbacombe. It wasn't just a case of understanding what was going on and feeling reasonably at home on an RAF station, he also had a fair grasp of many of the subjects, even down to the dreaded square bashing. He could already strip a rifle and several kinds of machine gun, he knew a bit about aircraft and a lot about aircraft recognition and he had a modest grasp of Morse code and elementary navigation. It may have been this slight edge which gave him the confidence to volunteer for the subsequent specialised courses that were probably responsible for keeping him alive. They were to lead to an unusually protracted period of training that kept him out of Europe during the bloody, dreadful, winter bombing campaign of 1943/4.

By this stage in the war a worried Air Staff had realised that the RAF didn't know nearly enough about navigation. In 1941 Mr Butt, an Air Ministry civil servant, had conducted an enquiry that showed that very few of Bomber Command's aircraft delivered their load within five miles of the target, largely because they were unable to find their way about a darkened Continent. Navigation suddenly assumed a primary importance because however good their crews were in all other respects, if they couldn't find a target they couldn't hit it. The standard of training for navigators had to improve and it became increasingly obvious that they were going to need a lot more of them. Progressively the Air Force began to train their crews in narrower specialities and Allen, recruited as a multi-role Observer was one of a dying breed. Some would still be needed, the Beaufighters of the Coastal Command strike wings and the new two-seater Mosquito fighter-bombers only carried a crew of two but the generality of navigators were only trained for the one role, the night navigation of heavy bombers.

It was in fact at this stage and for this reason that the ITW cadets came to the first realisation that the process of selection didn't stop at the initial interview. The growth of the night bombing campaign had increased the demand for aircrew and forced the Air Ministry into rethinking their policy on training. The new four-engined bombers like the Stirling, Halifax and Lancaster needed a crew of seven and the heavy and ever growing casualties of the Big League over north-west Europe were putting impossible strains on the training programme. In short, aircrew were being killed faster than they could be replaced and something had to be done to speed up the pace at which recruits passed through the system. The solution was to break-down the crews into a range of more narrowly defined skills: pilots, navigators, bomb-aimers, wireless-operators, flight-engineers and gunners.

The RAF could no longer afford the luxury of a first and second pilot in their heavy bombers and made do with the quicker and cheaper alternative of training a fitter or rigger as a flight-engineer to assist the pilot by looking after the engine controls and the management of the fuel system. The multi-role observer was largely replaced by a combination of other specialists and the gunners were quickly and simply trained to do nothing more than man their turrets. By the time that Allen reached his ITW anybody who failed the navigation component of the course was promptly re-mustered as a bomb aimer and posted for the briefer further training required for this much less demanding role.

It wasn't just in this increasingly ruthless selection process that life began to make demands on the cadets, not only were they required to learn new skills but to do so while coping with an arbitrary set of requirements for which civilian life had done little to prepare them. For a lot of his fellow recruits, although not for Allen, the first introduction to the phenomenon known throughout the services as bullshit came as a bit of a shock. Everything that could be polished was, and if it couldn't be polished it was either painted or blancoed. People no longer walked, they marched and physical training entered their lives in a big way. Some of the ideas for fitness training verged on the mildly sadistic. Cadets, dressed in PT shorts and boots were required to run from their billets, scramble down the cliff paths and bathe in the sea. It was not an enjoyable experience in the Channel in late spring and God alone knows what benefit it was supposed to confer. After this they ran back in their wet shorts and towelled off before going on to the next training session.

It was a fairly domestic variety of hardship however. It happened in Babbacombe and not Fort Zinderneuff, the drill instructors were mainly disgruntled ex-public schoolboys rather than Foreign Legion NCOs, and normality kept breaking through. Despite the assumption made by the Air Ministry that among the brutal and licentious soldiery venereal disease needed to be kept in check by assiduous propaganda, the majority of the cadets at ITW were about as promiscuous as Boy Scouts. They were, after all, usually not much more than eighteen years old and their idea of a good time was a visit to the cinema, the pictures as they were known, a dance-hall or indeed anything that involved an opportunity for chatting-up the local girls. On half a crown a day (there were eight half-crowns to the predecimal pound sterling) pleasures needed to be cheap and the other traditional military pastime, serious boozing, was too expensive even if their tastes ran in that direction. Most of them experimented with scrumpy, the cheap but very potent locally made rough cider, and usually experienced the subsequent giggling instability, nausea, throwing-up and the inevitable hangover. This was not an experience that many of them repeated very often, and so sedate walks, a bit of inexperienced groping, the pictures and even tea dances tended to fill their off duty hours.

Allen like all of his friends was permanently hungry. They were young, they were leading a physically demanding life and service food, even by the inexacting standards of wartime Britain, was pretty appalling. There wasn't enough of it, the diet was monotonous and the last meal was served at about five thirty in the afternoon which meant that by about eight o clock they were ravenous. Breakfast usually consisted of porridge, bread and margarine and a pint china mug of tea. Lunch was likely to be something like fish, or more rarely, meat, lots of potatoes and sometimes swede, cabbage or sprouts followed by an inadequately sweetened suet pudding and custard. It too was usually followed by the inevitable pint china mug of tea or "coffee", a brown fluid made up of coffee or chicory essence, milk and a minute ration of sugar. Supper tended to be fried bread, tinned tomatoes and sometimes the rare treat of scrambled egg made with the powdered, reconstituted egg that was being shipped across the Atlantic from America. It too was topped off with the inevitable mug of tea. The knives, forks, spoons and mugs used in the messes were not provided. Each airman was issued with these articles on joining the service and they were expected to bring them along to every meal. The problem of washing-up was solved by providing a galvanised iron trough at the exit from every mess hall. Live steam was piped into the trough to maintain the temperature as close to boiling as possible and as the diners filed out from each meal they were expected to swish their implements, their "mug and irons" clean in the scalding water. This was something of a counsel of perfection as the live steam didn't last very long and the trough was soon filled with a lukewarm solution of what amounted to thinly diluted pigswill. Even when the system was working it presented certain imperfections. Vigorous swilling of implements tended to splash near-boiling water on the backs of nearby hands and things were all too often dropped into a boiling sump. Many an item of cutlery was lost and the cadets soon learned to celebrate the event with a traditional service ditty "Tinkle tinkle little spoon, knife and fork will follow soon".

Like most of his friends Allen was paired up with a local girlfriend and, being an engaging lad, was soon on very good terms with her family. Joyce and her parents soon came to terms with his appetite for food and every evening out was always preceded by fish and chips purchased from the corner chippy and a jug of bitter beer carried in from the Roughwood, the local pub. It is entirely possible that food, rather than sex, was the imperative drive among the ITW cadets but in any case, well brought up lads that they were, their girl friends were in no danger of anything worse than over-persuasion. By contemporary standards they were an incredibly well behaved group of young men, brought up by parents for whom respectability was an important aspiration rather than a tepid adjective. They had been sent, reluctant to Sunday school, passed the scholarship examination to their local grammar school, joined the Boy-Scouts saluted the flag on Empire Day and, after leaving school at the age of sixteen, had found themselves jobs in banks, insurance companies and offices all over Britain. Their notion of war and their models of behaviour were drawn largely from the cinema and as yet, the hideously intimidating arithmetic of the bomber offensive had not begun to dawn on them.

Over fifty years later the letters, the diaries and the photographs of the period still have the power to move me to tears. The photographs are especially touching, young men posing rather self-consciously in flying kit, very proud, not yet afraid and the majority of them destined to be killed before the end of the following year.

Given the end that most of them faced it would have been reasonable to expect that draconian discipline would be needed to keep them in order, that "eat drink and be merry" would be the order of the day. The reality was that failing the course and transfer to the comparative safety of the RAF Regiment was the awful threat that hung over their heads and for most of these boys the penultimate year of their lives was to be as blameless as the first eighteen or so.

Allen was to be no exception. He was pleasantly surprised by the general friendliness of the locals towards the aircrew cadets who had taken over their town and Joyce, the girlfriend who he had very rapidly found, had introduced him to a family that had made him very welcome. One of the things that surprised Allen was the degree of self-assurance that the family seemed to possess; they seemed to have access to a store of confidence quite out of keeping with their relative poverty or their social status. Somehow, despite all that he had achieved, he had this sneaking feeling that Southerners had been given a head start in life, an inside track conferred by virtue of nothing more than an accident of geography and a different regional accent. Despite the new found self assurance of his own aptitude for air force life he was still curiously diffident. Diffident or not, he had found his girl and set out to make the best he could of the available entertainment. Happily neither he nor Joyce had been given the opportunity to develop expensive tastes and half a crown a day gave him enough money to take her out to such fleshpots as Babbacombe offered.

Our own view of conflict has been largely been conditioned by remoteness. The Falklands campaign happened on the other side of the world and even the televised horrors of what was Jugoslavia or the collapsed Soviet Union are transmitted from the other side of Europe. Admittedly terrorists of one kind or another do plant the occasional bomb but, horrible that they may be, they are few and far between and are usually small by the standards of Hitler's war.

In Britain in 1942 things were very different, a formidable enemy was uncomfortably close, occupied Europe lay just on the other side of the North Sea or the Channel and the Luftwaffe, despite being otherwise engaged in Russia, was still capable of mounting continual nuisance raids. Even a sleepy seaside resort like Babbacombe was vulnerable to surprise attack. and Allen was to be on the receiving end of a raid within three weeks of his arrival at ITW.

It all happened very quickly. The days training was over and Allen and two of his mates were pottering around in their billet, a room on the top storey of the Babbacombe Bay Hotel which had been stripped down to bare boards and equipped with rows of cast iron bedsteads. Allen was standing at the window, a great Victorian sash affair that ran from the floor to the ceiling, and gazing out across the Channel. Suddenly he noticed two or three single engined monoplanes just skimming the surface of the sea and travelling very fast directly towards them. These were the first real ones he'd ever seen but he recognised them at once and announced the fact in a loud shout "Jesus! FW 190s! Get down!" The correctness of his identification was confirmed by a roar of engines, a deafening burst of cannon fire and the sound of the ridge tiles of the hotel being fragmented as the shells struck home. The raiders flying in at nearly four hundred miles an hour at an altitude of less than fifty feet were well below the sweep of the coastal radar and caught the defenders completely by surprise.

Fortunately for Allen and his room-mates the cliffs had forced the FWs to pull up so steeply that their shells had impacted high on the roofs of the buildings on the sea-front. For what was intrinsically a fairly low-risk operation their luck was even further out. An RAF cook, detailed for the day as air-sentry, was manning an antique, drum-fed, First World War, Lewis Gun which was pillar mounted on the sea front. All credit to him, confronted as he was by three of the Luftwaffe's latest fighters, each of which mounted four twenty millimetre Mauser cannon and two seven point seven millimetre machine guns, he stuck to his post and let fly.

The Lewis wasn't much better than a pop gun firing rifle calibre ammunition at six hundred rounds a minute from a thirty seven round drum but, it was to be the cook's day. It must have been a chance in a million but the burst hit one of the Focke Wulfes in the tail and with elevators shot away it hit the sea at full throttle. The airframe disintegrated and later in the day the cadets were treated to the grisly spectacle of medics paddling along on the edge of the surf and collecting the remains of the unfortunate pilot in a biscuit tin. It was stirring stuff. A good day for our side, but on reflection if that could happen to a fighter attacking a virtually undefended target without any warning, what was it going to be like making low speed sea level attacks on heavily defended convoys?

Happily for their peace of mind the thought never arose. Over a pint of scrumpy that night the flukiness of the shot was toasted and the overwhelming feeling was one of excitement, the war could even reach Babbacombe. The brief awareness of mortality, the transient thought that crossed Allen's mind "bugger me! I've only been in the air force for three weeks and they're trying to kill me already" had been dismissed as quickly as it came and the main thing that he remembered was the admiration of his mates for his ability to recognise an enemy fighter at a glance. In any case life was just too busy and the imperatives of the next test, the next parade, soon drove the prospect of sudden and violent death to the back of his mind.

That was to be the only bit of excitement at ITW. In general the world was made up of square bashing, navigation lectures, physical training, exams, more exams, endless training films, each preceded by the inevitable strains of You Are My Sunshine and the incongruous juxtaposition of that and all that goes with being young in a West-Country seaside resort throughout spring and summer.

By early September the course was over! Allen passed with some credit, and was rewarded with a travel warrant, a week's leave and a posting to Number One Signals School which was at RAF Cranwell in Lincolnshire, there the air force was going to try to turn him into a radio operator, an important skill for anyone who aspired to the prized Observers brevet. He had every reason to be fairly confident, he had coped with everything that ITW had thrown at him and so far he was a success in his chosen profession, he was still one of the privileged victims.

3. Dah, Dit and Polish

Allen's leave, like every leave that any serviceman ever had, passed with the speed of a video fast-forward, and on the 23rd. of September 1942, he found himself on a train bound for Sleaford in Lincolnshire, the nearest railway station to Cranwell. It wasn't an easy journey as there was no direct route from Darlington to Sleaford and he was burdened like a pack-mule, festooned with webbing equipment, carrying one kit bag and dragging another as he sweated between platforms and up and down stairs. The second kit bag was needed to carry the flying gear that he had been issued with at the end of the ITW course and it was stuffed solid with the bulky padded Sidcot suit, flying boots, battle dress, flying gloves as well as a mound of training manuals and note books.

As he approached the camp his heart sank a bit, for even in September the flat Lincolnshire landscape is pretty dreary and after the lushness of the Devon countryside and the almost domestic ambience of Babbacombe it seemed fairly forbidding. That first impression was not misleading, Cranwell, the home of the regular Royal Air Force College was the strongest surviving bastion of the old pre-war service. Number One Signals School may not have been part of the College but it was just as deeply rooted in that lost world of between-the-wars and its style and discipline were very different to that of the hastily improvised Initial Training Wing. Many, if not most, of the officers and NCOs of the instructional and disciplinary staff were regulars, one of them boasted a service number with only two digits and claimed to have been in the Royal Engineers Balloon Company when it operated Cody Kite Trains, hence though the resultant trade training was good, the discipline was ferocious and the bullshit equally so.

Allen, who had been promoted to Leading Aircraftsman on passing out of ITW, found that neither that nor the white flash of the aircrew cadet he wore on his forage cap cut very much ice and he was still pretty near the bottom of the heap in signals school. He was barked at by every passing corporal, was still sharing a billet with thirty nine other aspirant signallers and instead of the bull reducing now that more advanced specialist training had started it was becoming more intense. About the only real consolation that he could look to was at pay parade when he collected three times as much for every day, a princely three half crowns, seven shillings and sixpence per day.

They were billeted in the low brick buildings that had been built during and after the First World War and had made up the accommodation of the Royal Air Force College until the completion of the new building in the late Thirties. The barrack rooms were lined with rows of cast-iron beds which could be telescoped to halve their length and which during the day were piled with the three horsehair cushions known as biscuits that were combined to make up a mattress on each bed. This pile was in turn surmounted by a stack of blankets and sheets which were neatly folded into a sandwich of alternate layers and held into a firm box shape by another folded blanket. Each bed was flanked by a steel locker in which the occupant of the adjacent bed kept his possessions all of which were carefully laid out in an elaborate pre-determined order. To complete the welcome in a manner familiar to generations of servicemen, a small pile of folded squares of blanket material lay inside each barrack room door. These were to enable the occupants to place them between their boot soles and the floor and, by sliding over it on these improvised " pads," both polish and protect the surface.

The overall effect was not cosy and things went downhill from there. The corridors like the dormitories were floored with dark brown linoleum and both were shined to a mirror gloss. Every metallic object from bath taps and fire buckets to the studs in their boots was polished and after every inspection a champion billet was announced. As the promotion prospects of the NCOs was closely connected to the performance of the billets they were responsible for the cadets were under intense pressure to comply with the increasingly bizarre requirements of the disciplinary staff. Cadets were marched to training sessions and meals, parades were a constant punctuation to their lives and the days and nights passed in an incessant whirl of scrubbing, polishing, blancoing and the continuous hard work of an increasingly demanding training course.

At a more mundane level, the food hadn't improved any, Sleaford was a good deal less welcoming than Babbacombe had been, a few rather dreary pubs was the best that it could offer, and without the refuge offered by a civilian girl-friend's family Allen like his mates was forced back onto the amenities offered by the NAAFI, the YMCA or the Church Army canteen. To make things even more depressing the signals course was intensive and the cadets were worked until they dropped with an endless round of lectures and practice sessions. The Morse code is not the easiest of things for most of us to become adept in and before any really serious study of signalling could begin the cadets had to acquire a very high degree of fluency in both audio and visual Morse. They soon established the habit of translating just about everything that they saw written around them into dots and dashes and both the camp staff and the local civilians had long become accustomed to "dit happy" signals cadets conversing in a series of chirrups as they transformed advertisements, newspaper billboards and even comments about the local talent into the dits and dahs, the dots and dashes, of the Morse alphabet. The workload became progressively heavier, with the constant threat of failing the course and reverting to a ground trade hanging over their heads and cadets were worked until they went exhausted to bed only to be harried awake by the Tannoy and worked some more. Somehow, fifty years later, it seems incongruous that they put themselves through all this agony in order that their chances of living much more than another twelve months or so might be reduced to something less than one in two.

Allen was, and indeed is, not very technically minded and did not enjoy the wireless operators course. Amps and ohms, coils and valves, wavelengths and frequencies, trailing aerials, generators and batteries, all were mysteries that were mostly memorised rather than understood. He never really comprehended the principles that he was applying and contented himself with the ability to simply follow the drills and make things work. There was however one silver thread that ran clear through a fairly bleak experience, because at Cranwell Allen began to spend a good deal of time in the air, quite a few of his classrooms were situated at anything between two and ten thousand feet over the countryside that lies behind the North Sea coast and the Midlands.

His formal flying training really started when he and three other cadets were ordered to dress up in flying kit, draw an observer type parachute from the store and report to the tarmac hardstand, the apron that lay between the hangars and the airfield. When they arrived they found a large, twin engined, biplane. It was a De-Haviland Dominie (the military version of the pre-war DH Dragon Rapide short-haul airliner) which was to be the flying class-room in which they were to be introduced to the rudiments of the radio operators craft.

Their instructor helped them buckle themselves into their parachute harness and then chivvied them into the passenger cabin which contained, apart from half a dozen seats, a standard 1082 radio set and the usual paraphernalia of Morse key, trailing aerial winder, work table and a log book for each pupil. They sat down, feeling awkward and rather self conscious in their clumsy flying gear and were given a brief description of the equipment they were to use and an injunction to use the bags provided if they had to throw up. While this was going on the pilot was making it difficult to hear the words as he ran up the two Gipsy Queen engines that powered the machine and then with no further ado the throttles were opened, the Dominie bumped across the Cranwell turf and as the bumping ceased, unstuck and climbed out towards their exercise area. The instructor took them, one at a time through the drill as they wound out their trailing aerial, tapped out their call signs and learned the basics of establishing and maintaining contact with their base stations.

Signalling from the air was a complicated business in the nineteen forties, valve sets demanded a fair amount of current and were notoriously vulnerable to damage from vibration, damp or even abrupt temperature changes. These hazards plus the uncertain generators of the period made the operators business difficult and often frustrating as they wrestled with the uncertainty of not knowing which of their problems was caused by equipment failure and which by their own lack of know-how. As well as the inherent difficulties of the job the instructors fed in more and more simulated ones. Once the basic skill of learning and using the Morse code had been assimilated Allen found that his instructors were feeding louder and louder interference into the circuit, then they started overlaying the signals with unrelated Morse transmissions and then finally with voice interference. This last problem was the hardest of all to cope with, as the ear naturally attends to the familiar patterns of speech and is easily distracted from its highly unnatural task of listening out for the arbitrary patterns of tone signals, the beeps and chirrups of Morse code.

As well as the signalling becoming more difficult so did the airborne environment in which it was being done for, after four hours in Dominies the sprog wireless operators were told that they were going on to Proctors. The Percival Proctor was a single engined, low wing, four seater monoplane, built by the team that had produced the Gull and Mew Gull racing machines. They had specialised in squeezing an amazing performance out of a relatively small power unit and the Mew Gull, for instance, had out performed the early Hurricane fighters despite having a fixed undercarriage and less than a third of the horse power generated by the Hurricane's Merlin engine. The Proctor was therefore, in Allen's words, "a fairly hairy little beast" and its intrinsic hairiness was substantially added to by its pilots, who were tour expired Polish fighter crews.

It was not an ideal situation. The Poles didn't want to do the job which they regarded as an irrelevance compared with their chosen vocation of trying to kill Germans and consequently chose to use the aircraft to attempt impromptu aerobatics rather than train signallers. Allen would be allocated to an aircraft for a training task only to be totally ignored by the pilot who barely acknowledged his existence. The best that he ever got out of his driver was a grunt of acknowledgement when he arrived and a nod in the direction of the cockpit to tell him to get aboard.

The Proctor had an enclosed cockpit with a nominal two seats in the front and two in the back but for radio training one of the rear seats was removed and the other one reversed to face a big 1082 transmitter receiver and its peripheral gear, just like the one fitted to the Dominie used for initial flying training. Allen therefore sat with his back to the pilot who was, in any case, taking absolutely no notice of him. As soon as the aircraft was airborne Allen was supposed to wind out his trailing aerial and carry out a set task but this was complicated by the pilot's fixed determination to wring out the airframe to the verge of disintegration by pulling every aerobatic manoeuvre in the book as well as improvising a few originals. Allen, with his galvanised guts was able to cope but those unfortunates who were prone to air sickness had a pretty miserable time. However, despite the efforts to kill him made by several airborne egotists, he survived, as did curiously enough all of the other members of his course. In an air force that was accepting casualty rates in training that sometimes approached twenty five per cent, Allen does not remember a fatal accident taking place at Cranwell.

So the training went on through the Autumn of 1942 over Christmas and into January 1943. In the Western Desert the Eighth Army delivered Montgomery's victory at El Alamein, the Russian and German armies fought to the death at Stalingrad and in the Pacific the Americans began the long fight back from Pearl Harbour. The cadets at Number One Signals School were barely conscious of all these crucial changes in the tide of the war, preoccupied as they were with ground classes, trying to transmit and receive Morse from the claustrophobic confines of the back seat of the Proctors as they cavorted about the sky and the endless, endless, bullshit.

Cranwell came close to being a self contained township with its own NAAFI canteen, Astra cinema, churches, chapels, barber's shop and library. Allen had never lived on a big permanent peace-time base before and at first it had a certain novelty value but before long cabin fever began to set in and he caught a bus from outside the camp gate to Sleaford. The experience was not enjoyable. That first impression gathered from his journey from the railway station was essentially correct and the town was a dead and alive place with little in the way of entertainment and even less charm. The next time he ventured out he went as far as Lincoln but it didn't make much of an impact on his memory, as fifty years later he can recall absolutely nothing about it. To be fair to both the town and the city they may well have been perfectly OK but the continuous dulling impact of the training left Allen and his mates very little surplus energy and it is entirely possible that the immediate proximity of Venice, a distillery and *complaisant houris* would probably have failed to excite them very much.

Happily nothing lasts for ever and in the last week of January 1943 Allen was awarded the bundled spark badge of the RAF signals branch and left Cranwell as a fully qualified wireless operator. He went through the tedious routine of clearing a station, confirming that he was not trying to abscond with anything belonging to the unit that he was leaving by binding around with his clearance card. On this document he secured signatures from the bedding store, the bicycle store, the anti-gas store, the library and every other conceivable office, until he was finally given a leave chit, a railway warrant and told to report to RAF Heaton Park in Manchester after his leave, in order to await a posting which would probably take him overseas for the next stage in his training.

4. Old World, Winter 1943

On the journey home Allen travelled across a country which in many ways was as alien to the England of today as pre-Columbian America. Even the landscape looked different: the fields were smaller, most of them were hedged and the pastures, as yet largely untouched by herbicides, still contained a proliferation of wild flowers in their season and had not been battered into sameness by the continual planting of fodder grasses and applications of nitrate fertilisers. The hedgerows surrounding the fields were frequently punctuated with trees and, as their timber was of little commercial value, towering Elms were often a dominant feature. Mechanisation had not made much of an impact on British agriculture and the substantial numbers of men and women now working in those fields were often using either hand tools or horse drawn equipment. There were fewer power pylons in evidence and those that could be seen were much smaller than the giant structures that traverse modern Britain. The train in which he travelled was steam-hauled and ran on a network that connected almost every town and many of the villages in the kingdom with a web of main line routes which were serviced by innumerable rural branch lines. As his train rattled over bridges and level crossings it crossed roads and lanes that carried a tiny fraction of the motor traffic that now exists, as private cars, relatively uncommon before the war, had virtually disappeared from the scene and commercial freight haulage was still mainly rail borne.

The small towns and villages through which the railway ran were pretty shabby and the tracks, like the canals, tended to come in through the seedier outskirts of communities rather than the more imposing main road frontages. As the locomotives slowed to traverse the points and run through the stations they usually passed the sewage farm and the gasworks and trundled between the allotments and gardens of the unfashionable end of town. By this stage in the war building materials were in desperately short supply and food rationing had replaced lawns and flower beds with vegetable plots and chicken runs. As a result the houses and gardens were looking unkempt and almost anything available was being pressed into service to make do and mend. It sometimes seemed that the most popular fencing material was the redundant bed frame, and sufficient brass bedsteads to cater for the combined needs of post war Hampstead and Islington were used to defend the boundaries of cultivated land in almost every village in England.

Most domestic heating was provided by open coal fires and the smoke from these, combined with that from the steam locomotives, blackened brickwork, roof tiles, trees and garden hedges with a ubiquitous layer of soot. As a result the dominant green of the English countryside was replaced by an overlay of black in any sort of built up area and the cities, particularly the big industrial communities, often looked as if they had been constructed of coal rather than heated and powered by it.

The nose as well as the eyes would have received a very different impression of Britain in 1943, for a country in which both passengers and freight were still largely hauled by steam engines fuelled with raw coal and houses were mainly heated with the same fossil fuel, smelled very different. The reek of coal smoke and the eggy odour of the sulphur dioxide belched out by the locos filled the air and from the train the pungent odour of sewage added a grace note. The lavatories on the trains were vented directly onto the track and the permanent way was frequently spattered with an noxious blend of toilet paper and human excrement.

As well as being slow, cross country rail journeys were both boring and guaranteed to generate anxiety. Signboards had been removed from stations during the invasion scare, as part of the general effort to confuse the advancing Wehrmacht, and if you were asleep or failed to hear the porters calling out the station's name you didn't have a clue where you were. Nor could you see very much from the carriage window as they had been obscured with fabric netting stuck onto the glass to prevent it shattering in the event of an air raid or a strafing attack and only small portholes in each pane allowed a view of the outside world, nor was opening the small sliding window at the top a good way of seeing out as it was likely to admit smuts, cinders and other flying fragments of soot from the locomotive funnel. Steam engines belched out sufficient debris to ensure that the entire train was sprayed with fragments of unburned coal and the manpower shortage meant that they were cleaned so infrequently as to be permanently filthy.

As his journey neared its end the Winter darkness fell and Allen, who daren't sleep in case he missed his station, tried unsuccessfully to read in the dim blue light that illuminated his compartment. Eventually he began to recognise the stations and the odd trackside building until his train finally pulled into a blacked out Darlington station. He dragged his kit into the corridor and with some effort got it out onto the platform and piled out of harms way under the station canopy. Once the train had pulled out and the platform had cleared a bit he struggled into his webbing, shouldered one kit bag and, dragging the other one behind him, made his way out of the station and headed for home. Darlington station is set up a cobbled entrance road flanked by brick walls and his first task was to get clear of this dark, sooty, canyon and out into the main road.

The urban landscape would have seemed peculiar to us. For a start it was plunged into something approaching total darkness with no street lights, no light showing from the blacked out windows of shops and houses, and the few motor vehicles about driving on lights that were shielded by headlamp masks which only allowed a chink of light to emerge from the narrowest of slots. The mudguards of these cars and lorries were painted white, every street corner was marked with white stripes and every tree, street lamp, telephone pole and pillar-box was banded with white paint or whitewash. Everything possible was done to make obstacles as visible as possible but without a glimmer of moonlight or some kind of illumination it was only too easy to collide with them. There were plenty of people about however, the pubs and cinemas were still open and with almost every factory working round the clock on three shifts it was hard to believe that this had been one of the lesser unemployment black-spots of the

Thirties only three short years before. There were men in work clothes with mufflers and cloth caps, men in suits, men in boiler suits and among them, in overalls topped with bright print turbans, a host of women factory workers were going on or off shift, dodging between darkened shops or queuing outside theatres or cinemas. Darlington may have been darkened but it was neither silent nor deserted.

There was no hope of getting a taxi, in any case there was nothing in Allen's background that would have caused him to consider it, and he didn't fancy trying to board a bus with his mountain of kit. In the event he elected to walk and, shouldering his kit, he set off through the darkened but familiar streets. After four years of war even the notices painted on the buildings were familiar to him : ARP Post pointing to the place where the wardens and rescue teams were waiting for trouble, Static Water Tank painted on the side of a fifty foot diameter cement-rendered structure which was kept full of fire-fighting water in case ruptured water mains made it necessary to draw on it, Decontamination Station directing people to a place in which they might clean off traces of toxic liquids in the event of the gas attacks that never came. A host of painted divisional signs and assorted military notices also pointed the way to the multiplicity of units that were now billeted in the area and the various offices and police posts that they brought in their train.

At last he came to a familiar white banded tree on the corner of his street and, turning into it, soon reached the equally familiar front door of the large early Victorian villa that had been his home ever since his parents had agreed to look after it. He mounted the steep front steps and knocked on the door which opened quickly to reveal his parents standing in the darkened hallway. After a hasty greeting the door was shut and, with the blackout secure again, the light could be switched on and they were able to say a proper hello before retreating into the warmth of the kitchen below.

It was nice to be back among the familiar sights, smells and sounds of home; the same pictures on the wall, the same wallpaper, the aroma of cooking, the pungency of his Dad's pipe tobacco, the wireless tuned to the BBC ready for ITMA or Grand Hotel and his Mum's voice murmuring away gently as she brought him up to date with the events that filled their small private world. It was equally good to sleep in his own room and his own bed after all those barrack room nights filled with the coughs and snores of the other occupants. He woke fairly early in the morning, conditioned by nearly a year in which the Tannoy had shocked him into wakefulness at "o six hundred hours" and with a grunt of relief turned over for another hour before breakfast.

Once up he made a hurried transit through the unheated bathroom before dressing quickly in a bedroom that was equally chilly and speeding down to breakfast in the kitchen, the only heated room in the house. This wasn't quite the indicator of poverty that it might seem, as central heating in the England of the time was almost unknown and most working class homes only heated one living room with an open fire or sometimes a kitchen range. The best room only had a fire lit at Christmas or New Year and bedroom fireplaces were only used in the event of illness.

Breakfast was a fairly leisurely meal although rationing meant that fried bread, fried tomatoes and potato cake were the staples but the tomatoes and potatoes were home grown, they were well cooked, the tea was hot and fresh and two weeks of leave stretched before him. It was, by any standards, a good leave. The never ending bullshit of Cranwell and the uncongenial wireless operators course were behind him, he had two weeks at home, and the future held the adventurous prospect of going overseas to one of the attractive postings offered by the Commonwealth Air Training Scheme. In retrospect it was probably the high spot of his service career. There were better experiences to look forward to, there was a degree of glamour and excitement that would enter his life, but this was the last time that he would look forward to change without a growing awareness of the price that was to be paid.

Few of his old friends from Darlington Grammar School were still about, as to a man, they had all volunteered for the services and most of them were by now either in training or in operational units. There were however plenty of unattached girls in evidence, ready and willing to be squired to tea-shops, dances and cinemas, although pubs were still considered to be slightly sinful places and were in general not much frequented by nice girls.

The cinema, the "pictures" was still the most popular place to go and most cinemas had crowds queuing outside if the film showing was anything other than a certified stinker. In the main escapism was the order of the day, the big Hollywood movies were sure-fire crowd pullers, although the British film industry had something of a renaissance in the nineteen forties. If the film was any good a period of queuing was inevitable and as films were shown on the basis of a continuous performance you became adept at picking up the plot from the point at which you came in, holding it in your mind throughout the B-feature, the news and the shorts and following the main feature with increasing understanding until you reached the point at which you came in. You were then faced with the choice of seeing the film through to the end again, leaving to seek out a drink before closing time or fish and chips before going home. The choice that you made frequently said much about the quality of the film that you had just left. Incidentally, a sojourn in a war-time cinema frequently left you smelling as if you had just slept in an ash-tray. Most of the adult population smoked and cinema goers were used to viewing the screen through clouds of cigarette smoke and glancing up to see the beam of the projector outlined with wreaths of the stuff. Sweets however were rationed and hard to come by and so the sound of chomping jaws and the rustle of chocolate wrappers was not a major irritant at the time.

Cinemas, dances, visits to the pub and the quiet satisfaction of simply being at home, all contributed to as good a time as it was possible to have in war time Britain. and his parents were patently delighted to have their eldest son home for a while. They obviously worried about him but they didn't say a great deal and Allen was never quite sure how much they understood about the dangers of wartime flying. His Dad, already plagued with heart trouble, hadn't served in the First War but his three brothers served from 1914 to

1918, two in the infantry and one as a field gunner and very much against the odds, all of them had survived. The family had been a statistical freak but it is hard to believe that anyone who had lived through those years did not have a shrewd idea of the dangers of active service. The only thing that may have relieved them of some of the worry might have been simple ignorance, for from the time that he went to Grammar School they had come to regard his interests as a mystery and him as something of a prodigy, and the complex skills and numerous hazards of flying were way outside their experience. The fact that he was merely training might have given them some reassurance as they were unlikely to have been aware of one statistic that the RAF kept very quiet, the fact that training very often resulted in casualties very nearly as high as those suffered in operations against the enemy.

However, if his parents were unduly worried they kept their concern to themselves and his leave was untroubled by any notion that his parents might be losing sleep on his behalf. The leave, like the last one, seemed to pass with unbelievable speed and at the beginning of February 1943 Allen found himself on his travels once again, this time on a train bound for Manchester and the Aircrew Holding Centre at Heaton Park.

5. North Atlantic

Royal Air Force Heaton Park was just what its name said, a damned great municipal park served by a local railway station and situated in the northern suburbs of Manchester about three miles from the city centre. In the summer it must have been a relatively pleasant spot but in February its charm wasn't immediately apparent. The north west of England is wet at the best of times and the great industrial conurbation that lies around Manchester, Salford and the industrial towns of the Pennine seemed permanently shrouded in low weeping clouds. Once inside the perimeter fence Allen was confronted with acres of churned up turf crossed by ribbons of cinder paths and dotted with the humped corrugated metal shapes of nissen huts. There were a few paved roads and ominously, a large asphalt square flanked incongruously by a rather fine Victorian band-stand and a flag-staff.

The billets were cold damp and uncomfortable. There were twenty iron framed beds lining the curved walls, lavatories and wash basins were in another block that had to be reached by slopping along a muddy path and the mess halls, instructional and administrative blocks were ten minutes walk away along equally muddy tracks.

Condensation dripped from the uninsulated ceilings and the two small cylindrical coke stoves didn't do much to warm the place up. Fuel was in short supply and even when they were lit they only managed to heat the space immediately around them.

Apart from kitting out there was little for them to do but drill, watch training films for the fifth or sixth time and strip Bren, Browning and Vickers machine guns until they not only could have done it in their sleep but probably did.

It should have been a formula for near suicidal depression but Allen and his mates were philosophical. There wasn't much in the way of bullshit and they knew that they wouldn't have to endure it for very long anyway. Every day the inhabitants of the transit billets were paraded in front of the bandstand and the names of the various drafts and their destination were read out. They were bound for a variety of exciting sounding destinations, flying and air navigation schools in Canada, South Africa, Rhodesia and a smaller group of cadet pilots would go to the United States of America.

On the 18th February 1943 Allen heard his own name announced with a draft ordered to Number Eight School of Air Navigation in Hamilton Ontario. He was bound for Canada but not only that, he was going to the one part of the old Empire where he actually more or less knew someone. Ever since he was at Darlington Grammar school he had been exchanging letters with Margaret, whose father was a doctor in Hamilton. It was quite a coincidence, but that casual schoolboy decision to write to a pen-friend was to prolong his stay in Canada and probably started a chain of circumstances that eventually saved his life.

Once the draft was announced he was confined to camp and forbidden to write to his parents, presumably in case they should accidentally pass his destination on to Admiral Doenitz. Forty eight hours later he found himself on a train packed with aircrew cadets and bound for Glasgow. On arrival they were decanted into trucks and from them to tenders, small boats which carried them out into the Clyde where they boarded an enormous liner, the 27,000 ton Canadian Pacific steamship Empress of Scotland. The ship had incidentally, been named the Empress of Japan when she was launched in 1929 but in 1941 Pearl Harbour and the invasion of Malaya made a change of name seem like a good idea.

It was an enormous vessel with acres of decks and once below it was like entering a vast badly run down multi storey hotel. The public rooms and stairwells had been stripped of their marble cladding and panelling but traces of magnificence were still visible. Allen and his group were led below until they reached a cabin which was about twenty feet square, filled with tiers of steel framed bunks and apparently well below the water line. Their kit was soon stacked around them and they were summoned on deck for what they expected to be the first of many parades.

At that first parade they were allocated lifeboat stations, given instructions as to what to do in a variety of emergencies from air attack to reporting sick and then, by the simple expedient of calling the names of all those cadets with surnames beginning with the letters A to C a cookhouse party was detailed. Allen thought that he had drawn the short straw. Toiling in the galleys and waiting at the officers mess tables was not what he had joined the air force for. At first he bitterly resented it but after a short while he realised that things could have been a lot worse. Working in the galleys gave the fatigue parties ready access to plenty of food and all those detailed to these apparently menial tasks were excused lookout and picket duties for the duration of the voyage. It was a damned sight warmer in a nice cosy galley than it was searching the skies for aircraft on the upper deck.

The voyage was also something of an educational experience. The Empress liners had always worked the eastern sea routes and as a consequence most of the crew were Lascars, Indian sailors recruited mainly in Bengal. The galley crew were equally exotic, Chinese cooks recruited from Hong Kong or the Treaty Port of Shanghai. Not only were they Chinese but they were Chinese speaking Chinese which caused certain communication problems between them and their cadet assistants. Lack of a common language however yielded fairly easily to goodwill and good nature. The cadets were a cheerful bunch and the cooks were equally friendly. Pidgin English and sign language went a long way and the two groups were soon chuntering away amicably. The cooks even passed on some fairly exotic local knowledge and Allen was soon given the kind of Geography lesson that had never featured on the curriculum of Darlington Grammar School. He was drinking tea and chatting companionably with one of the cooks who was trying to give him a few helpful hints for travellers.

"Singapore," he said, "plenty jig-a-jig". "Bombay," he added, "plenty jig-a-jig". He gazed thoughtfully at the deckhead for a moment and drew deeply on a cigarette. "Liverpool," he continued, "plenty jig-a-jig" and then, frowning disapprovingly, "Capetown … no jig-a-jig". It was kindly meant and an interesting notion – world geography in terms of the ability of travellers to find cooperative whores.

It seemed a funny old world to Allen, cooped up with several thousand other young men, deep below the waterline of a liner which was travelling at very high speed (21knots), unescorted and zig zagging furiously. Most of them were sea sick and none of them lay down at night without wondering what their chances would be of making their way to their life boat stations if the ship were torpedoed. Inevitably there were rumours of submarines, surface raiders and air attack but none of them resulted in any visible danger and after a week at sea they realised that they were approaching land. Maritime patrol aircraft appeared in the skies, other shipping began to converge on their destination and then the coastline came clearly into view.

They had not been sure of their exact destination but before long they realised that they were sailing towards a familiar skyline. They had seen it on a hundred films, they were sailing up the Hudson river, past the Statue of Liberty turning round Manhattan Island into the East River and with a great flurry of activity the ship was being moored at the transatlantic terminal, Pier 17.

As soon as the gangplanks were in position armed US Marine sentries filed up to guard the landward side of the decks and the quayside was similarly sealed off. The passengers were a bit puzzled as the guards seemed more interested in keeping people on the ship than preventing boarding but after nearly four years at war the actions of authority had long ceased to surprise them. Anyway the whole experience was so new and exciting that nothing much would have either surprised or worried them. They were in America and for most of them the next stop was to be Canada.

6. New World

After some hours of queuing, humping kit and endlessly answering to their names while worried men scribbled importantly on clip-boards, the cadets eventually filed down the gang planks and formed up in a column of three rather untidy ranks.

Then, burdened like pack mules with their kit and still accompanied by their marine guards, they marched off through the streets of Manhattan. New Yorkers are supposed to be blasé but the locals seemed nearly as fascinated by the sight of RAF uniforms as the boys were by the sights of the city. Allen, reared on a diet of Hollywood, was entranced. Despite the grey wintery sky the overall impression was one of light, for the city was brightly lit with shops and apartment buildings spilling illumination in all directions. New York was a new experience in itself but Penn Station was almost surreal. Its architect had been heavily influenced by the design of the Roman Baths of Caracalla and as a result it looked like a florid hybrid of Paddington Station and the Hanging Gardens of Babylon.

Before they had any real chance to savour it they were ordered to board their train and all their efforts for the next fifteen minutes or so were devoted to finding seats and stowing kit. The rolling stock that they had boarded seemed very much in keeping. with their exotic surroundings, antique wood panelled parlour cars with seats down both sides, a narrow aisle in the middle. and curtained overhead bunks that let down from the sides to give sleeping space to the passengers.

The train rumbled off through a snowy winter landscape chugging along at a steady thirty miles an hour through New York State, Connecticut, Massachusetts and Maine. It was very different from the England they had left behind. The snow was deep, the woods seemed endless and after dark the scattered towns were bright with street-lights, lamplit windows and illuminated shop fronts. Once they left Massachusetts habitation almost disappeared and they began to realise that there was an awful lot of North America and some of it was pretty sparsely inhabited.

Sleeping on the bunks was not comfortable in spite of the fact that they had long ago learned to sleep almost anywhere and in almost any posture. Even when wearing greatcoats gloves and shoes the brown leatherette surfaces were uncomfortably cold and the antiquated train heating was not really up to coping with the outside temperature of a New England winter.

The cold however, didn't seem to deter the local children who had obviously learned to recognise RAF blue, because they lined the trackside whenever the train stopped at a station and begged for English pennies as souvenirs.

Eventually the train crossed the frontier into Canada a hundred miles or so north of Bangor Maine and about five hours later they finished their six hundred mile journey and arrived at their immediate destination, the big transit camp in Moncton, New Brunswick. They had apparently followed a pretty roundabout course, as they were still well south of the St Lawrence River, but of course a winter journey to Canada couldn't be routed through the Gulf of St Lawrence and westward to Quebec, as ice closed the Gulf to shipping until well into the spring..

Allen didn't mind a bit, a diversion via Manhattan was just fine with him but Moncton proved a little less welcoming. The actual camp was comfortable enough by the fairly inexacting standards of the war-time air force, centrally heated wooden huts, showers with lashings of hot water and, a refinement new to Allen, urinals freshened with those little tablets of disinfectant that are now almost universally used. The food too verged on the luxurious with the fresh fruit, meat, eggs and canned goods that had almost vanished from strictly rationed England.

Moncton was probably fairly bleak at the best of times and in late February it was positively arctic but so brief was their stay that it made little impression. What did rather sour things was the surprising hostility of those men of the Royal Canadian Air Force who made up the permanent staff of the base. It was fairly low level stuff, boorishness rather than any sort of serious attempt to make life uncomfortable but it was unexpected and it did rankle. It was also mildly educative in a curious sort of way, as it was a raucous Canadian corporal who first introduced Allen to the term cocksucker. With the benefit of hindsight their antipathy is fairly easy to understand and was not a million miles removed from the attitudes of British servicemen to the Americans stationed in the UK. That was however, a degree of empathy that would have been hard to achieve at the time. Nobody actually enjoys being disliked and the cadets were not sorry when, a few days later, their turn came to move on. Allen's group were shipped out in a further troop train on the long circuitous journey through New Brunswick and Quebec to Hamilton in Ontario where they arrived on 5th March.

Number Five Air Navigation School, Mount Hope, proved to be a very workmanlike sort of place with paved runways and aprons, hardened perimeter tracks and roadways, a proper control tower, hangars, sophisticated Drem approach lighting and a small township of barracks, mess halls, administrative blocks and all the amenities needed by the several thousand airmen that inhabited the base. All these were enclosed behind a perimeter fence of chain linked wire and entered via a check-point with guard room and a knife rest barrier to control the stream of cars and trucks that constantly entered and left.

Curiously enough it was largely manned by men of the Royal Air Force, expensively and hazardously shipped across the Atlantic to provide the host of fitters, riggers, cooks, clerks, armourers, medical orderlies, administrators, padres and instructors that a big military training organisation requires. They too were frequently less than welcoming to the trainees flooding into the system and before long it became obvious why this was. It also went a long way towards explaining the hostility of the Canadian airmen they had encountered. The aircrew cadets were seen as a fairly exotic species by the local girls, young heroes removed briefly from a blitzed island and soon to be thrown into action over Germany. The permanent staff of the unit had originally benefited from this vicarious heroism but once the flow of cadets was well established they were soon seen as having arrived at a safe and cushy billet for the duration of the war. It wasn't long before their carefully nurtured social life began to be disrupted by the more glamorous inflow of newcomers and they would have been unusual had they not resented it. Far away from the action many of them would have had little notion of the price these young men were going to be required to pay for their transient popularity with the local girls.

Allen was even more fortunate than his mates. In his pen-friend Margaret, he had a ready made partner living in Hamilton although an outbreak of German Measles confined the draft to camp and delayed the meeting for another fortnight.

The delay didn't prove too onerous as the training programme, once started, was fast, furious and intensely interesting. Classroom sessions revised the early work on dead reckoning started all those months ago at Initial Training Wing and soon the cadets were learning to cope with the basic problems of speed, vector and drift. Flying-mad as they mostly were, the good thing was that much of the training was carried out in the air.

On their first morning they were marched over to the apron, the hardened marshalling area outside the hangars, and introduced to their aircraft, a row of twin engined Avro Ansons.

The Anson was a low winged monoplane powered by two 350 hp. radial engines. It was the first aeroplane in RAF service to be fitted with a retractable undercarriage, could achieve 188 mph. at 7,000 feet, rather better than that downhill with a following wind, and had started the war as a reconnaissance bomber. Some of them were still fitted with bomb racks and a mid-upper turret and they seemed remarkably business-like aeroplanes to Allen. As he grew older and wiser, and if one survived to grow older one was likely to grow wiser in the war-time air force, he also realised that it was also phenomenally reliable and would hold height on one engine, both life extending qualities!Allen and another cadet were first on the flight-line, burdened with bulky green canvas nav-bags, and parachutes and muffled in heavy flying gear to cope with the icy cold of the Canadian winter. They climbed in through the door aft of the trailing edge of the wing and settled down at the two navigation tables that occupied part of the roomy rear fuselage. The fuselage itself was a welded steel, fabric covered structure, with large rather flimsy plastic windows on both sides running as far back as the trailing edge of the wing. There was no insulation, freezing draughts whistled through every joint and crevice and even at cruising power it was deafeningly noisy. The Anson also provided its crews with a good deal of healthy exercise. Although fitted with retractable mainwheels the designers had rejected such fancy notions as electrical or hydraulic systems to work the gear. It was necessary to wind them up and down manually with innumerable turns of a large handle.

They flew in pairs, working with staff pilots who usually also had a fair degree of expertise as navigators. One trainee navigator calculating courses by dead reckoning on a Mercator chart while the other peered out of the windows and kept a visual plot with the aid of a simple topographical map.

The concept of navigating by dead reckoning is easy enough. A line is drawn on the chart marking the desired track and the required airspeed of the machine is decided. The speed and direction of the wind is factored into the calculation and the aircraft steered on a heading allowing for it. An aeroplane intending to track due north in a westerly wind, that is a wind blowing from its left, would steer rather west of north, that is aiming off to the left a bit. With a skill and a certain amount of luck the degree of aim-off would be just enough to compensate for the drift and keep on the correct path over the ground. Needless to say, actually doing it was rather more difficult. Wind speed and direction could change randomly and it was not easy to judge to what extent this was happening. Happily, the other cadet would be keeping a keen eye on the landscape and maintaining a visual plot on his map. The clear skies and good visibility usually experienced in Canada, the fact that major roads and railways in those parts ran east : west, while lesser ones ran north : south and the custom of painting the name of a town or village on the grain elevators usually made his task relatively simple.

For the plotting navigator the work was hard and continuous. The intended track line was drawn on the map, an initial drift calculation was made and a heading line ruled. As the aircraft flew on at a planned airspeed ground fixes were found by looking out of the windows and looking for known landmarks. Once the fix was established a new calculation for groundspeed and drift could be made and the speed and heading adjusted accordingly.

The permanent staff were not easy to please. On only his third trip Allen had passed the customary chit to the second pilot giving an estimated time of arrival over Kingston, Ontario. The pilot glanced at it and snapped "We're one minute off ETA, where's Kingston?" Allen glanced up. From 8,000 feet the town was clearly visible just out to the right. "There it is" he said. "Alter course 30 degrees starboard". "When?" asked the pilot bleakly "Now!" yelled Allen, by now a little irate, "and make it 35". The instructors face remained fixed in a frown. "Aren't you going to give me a chit?" he asked. Allen scribbled the new course on a scrap of paper and thrust it into his hand without comment. Technically speaking the instructor was right of course. Navigation changes were supposed to be confirmed in writing, as in the noisy environment of piston engined military aircraft it was possible to misunderstand spoken instructions. He was however, being a bit regimental, given the fact that the turning point was in clear sight, the aircraft was not only on track but on time and Allen was only on his third training flight in the job. Later on in his career he discovered that apart from being mildly unreasonable, the instructor had revealed a streak of petty officiousness and had filed a report criticising his change of course procedures.

This however was a very minor irritant and with increasing experience his confidence grew. As well as airborne training he spent hours in the classroom. The training schedule had been well thought-out and its planners had recognised the value of frequent repetition as a means of making navigation drills second nature. To put the student under pressure in ground exercises the clock was speeded up to halve the actual time available and most of the cadets soon developed the knack of careful plotting and rapid calculation with the Dalton Computer, which was a kind of circular slide rule.

Then came night navigation exercises which in European conditions would have been very much more difficult but, with clear North American skies and brightly lit towns, were not much of a challenge to their rapidly growing abilities. Night flying also gave them a chance to practice astro-navigation. The cadets would stand in the astrodome of the Anson, hang the sextant from the gimbals fitted, centralise the bubble in the spirit-level and line up the scope on the desired star. When the button was pressed a clockwork motor registered five positions and the average of those was taken as the star sight. Once again, with a bit of luck it was possible to establish a reasonable position fix, but it worked rather better in the clear skies of Canada than it was to on operations. In the cloudy conditions of north-west Europe, haze, turbulence and evasive action made it a great deal more difficult and astro-navigation was to prove of fairly limited value as a target seeking aid.

The course ground on and the cadets were to spend over twenty hours in the air, many more in the classroom and were subjected to a gruelling regime of tests, assessments and examinations. It wasn't all navigation either. One day they were re-introduced to the machine-gun and drilled in the intricacies of the 303 Browning and the Vickers Gas Operated gun. In the classroom they grappled with the concepts of deflection and bullet drop – in plain English, the need to aim in front of a moving target and above a distant one. They dealt with stoppages, stripped and cleaned the weapons and eventually took them out to a range and fired them. They brushed up once more on aircraft recognition and finally were put through an air firing course. This involved flying in one of the Ansons which had retained its turret and firing at a drogue target towed by another aircraft flown by an apprehensive instructor. The turret was pretty primitive, hand traversed and fitted with a single, pan-fed VGO,[1] but the gun made a highly satisfying clatter and produced clouds of exciting smelling

[1] Vickers gas operated.

cordite smoke. It was great fun but the difficulty they experienced in hitting a slow towed target at fairly close range was thought-provoking. What was it going to be like attempting to defend their aircraft from attacking cannon-armed fighters? But this thought was very much at the back of their minds, for the moment the course was exciting and the world was their oyster.

At last, after two weeks confined to camp until the quarantine period expired, the cadets were allowed out on local leave. The people of Hamilton were extremely welcoming generally but the luck that never entirely deserted Allen had sent him to Margaret's home town. Their first meeting was not a disappointment. She was eighteen years old, remarkably attractive and extremely likeable. What is more she was not remotely disappointed when they actually met and seemed to like him, so they were destined to spend a great deal of time together. Untypically for the daughter of a doctor, she had elected to leave school and work in a shop so she had plenty of spare time during evenings and week-ends. Happily and perhaps surprisingly, her prosperous middle class Canadian parents were content to see the friendship develop and treated their daughter's new boy-friend with an unforced and casual kindness.

By English standards, particularly those of the time, a considerable social gulf would have divided them. On one of their earlier meetings Margaret's father was amiably chatting, when he asked Allen if his father was a mason. Taking the question literally Allen said that he was a gardener, until he realised what he was actually being asked. The matter was passed off with good humour but it was fairly obvious that the good doctor was a freemason himself. However the question was clearly inspired by curiosity rather than unease about his social status which didn't appear to worry them one whit.

Their life style made a great impression on Allen. After the social rigidity of pre-war England the openness of Canadian society was exhilarating. Margaret didn't feel ready to go on to college yet and it was perfectly acceptable for her to work in a shop.

Her boyfriend was a fairly callow working class English lad but they took him at his face value, as an intelligent, articulate young man training for a difficult and highly dangerous occupation. Not only was he made very welcome in their home but Margaret was given fairly frequent use of the family car and allowed to show Allen the tourist sights, as well as visiting the movies, dancing and all the things that young couples did at that time.

It was in all senses a new world to Allen. He had grown up in the narrow, impoverished culture of working-class Darlington in the Thirties. Grammar school had widened his horizons a bit but he had still wound up on an office stool, a railway clerk working in conditions that hadn't altered much since Victoria was on the throne. Then came the war and for all its louring threat everything changed.

For his father's generation, a steady job was all that a man could hope for. A position in a bank or a drawing office was held up as a golden chance, with a regular salary and a pension after fifty years. To dream of flying aeroplanes was schoolboy fantasy, the real world was a much more serious place.

He had been faced with this grey prospect but the war changed everything. After a good deal of struggle he was presented with an all expenses paid trip to the New World and and then actually paid to do the things that he had never thought of as remotely possible. Even after the passage of more than fifty years the excitement of the whole experience shines through Allen's reminiscences.

As the long Canadian winter shaded into spring, Allen was shown the sights and at one of these realised that the Dominions had their own perspectives of history. We tend to see the American War of Independence through a face-saving haze, as a fairly good natured joust between cousins, a regrettable but understandable difference of opinion. The Canadians saw the war rather differently! Margaret had driven him to Niagara Falls, hard up against the United States border and they were wandering around admiring the scenery. The falls were a pretty impressive sight and Allen was duly impressed. Fascinated by the scene he studied every detail and noticed a tall Corinthian column with the figure of what seemed to be an eighteenth century sailor on its summit. "Who's that?" he asked Margaret. "It looks just like Nelson's column in London". She was genuinely taken aback at his ignorance. "It's General Brock" she said, as if that were sufficient explanation. He persisted with his line of questioning. "Who's General Brock?" Margaret could hardly believe his ignorance but it was patently genuine, so she explained. "He is why you're here" she said. "If he hadn't defeated the Americans this would be part of the USA". She went on to to tell him that the Americans had made a very determined attempt to conquer Canada after their earlier victories in the War of Independence and that it had been very bloodily repulsed. The history lesson was over, they went on their way but Allen realised that he had a lot to learn about Canada.

By the end of July, 1943 the course was finished and it had been a good one. Only one cadet was washed-out and although he was bitterly disappointed he was in no sense a failure, he merely developed a medical condition that prevented him from flying. He left for England cursing his luck, as having been released from the Metropolitan Police to volunteer for aircrew duties, he was obliged to go back to the same job.

The ANS training had been good enough to ensure that less than five months after the first shake-down flight Allen was awarded his flying brevet. There was something of a flurry of brass polishing and shoe cleaning before the wings parade but on the big day he found himself standing there with three stripes on his tunic sleeve and a brevet being pinned over his left breast pocket. To his surprise, instead of the single winged N that he was expecting, he was given winged O , an Observer's badge, the original and oldest flying badge in British military service. Because he had been enlisted as a Navigator/Wireless Telegrapher and destined for the observer's seat in a Coastal Command strike aircraft, he qualified for the historic "flying arsehole". What is more, although he was ordered to sew a navigator's badge on to his battledress he was able to wear his observer's badge on his best blue for the rest of his service. For a man with a keen sense of history it was very satisfying.

It was only after the parade and the subsequent celebrations that a mildly disturbing thought crossed his mind. Here he was in this fascinating place, summer was approaching with all the prospects of picnics and parties that Margaret had told him about, but he was due to go back to Europe. He lay on his bed and reflected on the problem for a while. The war wasn't going to end overnight, there would be more than enough to go round so far as the RAF was concerned, so could he find a way of spending a bit more time in Canada?

There was no point in messing around speculating so, with that decisiveness that was to eventually save his life on a bleak November morning a year and a half later, he put on his forage cap and strode off to the orderly room. After a few enquiries he found the NCO in charge of postings.

"Are there any more courses that you can volunteer for in Canada?" he said.

The sergeant looked at him slightly quizzically.

"Why? Don't you want to go and fly on ops?"

Alan was a touch taken aback. He hadn't thought that anyone would construe his request in that way.

"Yes of course I do," he said, "that's why I went to all the trouble of earning this bloody badge, but I've got a girlfriend out here and I'd like to see a bit more of her before I go back".

The postings-wallah relaxed and his face broadened into a grin.

"You could have put that better," he said, "but I know what you mean". He rifled through the files on his desk and offered a suggestion. "There's the GR course. Six weeks flying Ansons over the oggin[2] from PEI".

Allen looked suitably baffled.

"What," he asked "is a GR course and where the hell is PEI?"

"GR is General Reconnaissance and PEI is Prince Edward Island" was the reply. "It's a bloody awful place and you won't like it".

Allen didn't hesitate for many seconds. Six weeks wasn't very long, there would probably be leave at each end of the course and two more weeks of leave in Canada seemed worth the price. Without wasting any time, he volunteered. The die being cast he ambled back to his billet, lay back on his bed with hands firmly locked behind his head

---

[2] The sea.

and reached out to switch on his little portable radio. It had been raffled by a newly qualified navigator going home from an earlier course and to his surprise he had won it. Somehow it rather symbolised North America for him. At six inches by four inches it was, for a valve set, tiny by the standards of the day. It seemed the latest thing in transatlantic technology and as he lay there and listened to the music of one of the big swing bands he was very content.

After a very happy week of leave spent in and around Hamilton he packed his kit, boarded a train and took the slow journey up through Montreal, Quebec and Moncton to board the ferry for Charlottetown, the provincial capital of Prince Edward Island.

7. Victorian Values

The Maritime Provinces of Canada proved to be a bit of a shock and Prince Edward Island, the smallest province in the Dominion, was like falling into a time-warp. Suddenly he appeared to have been jerked back seventy or eighty years in time and transported to the east coast of Scotland. The weather, the landscape, the culture and the people were as far removed from his memory of a laid-back Americanised Ontario as it was possible to be. The rain squalls, the small farms, and the prevailing dour Protestantism opened up a forbidding prospect. Worst of all, for a young man rapidly acquiring a taste for the demon drink, the entire province was dry. Prince Edward Island continued to impose total prohibition of alcohol.

The base to which he was posted was just outside Charlottetown but that did not mean proximity to the bright lights. There were no bright lights on Prince Edward Island. unless you counted those that illuminated the airfield runways in bad weather. The camp itself was ordinary enough. It was a standard Canadian construction from the shingled timber huts to the mess halls, headquarters-block and hangars. The airfield had the usual paved runways and hardened manoeuvring areas with a number of camouflaged Ansons parked on the apron. This was in itself something of a departure from ANS where the training aircraft had been painted a bright highly visible yellow. A closer inspection showed that they were also fitted with mid-upper turrets and as two of them roared off down the runway on patrol he noticed that the under-wing bomb racks were loaded with depth charges.

The sergeant in the postings office in Hamilton had been absolutely right. Allen did not like Prince Edward Island one little bit. The only place to buy beer was in the sergeants' mess and that only by virtue of a special dispensation to the RAF, the RCAF base down at the other end of the island was dry. The girls were by any standards pretty quaint and buttoned up and to crown it all he didn't like the course very much.

A very great deal of the GR course was concerned with ship recognition and, as he was soon too discover, almost every capital ship was different from every other capital ship. He spent days in the classroom studying photographs, silhouettes and models and remembering that the *Scharnhorst* had a crane mounted on one side of the stern while the *Prinz Eugen* had a catapult mounted midships and to starboard. He had always been fascinated by aeroplanes but warships left him cold and the whole process proved mind-bendingly dull. It was however to prove fairly illuminating for someone who was later to take a keen professional interest in training, as it enabled him to understand the problems of aircraft recognition for those who had no previous interest in aircraft. It also suggested that his instructors probably knew what they were talking about when they assured him that he would be totally baffled for five of the six weeks of the course but that it would all fall into place for the final week. That is almost exactly what did happen and by the end of the sixth week Allen was able to identify his targets with a very high degree of accuracy.

The practical side of the course, some ten or twelve hours a week, involved flying out into the Atlantic on patrol and identifying and reporting everything they saw. Convoys going into the St Lawrence were constantly traversing their area and so they had plenty to go at. What is more, U-boats were operating as close inshore as they dared and so there was always a real possibility that they might sight and attack one. It wasn't very likely, the Ansons were not radar equipped and an alert submarine lookout was likely to see them long before they saw him, but it was possible.

The Royal Navy even provided them with their very own sample U-boat to attack. HMS Graph, originally U570, had been a German submarine which was depth charged to the surface, boarded and captured. It was, I think, the only one of its kind to fall relatively undamaged into the hands of the Allies and was used in the development of tactics to counter German underwater attacks. Allen was destined to give her new masters almost as big a shock as her original owners had suffered at the time of her capture. On this particular day the GR Ansons were briefed to fly to a rendezvous with the Graph, have a good look at it, observe the problem of even locating the slim hull of a surfaced U-boat and finally to attack it with nine-pound smoke bombs.

The task proved as difficult as they had been told. HMS Graph was hard to spot, and as they roared in at something approaching their maximum dive speed of 200 miles an hour it looked like a pencil in the water, an impossible target for the old fashioned course setting bomb sight. Allen, wearing his bomb-aimers hat, peered through the cross wires and eventually pressed the bomb release. Anything within fifty yards of the target would have been highly creditable but this was the shot of shots. With the wildest of flukes the little bomb bounced off the inside of the conning tower (thus inducing an immediate change of underwear for the lookout and the officer of the watch) ricocheted round and round, fetched up against the periscope standard and belched white phosphorous smoke in all directions. By a further miracle absolutely nobody was hurt but quite a few people were given the father and mother of all frights. This was to be his last effort at bomb-aiming and working on the principle of quitting while he was ahead this was probably no bad thing.

Social life in Charlottetown proved fairly limited. Although it was the provincial capital it was a very small town, probably much the same size as Richmond in Yorkshire or Bodmin in Cornwall and it, like them, did not offer a great deal of sophisticated entertainment. The favourite pastime of the young seemed to be parading round and round the central square. At the same time as the younger element engaged in this exciting pursuit their elders sat in their cars, which were parked nose to kerb, and watched them do it. There was of course the town's principal eating place, a cafe called The Old Spain, but although it offered a cuisine containing such exotic (to the English palate) things as hamburgers it too was dry and hence it had a fairly limited attraction to Allen and his friends.

With several hundred young men in search of amusement the RAF did what it could to cheer things up a bit and every so often the camp entertainments committee organised a dance. These could be fairly surreal events, as the local girls appeared to insist on bringing along their fathers and brothers to chaperone them. As an apparent consequence of this insistence, on the day of the dance immense queues of young and middle aged men and their sisters and daughters wound back from the camp gates and along the perimeter fence as far as the eye could see. It seemed that the airmen would have their style severely cramped, given that the girls were a fairly inhibited lot in the first place, but in practice the apparently anxious parents and siblings did not impose many problems. They had come, not to protect the virtue of their sisters and daughters, but to drink as much as possible as quickly as possible. As a result of this ambition they usually rendered themselves incoherent and incapable with truly amazing speed.

One week-end Allen and a mate got into conversation with a couple of girls who seemed to be holiday-makers. They were dressed in the kind of casual gear that they had become familiar with in Ontario and were a great deal more approachable than the local talent. Their accents too were obviously not local and they soon identified themselves as American tourists. They were both workers from the shipyards in Quincy, Boston and had come to Charlottetown because of its reputation for quaint, faintly rustic charm. At the time the boys wondered what sort of a place Quincy was if Charlottetown was seen as an improvement on it, but with the benefit of hindsight the Americans were right. It merely goes to show what a different gloss a few years experience can put on our opinions. In any case the girls proved very congenial company for a while and they eventually parted with the usual expressions of goodwill.

The six weeks, although it sometimes seemed like an eternity, soon passed and Allen was now technically trained for operations with Coastal Command.. In the normal course of events he would have been posted back to the UK and onto a squadron but by good luck he heard of something which was to change his plans yet again. Navigators were being sought to join yet another course at Patricia Bay on Vancouver Island where a Coastal Command Operational Training Unit had been established. Vancouver Island was on the Pacific west coast of Canada and in order to get there it would be necessary to cross the Rockies by train. Not only that, there would be leave at each end of the course and with a bit of luck he would be able to spend Christmas with Margaret. He acted with increasingly characteristic decision, took himself off to the orderly room and volunteered for the course.

8. Go West Young Man

He was faintly uneasy about the reception given to his application to join the Coastal Command OTU, which seemed to be a curious combination of respect for his keenness and doubt as to its wisdom, but it was granted with alacrity. He was told to collect a pass and necessary railway warrants for a weeks leave, told that he had an additional week in which to make his way to Patricia Bay and sent on his way rejoicing. Or, to be more exact he wandered off back to his billet to pack his kit wondering quite what he was letting himself in for. On the face of it an overland trip across the entire continent and three months on the Pacific coast was too good to be true, but why wasn't everyone volunteering? "Well, what the hell", he thought, too late to worry about it now, and in any case the up-side of the deal sounded pretty good.

The following day he was on his way to Hamilton and the happy prospect of a whole summer week of leave with Margaret and her family. As such things do, the week flew by, and in mid September 1943 Allen found himself on a local train from Hamilton bound for the Canadian Pacific Railway terminal in Toronto.

When he arrived at the rail depot the RTO informed him, to his mild surprise, that he was the senior NCO of the RAF party on the train. His duties did not appear to be too onerous and mainly consisted of being entrusted with a great roll of meal tickets which were to be used in lieu of cash to buy food on the four day journey. He accepted these cheerfully, and as the train was not scheduled to depart for a few hours, went off to investigate the train that was due to carry them westward.

For a railway buff it was the experience of a lifetime! The CPR was a steam hauled railway and the locomotives were enormous woodburners fitted with the kind of cowcatchers and smokestacks that he had seen in a hundred western films. The rolling stock was equally antique, wood panelled parlour cars with central aisles and let down bunks over the rows of seats. There was a buffet car with a bar and a restaurant car serving hot meals, it was absolutely wonderful and a very long way from Darlington County Durham.

Once the train was ready for boarding the airmen busied themselves for a while finding seats, loading the usual mounds of kit and rounding up the inevitable stragglers. Soon, after a good deal of kafuffle: shouting, whistling, jolting as the big locomotive struggled for traction, clouds of steam and the belching smoke and sparks, the train slowly lumbered forward and steadily gathered momentum. They were on their way.

It was not a very rapid progress. The speed rarely exceeded forty miles an hour and despite the fact that this was one of the two transcontinental links it was basically a single track operation with passing loops at intervals. On leaving Toronto large notices had actually proclaimed that they were travelling on Canadian Pacific's twin track route to the west but the twin tracks had soon petered out once they were clear of the city. The train rolled on through the relatively familiar pastoral landscape of southern Ontario then into a more rocky wooded terrain and then the wilder landscape of eastern Manitoba. There was a brief urban stretch as they traversed the city of Winnipeg before encountering the rolling prairies of Western Manitoba. The train's progress continued to be stately rather than swift, with pauses to double-head it with an additional locomotive if any sort of a gradient was encountered until they crossed into Saskatchewan where God seemed to have taken an iron to the landscape and flattened it into plains that ran as far as the eye could see.

The train picked up speed a little running past isolated farmhouses, small communities marked by great grain elevators and not much else. The sheer scale of the landscape was overwhelming and, confronted by this vastness, the imprecision of the railway timetable (which said things like Medicine Hat, Wednesday lunch-time. Kamloops, Thursday breakfast) became easy to understand. They stopped briefly at Regina, the headquarters of the Royal Canadian Mounted Police, where the famous red tunics were very much in evidence and then on through Moose Jaw westwards towards Alberta.

Sometimes they passed through areas which were dry, where prohibition was imposed, alcohol was forbidden and the bar was closed. This did not cause any serious inconvenience because they were warned in advance by a kindly conductor and were able to fill Coke bottles with Canadian Bourbon to bridge the gap. The train crews were very kind to them and although they were supposed to pay for their meals with Canadian Pacific vouchers, somehow these were forgotten and never collected.

Every now and again the train stopped to top up the fuel bunkers and fill the locomotive tender with water for the boilers. Allen would take advantage of this to wander along by the track and take a closer look at the little prairie community marked only by a water tower and the inevitable grain elevator.

On the third day the train crossed into Alberta and gradually the landscape changed from prairie to hill country and then into the beginnings of the Rocky Mountains. As they travelled from Medicine Hat to Calgary and Lake Louise the scenery became progressively more rugged. Sometimes the gradients were such that the train was hauled by three locomotives and even then the pace was so slow that it was possible to get out and walk alongside the carriages.

They crossed into British Columbia and when they reached the summit of the Kicking Horse Pass, the pass that took the track across the Rockies, they were over the watershed. From there onwards the rivers drained into the Pacific. The train pressed on westward, slowly gaining sped as the gradients eased. After four days the train arrived in Vancouver and the most impressive journey of Allen's life was over. He had seen some of the most spectacular landscapes on Earth, as well as lumberjacks in checked shirts and miners and cattlemen looking like extras from Western films. There had been Native American lodges (although in an age before political correctness he called them Red Indian tepees) fantastically carved totem poles, log cabins and Mounties in scarlet tunics. Talking about it over fifty years later the excitement still comes across with an intensity that you can almost taste.

From the railhead in Vancouver the RAF party and their small mountain of kit were loaded into trucks and driven down to the ferry terminal on the waterfront. At the terminal they boarded the ferry that was to carry them on the short sea journey across to Vancouver Island and after the usual period of frantic activity while kit was hauled aboard they were at leisure to sit on the deck and admire the view. Vancouver seemed a fairly typical North American city, fairly new, architecturally unexciting and busy but its setting directly under the coastal mountains was spectacular. Facing the other way, to the west, they could see Vancouver Island while to the north was the long strait that separated it from the mainland. To the south the strait of Juan de Fuca curved round to where Cape Flattery marked the north western extremity of the USA.

The ferry threaded its way between a host of small steep-sided wooded islands and as they steamed steadily towards their destination they were soon able to make out a rather gentle coastline backed, in the distance by a further range of mountains. As the ship curved in towards the bay fronting the provincial capital of Victoria they could see small seaside villages running along the coast. It was a strikingly beautiful prospect and Victoria, with a host of Victorian buildings, looked almost as if it had strayed from somewhere on the south coast of England. Dominating the waterfront as they moved nearer were the great granite legislative buildings and the equally impressive Empress Hotel which looked rather like a vast ivy-covered chateau. Allen, who had learned to recognise the Canadian Pacific hotel style, fingered the great roll of meal tickets left over from the journey and wondered. Perhaps they could be exchanged for a meal in the hotel restaurant? It would certainly be worth wandering into town at some future date to make enquiries. He turned to one of his mates and nodded at the building, "I bet we could eat very well in there" he said. A certain amount of ribaldry ensued at the thought of a bunch of hairy sergeants turning up at such a posh location but Allen was not intimidated and filed the notion away for future consideration.

Speculation about hotel meals came to an abrupt end in the confusion of docking. Kit had to be assembled and carried down the gangplanks to be loaded onto the usual trucks. They were soon on their way through the small and very English looking city headed toward the RAF training base at nearby Patricia Bay. The curious Englishness of the place was complemented by the traffic. Many of the cars were English; Austins and Rileys, Rovers and Morrises, quite unlike the American Fords, Chevrolets and Buicks that dominated the roads in Ontario and the eastern seaboard. Surprisingly until just before the war they had even driven on the left which must have been extremely disconcerting to North American tourists.

A few miles out of town the trucks passed through the little town of Sydney and swung in through the gates of a good sized airfield complex and as soon as they saw it they realised that they were not going to operate from the sort of rather drab but familiar military base they were used to. The airfield at Patricia Bay was built on a peninsula, the Saanich Peninsula which jutted out into the bay. The runway, which looked uncomfortably short, ran across a fairly narrow spit of land and offered no prospect of a safe over or undershoot. If you landed short or failed to stop in time you finished up hitting the water. Flying boats and float planes were moored in the bay and a slipway was evidence of an extensive servicing facility. Terminal buildings and the presence of some large civil aircraft showed that it was also the main civilian airport for the island and it proved to be the main Trans Canada Airways terminal on the West Coast.

In the bright Pacific sunlight the scene looked more like a shot from a travel film than an operational training base. The sky was blue broken by streets of piled cumulus. The sea was blue-green with windrows of small white capped waves. The straits beyond the bay were dotted with the steep shored densely wooded islands that they had seen from the ferry and busy with small boat traffic.

Their attention was diverted from the scene as the trucks turned away from the airfield into a more familiar hutted domestic site. Eager to be out they climbed over the tailboards and were soon dumping their kit into a series of small individual rooms. After the usual weary business of arriving at a new posting; drawing bedding, signing on with the medical branch, the chaplain, the anti-gas stores, the bicycle stores, the registry and all the familiar rigmarole, they were at last able to get something to eat and get some sleep. After four nights on a train Allen and his mates slept like logs

The next day they were crewed-up. It was a singularly unmilitary procedure and I think, unique to the RAF. A group of pilots, navigators and air-gunners were assembled in a hangar and told to sort themselves out. They milled around with a good deal of talking going on and in half an hour or so they had formed groups of two gunners, a navigator and a pilot. It may have seemed a funny way to choose the people that you might trust your lives with but it worked well enough.

9. A Dicey Business

The crew was the sort of Commonwealth mixture that was common in the war time RAF and seems so striking now. Jack Brightwell, the pilot and captain was a New Zealander. Allen the Navigator and radio operator was English. Bill Pitt the wireless-operator/air gunner and Parky Parkinson the gunner were respectively an Australian and a New-Zealander. Once a crew was formed there was a tendency to spend a fair bit of time together and Allen's was no exception. They had a couple of hours to kill between crewing-up and their first briefing for the course and they wandered off together to have a better look at the airfield.

The aprons were crowded with aircraft of all sorts but their first interest was in the machines they were going to fly on the course. There were a row of Lockheed Vega Venturas parked prominently on the tarmac but camp gossip had already told them that these had only just arrived and wouldn't be ready for a few weeks. The nearest Venturas were all still in USAAF markings and they were initially fascinated by the giant cartoons painted on the big twin-engined machines. Nose art was rare in the RAF and the prominent Mickey Mouse and Donald Duck motifs looked very exotic. A closer look revealed interior fittings which were decidedly plushy by the standards they were used to. Sound insulation in the cockpit area, cigar lighters on the instrument panel, a wardrobe with hanging space and, luxury of luxuries a chromium plated chemical lavatory. This last item really caught the fancy of the entire crew "a chromium plated bog" they kept muttering "bugger me!" A little further along the line harsh reality began to intrude. Riggers were busily spraying them in drab camouflage colours while airframe and instrument fitters were tearing out the wardrobes and fitting a drift sight where they had been. They looked regretfully at all this new equipment, wishing that they might have used it but as it happened they were wrong. Despite the success of its predecessor, the Lockheed Hudson, the Ventura was to be a catastrophic failure in service.

They wandered on and gathered around a line of parked Bolingbrokes, Canadian built Mk IV Blenheims powered by American radial engines. They sucked their teeth speculatively. Despite a fairly evil reputation for vulnerability these were proper aeroplanes but there didn't seem to be many of them, certainly not enough to equip a course of twenty crews.

Then they saw in front of them a range of parked Handley-Page Hampdens, machines which by mid 1943, were getting a bit elderly. The Hampden was originally designed as a fast day bomber but fast was by the standards of 1932. The designer had done everything he could to reduce drag and his solution involved building a fuselage shaped like a deep, narrow suitcase with a flimsy looking twin tail assembly carried back a further twenty feet or so on a slim single boom. The forward fuselage was only the width of a single-seater fighter. The solitary pilot was perched above the bomb-bay and behind the navigator, who sat right forward in the glazed nose section. On top of the fuselage and behind the pilot was a small glazed gun cupola which carried a power traverse for a pair of Vickers gas operated guns. Below this cupola was a lower emplacement mounting a further hand held VGO. The navigator/observer had another flexible VGO in the nose while the pilot could fire a fixed Browning gun mounted in the upper part of the front fuselage.

They looked apprehensively at the parked aircraft. The twin 1000hp Pegasus engines seemed okay, nice reliable power units but the machines looked decidedly tired. The paint was peeling from them, the cowlings were dented and oil-stained and what they could see of the interiors had a very well used appearance. Jack uttered a few words that summed up the sense of the meeting, "Bloody Hell" he said and they wandered off back to get something to eat before their first briefing.

The briefing was a bit of a shaker. The wing-commander (flying) opened the proceedings by telling them they were to be trained as torpedo attack crews. "It's a dicey business" he said and went on to tell them quite how dangerous the training had so far proved to be.

There were twenty crews on a course, this was the twenty third course, and so far they had never lost fewer than five crews each time. "You're the last lot to train on Hampdens" he said. "The riggers and fitters are busting a gut to make sure the kites are in the best possible shape so please try to stay alive". This was the first and only time in his entire military career that any one ever told Allen to be careful and he was duly impressed.

As the briefing went on it became much clearer why torpedo dropping was so dangerous and why doing it in Hampdens made it even more so. A torpedo is essentially a small, gyro-guided, unmanned submarine, which carried a large high explosive warhead and travelled at about forty knots through the water. For a torpedo to drop and run successfully the speed and height of the carrier aircraft was critical. Too high or too fast and the torpedo would bounce and either break-up or go completely off course. Ideally they needed to be released when the aircraft was flying straight and level at a height of about ten feet, an airspeed that did not exceed one hundred and twenty miles an hour and at a range of not more than six hundred yards from the target.

Flying a large machine like the Hampden (It had a seventy foot span, was nearly fifty four feet long, stood nearly fifteen feet from the ground and weighed about nine tons) was dangerous enough at low level. With only two thousand horse power it was hideously underpowered by modern standards. What made things worse was its design. With the after part of the fuselage little more than a boom and the forward part a deep slab-sided box if it was flown out of balance it was very much out of balance. As a consequence it had a marked tendency to slip or skid in turns. Flying only ten feet or so from the surface a badly balanced turn would cause the machine to slip straight into the sea.

Allen felt his belly knot. If simply flying the aircraft in training had killed that many, what would it be like with the Kriegsmarine shooting at them? German naval flak was famously effective and they were being invited to fly straight and level towards the guns at slow speed before trying to break away by flying over the target at mast-head height.

The usual defence mechanisms took over. Anything could happen before they actually went on ops. Surely they would only use Hampdens for training and in the meantime they would cope. He was however feeling markedly more mortal as the wingco went on to explain the technicalities of the course..

After the briefing the crew split up to go to tea. Allen, Jack and Parky to the sergeants mess and Pitt, unusually for a wireless-operator/air gunner already a pilot officer, sloped off to the officers mess.

After tea they reassembled and caught a truck down to the outskirts of Victoria for a few beers. The pub, called the Four Mile House was a necessary four miles outside the city limits as Victoria was a temperance town and no alcohol was sold within its boundaries. That far out of town there was nothing else to do but drink and there was a distinct flavour of eat, drink and be merry about that evenings entertainment.

The next morning the crews were assembled on the flight line to familiarise themselves with the Hampden. It was not a reassuring experience. These were indeed very weary aircraft. Some of them appeared to be painted with the white finish originally applied for the Norwegian campaign of 1940. Most of the interior fittings were decidedly battered. The little canvas bags intended to catch the cartridge cases from expended rounds were either holed or missing and the various knobs, switches and levers were cracked and distorted from long hard usage. The Perspex was scratched and yellowing, the Spartan padding of the seats was torn and leaking and the interior paintwork chipped and worn.

Once they had been given the usual Cook's tour of their respective positions the next stage was to ensure that their pilot could actually fly the aircraft. There was no such thing as a dual-controlled Hampden as there was no room for a second pilot. Jack, who had never flown anything bigger than an Airspeed Oxford, which was half the size, was committed to make his first flight aided only by advice from a screened pilot (an instructor familiar with the type) perched on the top of the bomb bay behind him. With less than two hundred hours flying experience he was about to take off and land from a short runway with the sea at both ends and a steep shore uncomfortably close to his climb-out path.

The screened pilot gave him a last minute briefing while he tried to remember the contents of the pilot's notes which he had scrutinised the night before. He climbed in and did up his straps, ran through his cockpit checks and started the big Pegasus radial engines. The warm-up took a long time. Radials take a while to come up to temperature and it is easy to oil up the plugs if you are too hasty. He tested the magnetos in turn, did a power check and set the throttles to a fast idle before calling the tower to tell them he was ready. The tower showed him a green light and at that he slid the canopy shut, opened the throttles with a bellow of sound and released the brakes.

The crew watched anxiously as the big machine lurched forward and slowly gathered speed. It swung a little as it accelerated but he caught it, corrected and as the tail came up drove it squarely down the centre of the tarmac. The Hampden looked dangerously near the end of the short runway when it lifted off but the rest of the bystanders seemed unruffled and they relaxed a bit. There was a collective sharp intake of breath as the aircraft appeared to dip towards the sea but they realised that he was merely checking forward on the controls to let the speed build up a bit. After a few seconds it banked, perhaps a little steeply at first, but then continued to climb out uneventfully. So far so good!

One of the watching pilots grinned at them. "Wait until you do that with a dummy war load" he said "that will scare seven different kinds of shit out of you"!

The Hampden re-appeared in the circuit and once more they looked anxiously at its approach. They saw that the wheels and flaps were down as the machine lined up for finals. Speed and height looked okay, he flared, touched down on three points and with only the tiniest of bounces and a puff of black smoke from the tyres, was down. There was a blare of sound as the throttles opened for another circuit and the procedure was more or less repeated. This time he had been briefed to come to a full stop so he taxied back to the apron before shutting down the engines. The pilot's canopy rumbled back and after a few seconds the little hatch on the top of the fuselage popped open and the screen scrambled out. He stepped onto the wing root, leaned forward and yelled cheerfully at Jack. "That was okay" he said "just lead a bit with the opposite throttle to correct the swing and you'll be fine". "Now go and do three more circuits and bumps and these poor buggers can join you". With this valediction he turned round, walked to the trailing edge of the wing and sat with his legs dangling before jumping to the tarmac and walking to join the watchers. Jack gave a broad grin, elevated a thumb, slid the hood forward again and re-started the engines. Once the tower gave him the okay he taxied out to the runway threshold and after a brief power check opened the throttles for another take off.

Three times more the Hampden touched down and twice it accelerated away noisily before braking to a halt after the third landing and taxiing back to the waiting crew standing on the apron. After a burst of throttle to clear the plugs the engines idled briefly, the props slowed and spun to a dead stop. The hood slid back with a clunk as it hit the stops and Jack climbed out and stood on the wing root. "Come on fellers" he said "Your turn now".

Allen was first. The ground crew shoved an access ladder forward and he hoisted himself up it, over the trailing edge of the wing root and forward to the navigators hatch. This was a little square opening on top of the fuselage and just forward of the DF loop.

The aperture was about eighteen inches square, secured by a pair of little doors and enabled him to step down about four feet onto a padded cushion secured to the top of the bomb bay. He pitched his navigation bag and observer-type parachute[3] in first and slid after them.

---

[3] Most bomber crew men wore observer type chutes. This meant that they wore their parachute harness all the time but the actual parachute was con-

He shuffled forward, constricted by his harness and conscious of the chafing of the Mae West around his neck. He dangled his legs into the gap between the back of the pilot's seat and the front of the bomb bay, steadied himself with a grab handle and, craning his neck, peered forward over Jack's shoulders. The gunners followed the same route over the trailing edge but then entered the rear fuselage via the hinged top of the upper gun position. Once the four were in they plugged their helmets into the intercom and checked in. After this brief exchange the engines were re-started and after receiving a green from the tower they were off on their first brief shake-down flight as a crew.

The Hampden lumbered down the runway, unstuck, picked up speed in a shallow dive and then accelerated into a climbing turn. The nose dipped briefly as Jack retracted the flaps and adjusted the trim and then continued in the climb.

At two thousand feet Allen decided to enter the navigators compartment in the nose and had his first attempt at this rather complicated manoeuvre. He started by slinging his nav-bag into the chute that ran down behind the pilot's seat. He looked at his parachute pack and made the first really alarming decision of his flying career. There simply wasn't room for it in his crew position and in any case his only means of egress was by climbing back up that chute and making an exit either via the top hatch or through the pilot's opened canopy. He may as well leave it at the top. In any case it was unlikely to be of much use to him.

The next trick was actually getting into his place and this involved sitting at the top of the chute behind the pilot's seat, raising his hands above his head and simply slithering down into the lower nose compartment. He found himself sitting below and forward of the pilot in a space barely wider than his shoulders and glazed from vertically

---

tained in a separate pack which could be attached to the harness with king-sized snap fasteners in an emergency. This enabled them to move around without being encumbered by a clumsy parachute pack. Only the pilot wore a conventional seat type pack as he couldn't leave his seat in flight.

above his head to just in front of his heels. With the tips of the props about a couple of feet behind his ears and only separated from him by six inches of clearance and a thin dural skin the noise was deafening. On his left was a mounting designed to take a Vicker's gas operated gun which could be pivoted out and fired through a slot in the nose. To his right was a folding chart table. He swung it down, unfolded his charts on the top and tried using dividers, parallel rulers and his Dalton computer in the confined space available.

After a while Jack's voice came through on the intercom straining to be heard over the engine noise.

"How are you fellers?"

Pitt replied first. "I'd better not get too bloody excited. Parky's sitting between my feet and if I fidget I'll tread on the poor bastard".

Parkinson confirmed this and urged Pitto to mind where he put his bloody great feet. Allen said that he was fine but it might be hard to hold a dance in his office. Nobody was very surprised by the cramped crew stations. They had formed a fairly clear view of their positions before they ever flew in the kite but there was some sort of security in being asked.

Jack's voice on the intercom again. "We need to fly out towards the sea a bit. Can you give me a course for the Straits of Juan de Fuca?"

Allen glanced southwards, saw where the straits swept round to the west and gave a heading. The machine climbed slowly to about five thousand feet above the widest part of the inshore passage where Jack tried a few steep turns. These weren't too bad, although the way in which they were slung about suggested a pronounced tendency to slip and skid. Then the nose went down, the throttles went to the stops and the machine went into a fast shallow dive. The subsequent jamming of the heads into the shoulders as the speed was turned back into height was received in stoical silence. What did produce a few yelps of protest was the sudden slowing of the engine revs, the nose rearing up above the horizon and the sickening lurch of a stall. The nose dropped, there was a roar of sound as the throttles opened and the Hampden accelerated back to a normal flying attitude. "That'll do fellers" said the driver "give me a course for home", and with that they headed back. Half an hour or so later they contacted the tower again and swung into circuit for their first landing as a crew. For Allen it was an interesting experience. He had to stay where he was for the circuit as getting out of his station was next to impossible in the air. His fascinated eyes followed their progress from the eight hundred feet of the downwind leg to the final approach, as the big machine motored in. The white caps of the waves under the tilting nose of the Hampden, waves breaking on the shore line, a blur of tarmac under his feet, a jolt, a puff of burning rubber and the Hampden was down. A green light from the tower and they taxied to their dispersal, stopped engines and their first flight was over.

One of the ground crew shoved the ladder into place and they vacated their positions as best they could. The pilot and the gunners had a relatively easy route from their stations, on to the wing and down by the trailing edge again. Allen's was a more difficult exit. He had to turn round in his cramped little compartment, push his navigation bag up the chute and pull himself up from under the pilot's seat onto the top of the bomb bay, to make a final exit through the top hatch.

Once standing on the tarmac again there was a babble of conversation. Jack was quite pleased with the handling qualities of the Hampden and said so. The crew were a bit less impressed.

"What was the fancy flying for when we did the roller coaster impression" said Pitto?

"I wanted to check the stall," replied Jack. "The book tells you the speed when it's supposed to happen but all aircraft are a bit different, even the same types. I wouldn't like to find that the book was wrong and have her stop flying at fifty feet on approach. It could screw up our entire afternoon."

There was a general mutter of agreement and the crew wandered off to dump their flying kit and go in search of supper.

10. Panics, Picnics and an Andy Hardy Christmas

The Pacific coast of Canada was not the easiest environment in which to learn to fly underpowered torpedo-carrying aircraft. Patricia Bay was separated from the open ocean by Vancouver Island with its mountainous western fringe and crossing it could be hazardous. Usually the crews were briefed to fly south and through the Straits of Juan de Fuca but return flights could be well off course and only one of the valleys that faced the open sea went all the way across the island. Trying to cross the island at low level and picking the wrong valley was the kind of mistake unlikely to be repeated. The Hampdens couldn't climb fast enough to clear the mountains at the end and there wasn't enough room to turn within the valley walls. Nor was the climate ideal. The moist westerly winds resulted in the sort of cloudy rainy episodes that we associate with the west coast of the United Kingdom, with the added complication of thick orographic cloud forming on the steeply rising slopes.

The war was also a good deal closer than one might expect. The Americans and the Japanese were fighting a bitter campaign for control of the Aleutian Islands and Japanese submarines were making surfaced approaches at night to attack the convoys that the US Navy was running northwards along the coast.

After that first shake-down flight the crew were worked fairly hard. A good deal of the time was spent in lectures. Ship recognition for all of them, with a constant update on those enemy vessels that had been sunk or crippled and news of any known new building. The gunners got more range practice and aircraft recognition and Allen was given an intensive course in the techniques of low level navigation over the sea. Jack and Allen were drilled in the theory of torpedo dropping and the critical needs to keep speed, altitude and dropping range well within the very narrow limits laid down.

Almost every day they flew training sorties. The Hampdens were loaded, initially with eighteen inch Whitehead torpedoes but before long these were replaced by concrete castings of roughly the same weight and size. The torpedo dropping mechanisms, which involved detachable air tails and long spools of wire paid out from the dropping aircraft, were extremely fragile and simply couldn't stand up to the hammering handed out by the inexperienced crews of an operational training unit. The crude solution to the problem was to cut out any actual dropping and make the crews merely simulate the exercises in aircraft ballasted to the correct operational weight.

Day after day, once lecture schedules were completed, the Hampdens flew out, westward from the coast of British Columbia as far as the prudent limit of endurance (the point at which their fuel supply was just sufficient to get them home with a modest reserve for diversions) would allow. As well as the particular exercises for which they were briefed they were told to look out for enemy submarines. Apart from rifle calibre machine guns they had no means of attacking hostile craft even if they saw them but they were supposed to climb high enough to reel out their long trailing aerial, transmit a sighting report to alert the duty flight of Bolingbrokes and try to shadow the surfaced vessel. The Bolingbrokes were the only ones capable of dropping either depth charges or torpedoes and would be crewed by the screened instructional staff. Happily no surfaced subs. were sighted, none were shadowed and no attacks made. The probability of running out of fuel would have been significant and the chance of surviving the subsequent ditching in the chilly waters of the North Pacific would not have been good. Training flights were to prove frightening enough without the added hazard of naval flak or ditching.

The beginning of each sortie, departing from a hybrid military and commercial airport, was an almost surreal experience as the Hampdens lined up on the single runway with a mixture of Trans Canada Airlines Boeings and DC3s, Walrus amphibians, Lysander army co-operation machines the odd U S Army Air Force Tomahawk fighter and small bush planes of a variety of types. Just to add a little spice to the proceedings the seaplane base that lay next to the runway was operating at the same time and they could fly alongside Stranraer or Catalina flying boats and a variety of floatplanes on the climb-out or in the circuit.

Take-off in a Hampden, heavily laden with fuel, ammunition and a large dummy torpedo, was always exciting. Jack would line them up on the end of the runway and once give a green light by the tower would rev the engines hard against the brakes before starting his run. Acceleration was slow and a lot of runway was used before the wheels left the tarmac. Once airborne he would hold the nose down to let the speed build up before setting course for the straits at low level. Allen would drop down into his position and start his plot. Every few minutes he would take a look at the lie of the waves, the amount of blown spray and use his knowledge of the old Beaufort scale to calculate his drift. He estimated the wind speed by the amount of spume blown from the wave tops and established its direction by aligning the astro compass with the wind-lanes. To his surprise this seemingly crude navigational technique worked surprisingly well. He alternated this with straight-forward use of the drift recorder. Sometimes, to give the gunners something to do, he would drop an aluminium dust sea-marker and get them to check the drift with their sights. Less frequently he would alter course thirty degrees port, sixty starboard and thirty degrees port again to cross check the drift but the most reliable method was simply eyeballing the wave tops and the wind lanes.

After a few sorties Allen's confidence in his navigation began to grow. The endless drills that he had run through in the skies over Ontario had made it all second nature. Establish your initial position and plot a course. Estimate the speed and direction of the wind and adjust your heading accordingly. Look for landmarks to establish your track and readjust your heading if necessary. Once over the open sea the third step became impossible but this was to some extent compensated for by his new found ability to accurately estimate drift at low level.

It was however bloody dangerous. Most of the time they were flying so low that the slipstream was throwing up spray and the slightest inaccuracy in a turn or loss of concentration in maintaining height would have had them slap into the waves at nearly two hundred miles an hour. Dummy torpedo dropping sorties were carried out in the sheltered waters of the sound using small rocky islands as targets. The islands resembled ships in many ways with the major difference that they did not move or fire back. The absence of return fire was welcome but as the essence of effective torpedo dropping was the ability to make accurate estimates of the target's course and speed, the value of the exercise was fairly limited.

In spite of the absence of movement or return fire, attacking islands still produced a few close calls. Allen would peer through a crude optical sight which vaguely resembled a folding wooden coat hanger turned on its side. The resultant horizontal v would be widened or narrowed depending on the assumed speed of the target. This speed was to be calculated in reality by identifying the ship, looking it up in the recognition manual, reading off the maximum and cruising speeds and assessing its actual speed from the size of the bow wave and the wake. All this being done, Allen would hold the contraption in front of his face and line up a peg protruding from one end of the v with the assumed bow of the target. The angle between the two arms was opened or closed in accordance with the assumed speed of the target, the faster the target, the wider the angle. He would then steer Jack along a line which was produced from a peg protruding from the other end of the v. With a bit of luck, if they had judged the range and speed correctly, a torpedo dropped on that heading should reach the same bit of sea at the same time as the target. The whole thing demanded a high degree of cooperation between pilot and navigator and total concentration on maintaining the right speed, height and heading. Several times their Hampden flew into mist or low cloud and it was only by good luck or the grace of God that they didn't either fly into the sea or the target. Several times the wave hopping Hampden narrowly missed the upper works of a ship as it loomed up out of the mist. Allen had even more of a shock on another murky day. He was head down working on his plot when the throttles were rammed open, the stick was hauled back into a shallow climb and his head forced forward by the g-load. Just below him he saw what looked like a gypsy encampment in the middle of a timber yard. Little log shacks with smoking chimneys, hen coops and tethered animals, dotted the surface of a rectangular island. "Christ" said Jack "That was bloody close"! The startled Allen caught a glimpse of a big tug-boat as they banked away and he realised that they had nearly collided with a vast timber raft which was being towed to the saw-mills some hundreds of miles down the sound.

In contrast to their highly dangerous training schedule their off duty pursuits were curiously innocent. The New Zealanders in the crew positively detested being in Canada, regarding it as an irritating diversion from the serious business of getting on with the war and bitched about all things Canadian. They even moaned about the food which to Allen, after four years of rationing and a fairly spartan up-bringing, seemed sybaritic beyond belief. As a result they received food parcels from home and these were used as the provisions for picnics and boating expeditions.

For most of his time in the service Allen's social life revolved around the traditional military passions for wine, women and song....possibly not much song, and beer rather than wine but the principle held. In British Columbia the New Zealand contingent converted their crews to the outdoor life. Canoes, sailing boats and little power boats were hired and picnics, barbecues and swimming expeditions were their chief sources of entertainment all through the autumn and, with the exception of swimming, into the early part of the winter. It was all very Baden-Powell, very different to anything that happened to him in the air force either before or after but it was to be a very happy time for Allen.

Even more surprisingly the whole course continued to beat the odds; six weeks into training and no serious accidents. There were one or two close calls when aircraft came back with bent propeller tips after touching the sea or damaged wing tips in the same way but by some miracle none of them resulted in a serious crash.

One Hampden crew arrived back at the west coast of Vancouver Island a bit short of fuel, confidently decided that they knew where they were and elected to try to fly across the island by following the only valley that went right across. They were wrong and they soon found themselves confronted by a mountain slope far too steep for the sluggish Hampden to climb over, they would have been slap into the terrain long before their aircraft was able to reach a safe altitude. It should also have been impossible for the big machine to make a 180 degree turn in the narrow valley. A turn tight enough to clear the flanking slopes should have resulted in a high speed stall that would have rolled it into the ground. Happily a combination of jettisoning the dummy torpedo, a suicidally desparate diving turn and probably a slight widening of the valley allowed them to get away with it and a seriously shaken crew found themselves back over the sea. Even then they had to grope their way back to the straits and when they finally arrived back at base the needles on the fuel gauges were bouncing on the left hand stops.

Sometimes a note of farce tempered the hazards. One of the navigators on the course was a genial rather kindly Cornishman called John Ennor who liked to sport a Royal Canadian Air Force tunic. His reasoning was simple. He said that the initials RCAF stamped on the buttons stood for Royal Cornish Air Force and it was good to make those up-country buggers in London recognise the true importance of his native duchy. Ennor was a lovely man and a real gentleman but he was a somewhat indifferent navigator. His crew were briefed for an exercise that involved flying westward out to sea and climbing to some eight thousand feet before turning across the island and descending to near sea level for a simulated attack on shipping in the sound. After take-off the Hampden wheezed its way up to this unfamiliar altitude before turning through 180 degrees and running in on the coast. They didn't take a lot of notice of the wispy bits of cloud that were forming under them as they struggled for height as the sky ahead was still clear blue. John and his pilot were therefore a touch surprised when they completed their turn and looked ahead, to see that the sky to the eastward of them was filled with cloud, the brilliant tops of which appeared to come very nearly up to their cruising height. What is more, confident of being able to see the coast and establish his position visually, John hadn't bothered to maintain much of a plot and he was by no means certain where they were.

A faintly plaintive "what do we do now nav?" from the pilot jolted him back to reality. The first step was the fairly obvious one of steering east and looking for breaks in the cloud. With a bit of luck they would find a hole through which they could descend over the sound. The gunners were told what to look for and for nearly an hour they carried out a square search over cloud looking for a sight of the sea or the ground.

"This is no bloody good" said the skipper, "we could be stooging around up here 'til the fuel runs out." John agreed. "There's only one thing to do" he said. "The cloud belt is only on the coast, we can lose height over the sea and run in on the coast at low level". We're bound to recognise something on the way in and we can go back through the straits".

Just as they were about to start the descent a thought struck the skipper. " Oh Shit!" he said. "We forgot the bloody air firing". There was a chorus of groans. On every trip they were supposed to do so much air firing. Two pans of ammunition from each of the gunners, a pan from the navigator and a belt from the pilot's fixed Browning. Navigators loathed it because the spent shell collection bags were long since worn out and they were deluged with hot brass cartridge cases. The gunners loathed it because they rarely had any sort of target to fire at and all it meant was that they had to clean the guns again. "It's no good binding fellas," he said. "We'll only get a load of grief from the flight commander. Just fire the fucking things!" He booted the rudders and rolled level over the cloud sheet, while for a long minute the guns hammered away at nothing, hot shell cases cascaded everywhere and the kite filled with cordite fumes.

Suddenly there was a bang audible above the noise of the engines and a yell of alarm on the intercom from the top gunner. Before they could ask what the hell he was shouting about six small flame-centred black clouds appeared about a hundred yards ahead. Given that they had heard the explosion over the engine noise, the salvo that had scared the life out of the gunner had been a damned sight closer.

"We must be over bloody Seattle" said John. "Why are the Yanks firing at us, we're on their side?"

"They don't know that you silly bugger," said the skipper. "All they saw was tracer coming out of the clouds".

"Turn onto two forty degrees and go like buggery," added John and as they dived into the edge of the cloud sheet the gunners reported more salvos of flak bursts exploding above and behind them.

Soon they were in clear sky and over open sea. They continued their descent turning eastward and running in towards the straits at low level. They now knew exactly where they were and shortly afterwards were landing back at Patricia Bay. That evening in the sergeant's mess there was a certain amount of hilarity at John's expense and one or two accusations of line shooting at their claim to have come under fire from the American AA defences. The doubt was eliminated and the laughter redoubled the next day when the papers were delivered. There on the front page in great black banner headlines were the words... **LONE JAP RAIDER OVER SEATTLE**.

Late summer turned to autumn and still their luck held. Nobody got hurt and the worst thing that happened to Allen was the dreaded air firing exercises. They did fighter affiliation exercises, when US air force Curtis Tomahawk fighters made dummy attacks on them while Jack desperately attempted to prevent them getting into a firing position. Their own gunners were given very little practice at air to air firing. Towed targets like practice torpedoes or target ships were in very short supply and the gunners, eager to develop their skills before doing it the hard way, fired at seagulls and basking seals, something which, fifty years afterwards, still pricks Allen's conscience. As it happens they rarely hit much but every time they went through the exercise Allen was deluged with hot shell cases and choked with cordite fumes.

Eventually, in mid December, the course finished and unbelievably in the light of the previous history of the unit they had all survived. Course number twenty three had beaten the odds. The wingco's homily and the ground crew's efforts had been rewarded.

Once more Allen's luck held good. After a few formalities and a brief delay while postings were sorted out, he was given a rail warrant and a leave pass and told to report to the depot at Moncton after Christmas. The crew had a final drink to say goodbye to the gunners Pitt and Parky who, now that the torpedo Hampdens had been largely replaced by two seater Beaufighters, were destined to be posted to Bomber Command, and went through the usual weary chore of clearing camp.

They took the alternative Canadian National route on the journey south but unlike the luminous memory of the northward journey Allen remembers little of it. News of his contemporaries at ANS Hamilton had been filtering back ever since he left and all of it was bad. Old Charlie or Geordie or Chiefie Wallace, a host of familiar names, had already "bought it on ops". Now he was off to join the big league and he wondered how long it might be before his name would be added to the roster of those who had got the chop. Not surprisingly his thoughts were too preoccupied with what might happen in the future to pay as much attention to the scenery on this trip. However, before that he had Christmas in Hamilton with Margaret's family, the prospect of some home leave and who knew, it might not happen. Perhaps he would complete the two contracted tours unscathed. Somebody had to survive and it might well be him.

Four days later he arrived at Margaret's home in Hamilton and was made very welcome. Margaret might not have known the score but her parents did and they knew that this might be Allen's last Christmas. They had also invited his friend Norman Birkett, another Darlington lad who had just completed his training as a bomb aimer. They were determined to give the boys a good time and they succeeded. The Andy Hardy films were very popular in England and as a result both of the boys had a very fair idea what to expect from a middle class North American Christmas. The only difference was that they were enjoying the experience live and in colour and they had a truly magical time. Margaret's house was brightly lit, with a Christmas tree decorated with coloured lights in the front window and the lights reflecting in the clean snow outside. There was a garland on the front door which contrasted vividly with the snow laden front porch. The house was decorated with baubles and garlands and under the tree was a great heap of parcels wrapped in Christmas paper. Curiously enough it was the "bonny paper" that so impressed Allen. At home , paper chains would have been the best that they could manage, with a sprig of mistletoe suspended from the light fitting and any presents might be wrapped in brown paper.

Christmas in Canada was the stuff that dreams were made of and the boys enjoyed every minute of it It is good to know that they did. Allen's next Christmas was spent in an East Prussian prison camp and Normans was only to survive for one more. He was to be killed in March 1945 when his Halifax was shot down over the target.

After Christmas came the hard bit. The long and largely happy adventure was over and Allen had to say goodbye to Margaret and her family. He caught the train from Hamilton to the Moncton depot and after a brief three day stop was on his way again on a train bound for New York and a trooper bound for England. He was not destined to set foot in Canada again for forty years.

11. England Again

The trooper that Allen joined turned out to be the old *Aquitania*, once a luxury Atlantic liner, but by then pressed into service as a fast transport. Launched in 1913, by 1944 she was getting a bit elderly but at 45,000 tons displacement, with her enormous carrying capacity and high speed she could carry several thousand servicemen in relative safety from attack by submarines or surface craft. They may have travelled fairly safely but they certainly travelled in acute discomfort. They were packed in to spaces so congested that they barely had room to stretch their legs. Cattle carried in those conditions would have attracted the immediate attention of the RSPCA, but as these were only servicemen the situation was tolerated without comment. The fact that Allen and his mates were by then all sergeants, senior non-commissioned officers, didn't make much difference to their accommodation. Laden, as usual, with kit and souvenirs they filed up the gangway, through an entry port and then down several companion ladders to a large cabin completely filled with tiers of steel pipe bunks. Their possessions were stowed as best they could but they had little time to settle in before the tannoy demanded their presence on deck.

Once assembled they were issued with life jackets, allocated lifeboat stations and bombarded with information ranging from the horrendous penalties for showing any kind of light at night to the whereabouts of the mess deck on which they would eat their meals. With a high-speed North Atlantic crossing to look forward to, it seemed unlikely that many of them would feel much like eating, but it was nice to know that they could if they wanted to. By that stage in the war no serviceman took food for granted.

After the usual period of chaos, constant tannoyed messages and a great deal of bumping, hooting and manoeuvring by tugs, the ship was backed away from the berth. The hum of the main turbines became more audible, the propeller shafts started to turn and the ship slipped slowly down the Hudson River and out towards the open sea. If you were on deck the wind freshened as the ship gathered speed and you were soon driven below to escape the bitter January cold.

Most of the thousands of troops on board were Americans, either army reinforcements destined for units preparing for the coming invasion of France or replacements for the Eighth Air Force which was currently sustaining heavy casualties on daylight attacks on Germany and the occupied territories. Only about two hundred or so of those on board were from the Commonwealth and of those, less than thirty from the UK.

Once clear of the American coast the *Aquitania* worked up to her full twenty knots and zigzagging to make torpedo attack almost impossible went like a bat out of Hell eastward across the Atlantic. Despite the heaving of the ship and the stuffiness between decks the aircrew on board were relatively untroubled by sea sickness. If you have attempted to perform complicated tasks while your machine copes with turbulence or carries out violent evasive action your body becomes fairly well inured to irregular motion. The food was not good but by war time standards was acceptable and the worst enemy was boredom.

The RAF contingent whiled away many hours in telling tall stories to the Americans. Few, if any of these had been overseas before and most had little idea of where they were going or what they were in for. The war-time cinema had persuaded US cinema audiences that the British were a mixture of resolute but cheerful plebeians and gAllent aristocrats, the latter equipped with upper lips so stiff as to be in continual danger of fracture. The entire population was depicted as being under constant bombardment by the Luftwaffe and alternating between community singing in pubs, toiling in munitions factories and taking refuge in air raid shelters. "Mrs Miniver" was a great screen success in the United States and had done much to convey this curious view of war time Britain.

Allen and his mates made much of their opportunities for trading on the credulities of their fellow passengers. The pastime was known as line shooting and they made the best of their chances. It was harmless enough. The Americans would soon find out for themselves and as they were either destined for the anticipated invasion or were facing the prospect of making daylight bombing raids most of the listeners were unlikely to be of a nervous disposition.

The RAF contingent soon became conscious of the fact that they were being treated with a surprising degree of wariness by their fellow passengers. Putting out a few cautious feelers revealed the fact that they appeared to have a reputation for hair-trigger tempers and a propensity for inflicting grievous bodily harm. This was something of a puzzle at first. They were after all, a fairly amiable lot, young, by and large well brought up and not inclined to attempt even trivial bodily harm. They put out a few rather more direct conversational feelers and discovered that they had all been identified as New Zealanders and hence by definition ferocious fighters. There were some Kiwis among them but they did not wear a distinguishing flash on their uniforms until they reached the UK and anyone in blue was believed to be one. Why they had this man-eating reputation was something of a mystery to Allen. He had been crewed up with two of them and apart from a certain unreasoning impatience with Canadians and a contempt for most training as an undesirable delay on their getting into the war they seemed good natured enough to him.

He also discovered that the RAF had a reputation for stoicism largely based on their habit of getting into their pyjamas in order to go to bed. The US troops had been ordered to remain fully dressed, to wear life jackets at all times and seemed to don steel helmets whenever they were upright. It may in fact have been a reasonable enough precaution given that they were a prime target for U Boats, but four years into the war most British servicemen had learned to make their own assessment of risks and it didn't seem worth the discomfort so far as they were concerned.

Ever curious, Allen tried to explore the vessel but with every space crammed with bodies it was very difficult. It was however possible to find traces of the magnificence that had been a feature of the great transatlantic liners. The companion ladders between decks were more like hotel staircases and both on those and in what had been some of the public rooms, traces of art deco panelling and gilded pillars could be seen.

Congestion made sight seeing next to impossible however and after a while he fell back on the company of his mates, the shop-talk to which most flyers are prone and catching up with the fate of mutual acquaintances. It was a fairly discouraging business. As they fitted together scraps of gossip and fragments of letters from friends and family it was gradually borne in on them that an awful lot of their peers were already missing. Allen realised that the growing uneasiness that had troubled him on his homeward journey across the Rockies was only too well founded. The winter of 1943/44 had been an abysmally bloody one for RAF Bomber Command. 34 Major raids alone had resulted in the loss of 953 crews. In Bomber Command alone this meant that nearly seven thousand trained aircrew had been lost in these machines, as well as those who went down in smaller operations or were killed in aircraft that limped back with battle damage. The Coastal Command strike wings were even more dangerous. Only about eighteen per cent of their crews survived a tour of operations and most of Allens's contemporaries from the operational training unit on Prince Edward Island were long dead, shot down into the sea making low level attacks on heavily defended coastal convoys. The exact statistics were not generally known at the time but the kind of anecdotal evidence that groups of flyers swapped gave soon them a fairly shrewd idea of the situation.

For the first time Allen began to wonder if he wasn't paying too high a price for his love affair with aviation. He could have stayed in a reserved occupation with the railway. With his ATC background he could have joined the RAF in one of the ground trades and served out the war in relative safety. As it was, he seemed to have bought himself a one way ticket to the banks of the Styx with every possibility of making the acquaintance of the ferryman. It was however too late to worry about that, the die was cast and short of admitting that he had lost his nerve there wasn't much that could be done. What he did do was resolve that he would not stick his neck out any further than necessary. No more volunteering for Sergeant Clifford!

As the *Aquitania* drew nearer to Britain the weather moderated and it became possible to spend a bit of time on deck. Coastal Command aircraft were seen with increasing frequency and soon they saw the loom of the land in the distance. The navigators among them had a rough idea of where they were. They had skirted the north of Ireland and were coming down the west coast of Scotland with the Western Isles lying to seaward of them.

Allen noticed that the troops on deck were all wearing webbing equipment and steel helmets. He was standing next to a group of them when one of the GIs told him that they were under orders to dress this way now that they were in a war zone. Not unreasonably, given the ordered precautions and what the cinema had led them to believe, they were looking a bit apprehensive.

"Where are the bombers?" he was asked. "Aren't you scared?" He said that he wasn't scared and in fact was rather looking forward to going home after a year on the other side of the ocean. He explained that bombing was not a constant hazard all over Britain and that there were large areas where German aircraft were rarely seen. Indeed there were some areas where German bombers had never been seen. They took a while to digest this then one of them asked him what the nearby land was. Allen wasn't entirely sure but as it appeared to be about two miles long and surrounded by water he settled for a fairly vague answer. "It's an island" he said.

"Ireland" said his interrogator, he obviously knew about Ireland, but Allen said that Ireland was rather bigger than that. What they were looking at was probably one of the Inner Hebrides.

The seas about them began to become busy with small craft. Escort vessels and mine sweepers abounded and as they rounded the Mull of Kintyre into the Firth of Clyde a stream of tannoyed messages bade them prepare to disembark. Before nightfall they had docked in Gourock and as the warps were secured and the engines stopped Allen realised that he was nearly home. After the usual queuing, shuffling, picking up and dumping kit while uniformed clerks made marks on clipboarded papers, they filed down a gangway and were marched off to the grimy confines of a nearby railway station. There they boarded a troop train and one of the RTO staff told them that they were bound southward for the big aircrew holding depot at RAF Pannal Ash near Harrogate in Yorkshire.

His stay at Pannal Ash was extremely brief. He and Jack Brightwell were given emergency ration cards for a month and told that they could renew them at any local food office if they needed to. They were then sent off on indefinite leave and told that they probably wouldn't be needed for a month or so. They parted at the railway station, Allen en route for Darlington and home, Jack off to see something of Britain while he had the chance. As it happened they never met again.

As his slow local trains jolted their way from Harrogate to York and York to Darlington, Allen gazed about him, almost like a tourist from another country. After a year in North America the scale of the landscape seemed fairly cramped. England also seemed curiously down at heel. Not much by way of maintenance had been done since 1939 as neither the resources nor the labour could be spared.

Buildings were shabby and unpainted. Broken windows had been boarded up or glazed with plasticized wire mesh. Grass and weeds grew untrimmed around the bottoms of fences and everywhere lawns and flower beds had been turned into vegetable patches. The people were equally shabby. They were well nourished enough. Full employment and food rationing ensured that everyone enjoyed a reasonably balanced diet and the average Briton was better fed in 1944 than they had been ten years earlier. Clothing however was showing signs of the need to make do and mend and people looked grubby, grey and tired. Most British factories were working three shifts by this time in the war and the need to man the armed forces had forced most adults into employment. People were just over-stretched. The war had gone on for too long and everyone was getting a little fed up and weary. By the beginning of 1944 war production had passed its peak and almost the entire adult population was involved in some kind of war work.. Even home defence anti-aircraft batteries were crewed by women and the part-time soldiers of the Home Guard, so that able bodied gunners could be drafted into the assault forces gearing up for the coming invasion. Casualties could not be replaced by new drafts and from the summer of 1944 army units would only be kept up to strength by breaking up other formations.

In the smoky dark of a January evening Allen came home. Out of the cavernous red brick approach to the station, along the familiar streets and at last to the even more familiar front door. A cheerful rattle on the knocker, a babble of greeting, a dragging of kit through the blackout curtains and he readied himself for a nice long leave. He would start it gently. A few good long nights in a comfortable bed and a search for a few old mates. A month or two would be very nice.

Very nice it turned out to be although the food, even home cooking, was a bit of a let-down after his stay in Canada. At the beginning of March 1944 however, reality obtruded when he received an urgent telegram, "Return to RAF Pannal Ash for immediate posting". The war had caught up with him again.

On arrival at the holding unit he found himself with a number of other Navigator/Wireless Telegraphists expecting to be posted with their pilots to Coastal Command strike wings. "Sorry chaps," they were told. "There's been a big chop in Bomber Command and they need crews in a hurry; you are going to be needed there". There were, of course, a few protests. They were already trained, crewed up with pilots and didn't fancy flying with strange pilots in an unfamiliar role. "Tough" was the reply. "Bomber Command takes priority here and Butch Harris needs you". They had been trained in daylight low level dead-reckoning over the sea and were not familiar with the techniques of high altitude night bombing. "Fair enough" was the reply to that objection. "You will complete another Operational Training course to gen up on these things. You are all posted to RAF Wing in Buckinghamshire where you will join Number 26 Bomber Command OTU. Here are your railway warrants, on your way"!

12. Learning the Trade

A succession of trains took the rather resigned party of navigators to Linslade, the station for Leighton Buzzard, a small town just over the Buckinghamshire Bedfordshire border. A couple of hooded three ton trucks took them from the station and drove about a mile and a half south westward, through the little village of Wing and to the nearby RAF station which housed 26 OTU. It contained the usual domestic site with its mixture of huts, stores, administrative blocks and the inevitable station cinema. Adjoining this could be seen the big T10 hangars, on the edge of the airfield the distant humps of the bomb dump and, in the distance, the wooden towers of the transmitting station. Dotted around the dispersal areas could be seen the tall fins of what appeared to be a number of twin engined Wellington bombers.

They were greeted by a corporal who organised the usual formalities of joining camp, such vital details as the allocation of billets, the whereabouts of the sergeants' mess, the availability of bicycles, the proper day for the collection and return of laundry and the approved procedures for reporting sick. He also gave them an informal run down on the local bus timetables, the location of the best pubs and the degree of bullshit to which they were likely to be subjected.

That evening in the sergeants' mess they found themselves surrounded by aircrew of all sorts: pilots, gunners, radio operators, bomb aimers and more navigators. Some of these were sitting around in little clusters, obviously crewed up, but some were not. The significance of the latter group did not escape Allen and he examined them with more than usual interest. Somewhere among them were the men that he was finally going to fight alongside and making the right choices was to be literally a matter of life and death.

Bomber OTUs didn't have much spare time at that stage of the war. The heavy casualties of the previous months had to be made up and crews had to be trained as quickly as possible. The fresh intake was pitched, without pause, straight into a hectic instructional schedule. For the first week they were drilled in classrooms and each trade group was given some idea of the new techniques that had been developed in the hard school of operational flying. For the first time Allen was introduced to the notion of electronic navigation and guarded descriptions of such devices as Gee and H2S prepared him for the training to come. He was also warned of the difficulties that would be experienced operating at high altitude in the bleak weather and cold damp atmosphere of north west Europe.

The other aircrew groups were going through a similar experience. The pilots were warned of the problems inherent in the ageing aircraft in which they were going to train. All of the machines had been retired from operational squadrons and after hard usage were well past their sell-by dates. It was a commonplace that OTU casualties sometimes approached those of front-line units and the age and unreliability of the aircraft was a significant factor in this. They were, without doubt, not the sort of machines with which one could take liberties.

The radio operators, bomb aimers and gunners had a slightly easier ride at this stage they would only start working really hard once they started serious airborne training.

After this brief period of classwork they were told that they were to be crewed up the following day. It would be an informal procedure and the word was that once a group had agreed among themselves to form a crew they would be allowed to remain together.

The next morning they were told to report to one of the hangars down on the flight line and arrived to find a mob of aircrew milling around inside. It was composed, not just of those that they had seen the evening before in the mess but included another group of commissioned flyers, mainly Pilot and Flying Officers. Their status didn't seem to help them very much and most of them looked quite as lost as everyone else.

A Squadron Leader standing by a blanket covered table shouted for attention and told them again, that before they started the next stage in their training they would need to be organised as crews. Each crew would, to start with, be made up of a pilot, a navigator, a bomb-aimer, a radio operator and an air-gunner. At that he shouted "right-ho chaps, sort yourselves out!" before spinning on his heel and disappearing into a little flight office at the rear of the hangar. Their was a brief silence followed by a buzz of conversation and a hesitant shuffling about as the group of strangers struggled to size each other up. After a while Allen found himself talking to a pilot, a Flying Officer wearing the dark blue uniform of the Royal Australian Air Force. He remarked that one of his previous crew had been an Australian and his last skipper a Kiwi. The subsequent conversation led around to the fact that this was his second experience of crewing-up, that he had already trained for one operational role and was now re-training for another.

His new acquaintance introduced himself as Les, rank was not generally much of a barrier among aircrew and Australians took less notice of it than most. Les Hough turned out to be an ex-newspaper editor from Adelaide. He was 26, fairly elderly by the standards of the peer group and seemed pretty self assured. Allen, suspecting that this self assurance reflected a reasonable degree of technical competence, took rather a shine to him. Informal but competent, it was a good combination in a pilot. A navigator might have a reasonable life expectancy with such a man. Les probably had much the same idea. Allen's somewhat unorthodox progress meant that he was a good deal more experienced than most new navigators and a pilot might also live longer with him.

Les excused himself on the grounds that he needed to take a leak and a few minutes later Allen found himself in conversation with a very young looking wireless operator who seemed to have an even more youthful gunner in tow. Les returned to find a fairly animated conversation in progress. By now there were very few solitary figures in the hangar, the last to join them being one of them, a tall fair Flying Officer with a bomb-aimers brevet on his tunic. His slightly formal manner and vaguely cut-glass accent seemed to grate a little with Les but by now the rest of the inchoate mass of men with which they had started seemed to have formed themselves into crews of five.

Without appearing to make very many conscious decisions the Hough crew had sorted itself out as instructed.

The introductions were brief and informal. Les and Allen the pilot and navigator were the original pair. Harry Burnside, the wireless-operator, was 22 and came from Catford in east London. The rear gunner, Stan Lee, at 18 was the youngest of the crew and came from Bristol. John Baron, the bomb-aimer was 20, had started to train as a pilot but like many of his trade had failed the course and been re-mustered. As a middle class Londoner with a commission he didn't appear to have a great deal in common with the rest of the crew.

The squadron leader re-appeared and called them to order. "Okay chaps" he said "well done! Now that's over we can go and have lunch. Meet up in the briefing room at two and we'll tell you what's going to happen next". In this rather low key manner commenced a short, eventful and memorable relationship. Not even a marriage could have quite such an effect on your life chances as your choice of operational crew and the business was all over in less than the time that it takes to read a newspaper.

After lunch they all assembled as instructed and were confronted not just by the OC (Flying) but also by a group of specialist instructors. The OC gave them a general briefing. He explained that the purpose of an operational training unit was to take a collection of aircrew specialists and turn them into battleworthy crews ready for squadron service. They could expect a great deal of intensive training both in lecture rooms and in the air but most of their time would be spent in actual flying training. The various chief navigation, signals, gunnery and air bombing officers then said their pieces and all of them hammered away at a common theme, the vital importance of coordinated effort in a good crew. It didn't matter how good the pilot was if the navigator could neither find the target nor return to base. Similarly the best navigator in the world wouldn't be much use if his pilot couldn't fly his courses accurately. Wireless-operators could wreck an operation by failing to pick up diversion messages, bomb-aimers frustrate it by missing the target to which they had so pains-takingly struggled. Flight-engineers could abort an operation by mismanaging fuel or could kill all of them by failing to sort out in-flight mechanical emergencies. Even the most hastily trained crew members, the air gunners, could transform them into names on a war memorial by failing to spot an attacking night-fighter in time. Nobody in a bomber crew could afford to go to sleep on the job.

At this stage the crew broke up for individual briefings but not before arranging to meet in an agreed pub that night. With a crew that mixed commissioned officers and sergeants they couldn't share a common mess and a pub was the best compromise available.[4]

Like a marriage the relationship, for the NCOs at least, involved living together. They shared a room in one of the corrugated iron hutted billets that were so much a feature of air force life. From then on the crew spent a lot of their spare time together as well, and tempered by a shared adventure, the bond became social as well as professional. Les Hough, with the easy sociability of the Australian was largely indifferent to rank. He introduced himself as Les to the crew but like most pilots in Bomber Command he was known simply as Skipper, sometimes abbreviated to Skip. His crew were his crew, and so far as he was concerned nothing was too good for them.

Unfortunately that kind of flexibility did not seem to come easily to John Baron.

In the 1940s class differences were clearly defined in Home Counties England, Baron's accent, formality of manner and apparent lack of rapport with the other NCO members of the crew irritated his pilot from the start. It was to be the only irritant in an otherwise fairly happy collection of working relationships.

OTU proved to be remarkably hard work and Allen, apart from his pilot, probably had the hardest task of all in the Hough crew. Navigation in the wet, cold windy, skies of north west Europe was a very different proposition to finding your way about the clear dry atmosphere of Ontario or at low level over the Pacific. To start with, even if

---

[4] The all-Canadian 6 Group recognised the problems caused when crews who fought together couldn't easily mix socially. They established special aircrew messes where all ranks lived, ate and drank together.

you could see the ground it was almost completely blacked out and in the absence of moonlight it was very difficult to identify your position visually. These factors had rendered most night raids ineffective in the first three years of the war in Europe and it was only the development of a range of electronic aids that significantly improved the situation for Bomber Command crews.

The first few days that the crew spent together were devoted to exercises known as "gropes" in a kind of crude flight simulator. Their mount was a double-decker cubicle set with several others in a darkened hangar. The pilot and Navigator sat at the front of the top deck and the rest of the crew were seated below. Once in position they had to plug themselves into an intercom system and engine noises were fed into the circuit. They were then required to fly their machine to a German target reacting to a series of changes in wind and weather. Their progress was traced on a chart by the mechanical crab similar to those used in Link Trainers. To make the entire business a little more difficult the clock that they were working to was speeded up fifty percent. They did not find it easy. It was dark, noisy, stressful and for all of them except the pilot and navigator, rather boring. All that it needed to inject a note of added realism was intense cold, lack of oxygen and the constant fear of flak, fighter attack or flying into the ground.

After four days of gropes the really dangerous bit of the course started, the business of flying together as a crew, but first they had to be introduced to their aircraft, the Vickers Wellington. The Wellington had been the most effective heavy bomber in RAF service at the beginning of the war and remained the mainstay of Bomber Command until the new four engined heavies came into service. It was a large (Wingspan 86 feet, loaded weight of about fifteen tons and standing some seventeen feet from the ground at the top of the fin) twin engined monoplane powered by a pair of 1,400 horse power Bristol Hercules radial engines. It sported power operated nose and tail turrets each armed with a pair of belt fed 0.303 Browning machine guns and could carry a bomb load of some two tons. Its fairly conventional appearance masked a highly unusual structure. It had been designed by Barnes Wallis, a talented and original engineer, and utilised the principal of geodesy to produce a light but strong structure. Essentially the machine was a skeleton of interlaced curves of tubing secured at every join and covered with fabric. This geodetic framework was capable of taking a good deal of battle damage before it failed although it was vulnerable at places where openings had to be made in the structure or where attachments were fitted. The high aspect ratio wings, so called because the width or chord of the wing was very narrow in proportion to the span, were also very thin, indeed far too thin to contain fuel tanks. As a consequence, with the exception of a couple of small reserve tanks in each engine nacelle, they were located in the fuselage which meant that the Wellington was one aircraft in which it was genuinely not really safe to smoke. The wings in fact somewhat belied the Wellington's reputation for extreme robustness, as it was not too difficult to break them during violent evasive action.

Incidentally almost nobody in the air force referred to the type as the Wellington. It was invariably known as the 'Wimpey' in tribute to a character in the Daily Mirror's popular "Popeye" strip cartoon, a serial hamburger eater called J Wellington Wimpey.

The introduction took a little while. Each crew member was shown his station by an appropriate instructor and they were encouraged to find their way about the fuselage. It was only on the inside that the unorthodoxy of the design became really apparent. In some ways it was like going back in time to the days of wood and fabric biplanes. The main structure resembled a vast loosely woven basket with only a frail membrane of doped fabric separating the crew from the outside atmosphere. A narrow catwalk enabled them to walk along it and it was flanked by big self sealing fuel tanks. The double skins of these tanks were separated by a layer of uncured rubber and if they were holed by bullets or shell fragments the rubber would react, swell when mixed with petrol and, theoretically at least, seal off the leak. That is of course, if the hole was reasonably small and the fuel didn't ignite in the first place.

There were panels of clear plastic Cellon windows towards the rear of the fuselage which enabled them both to see out and al so to admire the geodetic framework from the outside as well. There were also a few additional holes where clumsy crew members had stumbled and put their feet or hands through the fabric as well as a range of obvious patches where such accidental damage had been repaired.

Despite this the Wimpey seemed a nice solid aircraft. The undercarriage was short and hence it sat low and square on the ground. Like most aircraft of the day it was a tail-dragger and hence the base of the rear turret glazing wasn't much above waist height revealing a functional looking interior. The crew compartment was roomy and communication between members was easy, although the main spar protruding a foot or more from the floor between the wings, was something of a hazard. The astrodome was large enough and perched midway along the fuselage promised to be effective both as a navigation and a fire-control position. The wireless operator and navigator had reasonably adequate space and the only real problem was the cold and draughty nature of the interior and the absence of effective heating. With a fabric covered fuselage it was also extremely noisy but that was true of almost all military aircraft of the period.

The first task was to ensure that the pilot could actually fly the aircraft. Les, like most bomber pilots, had trained on twin engined Airspeed Oxfords. The Wellington was twice the size and more than three times the weight and power of the Oxford. For a newly trained pilot with very limited experience it must have been a fairly intimidating prospect. It was also going to be fairly thought-provoking for the rest of the crew, conscious of the fact that their lives were quite literally in his hands.

There was, happily, one major difference between a pilot converting onto the Wellington and one converting onto the Hampden. The Wellington had been designed for two pilot operation and a screened instructor would be sitting at the controls in the right hand seat until Les was judged to be competent on type.

The next thing that they all did when left alone for a couple of hours was to find an aircraft that had been parked awaiting maintenance and crawl all over it. Les spent a good deal of time just sitting in the left hand seat judging the position and the appearance of the ground in take off and landing attitude. He then sat with the pilot's notes on his lap and tried to familiarise himself with the controls and cockpit interior. The others tried out their crew stations and practiced moving about within the confines of the fuselage. They knew that it would be a great deal more difficult when the aircraft was pitching and rolling and everything was blacked out.

That night, talking shop in the pub, the main topic of conversation was their first impressions of the Wimpey. They were in general favourable, although in reality they had very little experience on which to base that judgement. With the benefit of hindsight it was probably the fact that it was a real bomber and not long out of operational service that impressed them as much as anything.

The following day the weather was bad and they spent their time variously on the gunnery range, in the Link trainer, the bombing tutor or a variety of training classes. It was only on the day after that, they were briefed for their first familiarisation flight.

They drew parachutes and Mae Wests from the safety equipment store before a truck took them down to the flight line. They found the correct dispersal pan, a frying pan shaped concrete pad connected to the main taxiway by its handle, and waited apprehensively. It was to be a longish wait as it was mid morning before the machine that stood there was declared serviceable. As they waited they spent a good deal of time wandering around it, while various technicians worked on the engine, airframe and various bits of auxiliary equipment. To Allen's fairly untutored eye, apart from a generally shabby and rather weathered appearance and a tendency to drip a bit of oil, it looked perfectly normal. Les however was not going to take anything for granted, survival started there! With the crew at his heels, he inspected the outside methodically. He checked the tyres for wear and signs of creep(A tendency for the tyre to slide around the inner tube until the join with the valve failed). He looked at the brake lines for evidence of hydraulic leaks and the oleo legs for signs of leaking seals. He peered into the flap tracks, as well as any visible control hinges and linkages. He looked at the fabric covering, and at the condition of the perspex around the cockpit and the turrets, before turning back to the big cowled radial engines. All he could do about these was look for major oil or petrol leaks.

Soon after the NAAFI van had visited with its welcome load of tea and wads a small Hillman van drew up. One of the staff instructors climbed out told them to board the Wimpey while he and Les did the walkabout, the pre-flight inspection. The walk-about did not take long. The training schedule was tight and Les soon satisfied his mentor that he had already given the machine a thorough, if superficial, check.

By now a group of attendant ground crew had appeared and connected up a trolley-acc, a wheeled trolley carrying a bank of big lead-acid batteries and intended to take the load off the aircraft's internal power unit when starting. Meanwhile Les and his instructor were working through the start-up drill. Minutes later one of the fitters elevated a thumb, the starter motor ground noisily, the big three bladed propeller on the starboard engine swung over ponderously and with clouds of smoke, belching flames from the exhaust stubs and a great deal of noise, the cylinders began to fire and after a period of banging and rough running settled down to a steady roar. The trolley-acc was then disconnected, as once the starboard engine was started the generator was running and the internal batteries could cope with any subsequent loads. Next the port engine started with a similar degree of sound and fury and both engines were run up, turning over at a speed high enough to ensure that the plugs didn't oil up and the oil temperature brought up to operating level. The running up procedure took a long time. The instructor was showing Les how to manage the throttles, boost and pitch controls as well as a quick refresher course on the use of the flying control trim tabs.

The intercom crackled "pilot to radio operator. Get up into the astrodome Harry and be ready to give the ops caravan a flashing green when we're ready to taxi".

A few seconds later a flashing green from the caravan started their taxi run to the threshold. They checked at the halt point to do their power checks and then, on receipt of a steady green they swung onto the runway, opened the throttles and with a bellow of power from the twin Hercules were climbing away to start the exercise. The rest of the crew could only follow the progress on the intercom as Les responded to the instructors prompting. Without a warload the elderly Wellington climbed well and once it reached a safe height the flaps were retracted by stages and Les was able to try a few turns. Soon they were joining circuit again and as they dumped full flap at about three hundred feet on finals the Wimpey seemed to slow perceptibly. Les confided afterwards that he had been surprised by the trim change as the flaps went down. Despite the fact that he had been warned of the need to apply forward control pressure he hadn't anticipated the gorilla like strength that it would actually require. However the Wimpey was stable enough on the approach and they wheeled onto the ground and settled with a nice solid thump. They did a few more circuits and bumps before climbing away to do some steep turns at a safe altitude before trying a stall. The stall was impressive. The big aircraft became curiously quiet as the power was throttled right back but in the rear crew positions it was difficult to notice the beginning of the nose high attitude that they assumed. When it did become apparent it was followed shortly by a sickening lurch and a crescendo of noise as the nose dropped and the power was applied to assist the recovery.

By now an hour or so had elapsed and it was time to go back and let another crew have a go. One more circuit culminated in the aircraft braking to a halt and taxiing back to the dispersal. The engines were given a burst of throttle to prevent the plugs oiling and then the revs were progressively reduced until the mixture was reduced to full lean. Once the absence of fuel caused them to cease firing the magnetos were cut and they were switched off. The big props slowed and then stopped. The crew cleared the exit first while Les listened to what his instructor had to say and after a few minutes he dropped out of the hatch and joined them. It was a cold day but they noticed he was in a lather of sweat. First flights on type can be a fairly tense business.

Humping their gear and parachute packs they made their way back to the crew room. It had been curiously exhausting and they all had a good deal to think about. If it was like that simply beginning a type conversion what was it going to be like on ops? Les went off to his room clutching a copy of the pilots notes for the Wellington having first arranged to meet up in the pub again that night. John Baron ambled off in the direction of the bombing section while Allen, Harry Burnside and Stan headed off for the sergeants mess and tea.

From then on they spent a great deal of time in the air, the first milestone being reached when the screened pilot got out and Les flew the aircraft without that reassuring presence beside him. He only had about four hours on type before this happened and from then on, although he would fly with an instructor for regular checks, when learning to operate in the dark, or for learning the basics of evasive action, he was indisputably in charge of the crew.

From the very beginning Allen had to earn his corn. The Spring skies were more often than not overcast and it was always painfully easy to lose track of your position and have the very greatest of difficulty in finding the way back to base. The drill was simple and demanding. Once the machine was airborne he tried to fix his position every six minutes and maintain a running plot. Harry was able to help quite a bit in British airspace by seeking cross bearings from radio direction finding stations but Allen was uncomfortably well aware that this would not be possible on operations. The Luftwaffe signals organisation were hardly likely to cooperate with fixes, UK stations were out of range and any transmission could be used to home fighters onto the bomber stream. Strict radio silence was maintained over enemy territory with only the briefest of essential transmissions allowed. For the time being he simply had to learn to cope with dead-reckoning and astro navigation.

At first, Allen was largely on his own with the odd radio bearing from Harry Burnside and John Baron, equipped with a topographical map, to assist him. Initially, when they were only flying locally and in daylight, he found navigation hard enough. Once they started doing cross countries it became very hard indeed, but fortunately two things came to his aid. First his longer than usual apprenticeship paid off and second he was initiated into the mysteries of GEE. This new navigational aid relied upon three linked transmitting stations laying down an invisible grid of electronic signals. These were shown as oscilloscope traces which could be read off and translated into a position on a special chart. Although by 1944 it was widely jammed by Luftwaffe signals stations over occupied Europe it was highly effective over Britain. High level navigation never became easy, especially in the dark, but as in spite of everything he usually managed to achieve good enough fixes both to find their way back to base and present a reasonably acceptable plot to his navigation leader.

Once the Skipper was cleared for solo flying in daylight they embarked on an intensive programme of circuits and bumps, usually this meant circuits in which the machine made a final approach and once safely rolling on the runway the throttles would be opened and an overshoot initiated. This was not a good idea when flying a clapped out Mark X Wimpey. An overshoot could all too easily result in the big machine stalling as the engines failed to cope with the drag from the flaps, or dropping like a brick if the flaps were retracted too quickly. As a result they would land off each approach, taxi round to the threshold and initiate another take-off. Once he had four or five hours of circuit bashing under his belt they advanced to the next phase and started the serious business of bombing training in cold, wet, cloudy, European conditions.

To start with they made endless runs over Lincoln Cathedral, using the tower as an aiming marker for a simulated attack. They also dropped nine pound practice bombs on ranges in the Wash and John spent a good deal of time in a simulated bombing tutor on the ground. Most bombing runs came at the end of a long cross country exercise and the crew hours were steadily building up. They were also introduced to the stomach churning business of evasive flying. A staff instructor sat in the right hand seat and showed Les first how to carry out an effective banking search and then how to fly the famous Bomber Command corkscrew manoeuvre.

The banking search wasn't too bad. It was an attempt to cope with the fact that RAF bombers of the period were effectively blind to attacks from below. The retractable under-fuselage dustbin turrets of the early Wellingtons had proved impractical. They had caused so much drag as to seriously affect the performance of the aircraft and they were soon removed. Bomber Command then, in its wisdom, abandoned the idea of a lower defensive position and with it sacrificed the ability to scan the sky below and behind. The best that they could do was to develop a tactic in which the pilot would put the aircraft into a steep left and right bank every so often, or when called to by the gunners, and give them and the fire controller a chance to look out below. It was a fairly inadequate response and most of the bombers shot down by night fighters were attacked from below and never saw their attacker until the shells started hitting their aircraft.

The corkscrew was a very different matter. In it the pilot would almost bunt the machine into a steep diving turn through about five hundred feet which would be reversed and turned into a steep climbing turn of five hundred feet in the opposite direction. If this manoeuvre was carried out with sufficient violence a fighter would be presented with almost impossible deflection shots and in the dark would almost certainly overshoot as the bomber lost speed in the climb. It would also mean that every loose article in the evading aircraft was thrown all over the place and weak stomached members of the crew would probably throw up. In fact the manoeuvre as demonstrated in the Wimpey was fairly restrained. Those high aspect ratio wings had proved to be pretty fragile and instructors were well aware of the fact. It was not unknown to pull them off in an over enthusiastic corkscrew and no crew member was likely to survive that. Baling out of a violently spinning bare fuselage was impossible. The only real chance of getting away with it was to be thrown clear as the structure broke up. It was not an attractive prospect and as a consequence demonstrations were conducted with more than usual care. Later on, in other types, things would be different!

Once introduced to basic evasive action the next stage was to try it in daylight with fighters from nearby bases. The turrets were equipped with camera guns and after every exercise the cine films from both attacker and attacked were evaluated. It was not a cheering business. A corkscrewing bomber, even one using the rather restrained technique practised in the Wimpey, did not offer a very steady gun platform and the gunners found it very difficult to hold a fighter in their sights. It was also slightly unnerving to notice that they usually failed to spot attacking aircraft until they had come alarmingly close. They simply hadn't been flying long enough to have learned the art of seeing in the air. Denied the usual sight references they were still focussing their eyes on a point about fifty yards ahead of them.

In contrast the camera guns of the fighters were producing pictures distressingly full of close-up pictures of vulnerable bits of Wellingtons. They consoled themselves with the thought that it would all be different once they were operating under cover of darkness but they were whistling in the dark as well as looking forward to operating in it.

The sea change in Allen's thinking that had happened towards the end of his time in Canada, the realisation that this was going to be a fairly bloody business, became more and ingrained. The weather in the early months of 1944 was bad but in spite of the appalling conditions they flew if the cloud base was high enough for them to get off the ground. More often than not the skipper was on instruments from a couple of hundred feet above the runway. Allen was navigating on a combination of GEE, dead-reckoning and radio bearings and getting home involved hair raising descents into cloud that broke terrifyingly close to the ground. The injunction to take care with which they had been greeted when they went to Patricia Bay was a long time ago. It began to dawn on all of them that they were urgently needed to sustain the bomber offensive and that they had become expendable in the process. It was not a warming thought!

At the same time the quality of life had become a great deal less enjoyable than it had been in Canada. Britain in 1944 was a fairly bleak place in which to live. Bad weather, blackout, rationing and eternal shortages were taken for granted. There was enough food but the diet was monotonous. Fats like butter and cheese, as well as meat and sugar were strictly rationed. Shell eggs were a luxury, the staple alternative being the reconstituted powdered variety. There was no imported fruit, and even beer was in short supply. What was worse with sugar rationing and the need to conserve grain the brew that could be had was weak and fairly tasteless. Spirits were virtually unobtainable and the only readily available mood altering drug was nicotine. Not surprisingly most servicemen smoked like chimneys, a habit that in later life the survivors found remarkably difficult to kick.

After the good times and easy living of Canada it was a depressing sequel and the sense that they were on a rapidly moving conveyor belt taking them towards the probability of early and unpleasant death was all-pervasive. At one level their life was fraught with danger and they lived on surges of fear-induced adrenalin but paradoxically, boredom was also a problem.

Flying was still exciting partly because it was so hazardous. It wasn't all flying however, the weather was bloody awful, the ageing Wimpeys were frequently unserviceable and neither the Link trainer for the skipper nor the various ground tutors could fill all of the available time. Once the urgent pressure of training was relaxed there was time to think and too much imaginative reflection was simply terrifying. What they needed was diversion, fun, and the main problem with spare time was finding something to do with it. The local girls were not keen on investing their hopes in highly transient aircrews and Wing was not well situated for much in the way of entertainment.

The problem of entertainment was not peculiar to OTU trainees. In an age before television was more than an interesting curiosity there was, at the best of times, a serious dearth of accessible popular amusement. For most young people in Britain entertainment meant the cinema, the pub, dancing and the "wireless".

The cinema was in its heyday and most people with the necessary time and money would go to "the pictures" to see a film once or twice a week. Programmes, usually changed twice a week, were usually made up of a supporting B picture, commonly of pretty abysmal quality, a newsreel, a trailer for the next programme and the main feature. Then, as now, Hollywood dominated and British films were fairly few and far between. The British film industry was however seen by government as an essential means of boosting public morale. Such war films as *In Which We Serve, The Way Ahead, Target For Tonight* or *The First of the Few* were overt propaganda for the armed forces. Marginally more subtly, movies like *This Happy Breed, Demi-Paradise* or *Henry V* were vehicles for a notion of Britishness intended to encourage national solidity. Some of them were very good but escapism was infinitely more popular and American pictures usually attracted the most enthusiastic audiences.

Allen's crew, like almost everyone else on camp, saw almost every show at the station cinema as well as most of those showing in Leighton Buzzard. They would queue outside and once admitted would pick up the thread of the film wherever it happened to be. Cinemas of the time operated on a basis of continuous performances, during which films would be projected in sequence from opening to closing times with only minimal breaks in between features.

Pubs were another escape, they were great social centres and for a mixed officer NCO group like the Hough crew the pub was the only available substitute for a shared mess. Given the permanent shortage of beer it was the companionship not the booze that attracted them. For more serious drinking, mess parties were far more significant and they would be held a couple of times a week on average. Individuals would contribute ten shillings or a pound a head and drink their way steadily through the kitty as the evening wore on.

Dancing, although popular with the local civilians and with the permanent staff, did not feature much in the lives of the OTU crews. By definition a dance required a girl, and neither the station Waafs nor the local girls were really very interested in such transients. They were only there for a very short while, had little spare time and, an unspoken sub-text, were so short-lived that it was not a good idea to form a relationship with them. By that stage in the war the glamour of associating with flyers had largely worn off. All that remained was the knowledge that their lives were too ephemeral to make them much of a bet as partners.

Radio, the wireless, ran the cinema a close second as a source of fun, drama and all kinds of music. It was, if anything, even more popular than the cinema and much more accessible. Most families had a radio. They were not the small transistor models with which we are now familiar but usually big, solid, wooden-cased instruments with a bank of thermionic valves and a power demand that could only be accommodated by mains input or a big rechargeable lead acid battery. NAAFI canteens would have them, as would the various mess ante-rooms and a fair number of individual billets. Allen still had his little portable and he and the other NCOs in the crew would spend much of their time in their billet listening to it. The BBC enjoyed a virtual monopoly, now that the continental based commercial stations like Radio Luxembourg were closed down or broadcasting Nazi propaganda, with only the American Forces Network as a serious competitor.

There were lots of music programmes ranging from classical concerts to swing as well as a number of comedy shows. Some of these were essentially radio versions of stage variety theatre, a mixture of instrumental numbers, vocalists, comedy sketches and musical turns of one kind and another. The quality was pretty variable but by any reasonable standards pretty mediocre. Workers Playtime was a fair example of the genre, usually broadcast from a munitions factory canteen somewhere in Britain and usually featuring such gems as Ronny Ronalde whistling "In a Monastery Garden", Harry Hemsley with his imaginary family, Elsie and Doris Waters as a garrulous pair called Gert and Daisy and Ivy Benson's all girls band.

There was also an innovative streak of surreal comedy beginning to emerge in shows like Band Wagon in which Arthur Askey and Richard Horne broadcast from an imaginary flat on the roof of Broadcasting House or Itma , It's That Man Again, in which a cast led by a Liverpudlian comedian called Tommy Handley created a fantasy world populated by a range of lunatic characters like Mrs. Mopp the charlady, the bibulous Colonel Chinstrap and Funf the spy. Almost everybody listened to these and the catchphrases that they created entered into the language. Lines like "Can I do yer now sir? " or "Don't forget the diver" will still raise a nostalgic smile from most who remember the period.

The American influence was beginning to become fairly pervasive as well. Popular music was not something that the BBC did very well and the American Forces Network opened up a new world to the British public. The continuity announcer-cum-compere, sergeant Roy Mckinley, became a friendly and familiar voice to a generation of listeners to AFN. He introduced the music of the big swing bands like Tommy Dorsey and "Captain Glen Miller with the Band of The American Expeditionary Force". Less commonly he offered jazz and always a variety of recorded hits made popular by American radio and Hollywood screen musicals.

To all practical purposes live theatre was not available much outside London and the major cities. The ENSA network did bring concert parties to service stations but they were fairly rare and tended to concentrate on isolated units rather than those close to centres of population. The permanent staff of camps, who led a fairly safe but mind-bendingly boring existence, did organise dances, concerts and amateur shows but the speed with which the aircrews moved through the system effectively isolated them, and Allen has no recollection of ever ever attending any such thing. Once on the treadmill new crews passed between the pub, the cinema, the mess party and all too often oblivion, without making much contact with anything outside their private world.

In that private world the pace of training continued to quicken. The Hough crew flew more and more daytime cross-countries, made more and more dummy bombing attacks and became steadily more proficient. What is more, Allen's luck continued to hold. The grisly reputation of the OTUs seemed in temporary abeyance and nobody on the course was killed. There were a few close calls when aircraft wandered into balloon barrage areas or were shot at by gun defences. Several of them had narrow squeaks when they nearly flew into high ground or missed approaches in bad weather and just scraped in below the undercast before their fuel ran out. One of them even crashed on landing when the pilot told the bomb-aimer, who was sitting in the right hand seat, to "whip them up". He meant the flaps but the bomb-aimer construed this as the wheels and retracted the undercarriage as the Wimpey touched down at about ninety knots. This was a piece of sloppy RT procedure that should have killed them as the aircraft broke up and the tanks ruptured in a gout of flame. Happily, although the machine was a write off, the structure remained more or less intact and the shaken crew all walked away from the crash.

By now they had begun the process of learning to operate by night and once more the crew sat stolidly at their stations while Les, again flanked by an instructor, learned how to handle the big machine in the dark. First an hours handling, then a couple of hours of circuits before being sent off solo. Allen didn't have much chance to be nervous himself, he was too busy trying to plot their position and ensure that they could find their way back to the circuit. When Les did first fly the brute alone and in the dark he was too preoccupied to be even mildly apprehensive.

By the middle of April the first phase of the OTU course was over. Les was judged fully competent by day and by night, Allen's navigation was up to scratch, their bombing averages were satisfactory, there had been no serious problems with radio procedures and Stan's gunnery seemed to satisfy the gunnery leader. The air force was not generous with rewards, they were given a forty eight hour pass and told that they would be moving on to Halfpenny Green an airfield located about halfway between Stourbridge and Bridgnorth on the Shropshire Staffordshire border.

13. Nickels and a Gladiator

The journey from Wing was unusually straightforward. Like almost every posting in those days the trip was made by rail and they were able to pick up a train from Linslade to Birmingham and then a local service to Stourbridge, where they expected to find the familiar truck waiting for them. As the train headed westward from Birmingham on the second leg of their journey the first impression was not a good one. Even Allen, reared as he was in Darlington, found the landscape more than usually dreary. Les Hough, raised in the sunny suburbs of Adelaide, was rather more uncomplimentary. "Can't understand why the bloody Gerries wanted to invade this. I'd pay to bloody well stay away from it". One smoky, depressing little town seemed to merge into another and the pall of industrial smoke combined with a fine drizzle and a louring sky to limit their range of vision to a few hundred yards. The train was steam hauled and the smoke and cinders belching out from the locomotive funnel blended with the rain and swept along the carriage windows like dirty net curtains.

As they came closer to Stourbridge however the landscape began to open out into cultivated fields and through the gathering dusk they saw that they were running into a pleasant enough little town. They didn't have time to explore because the usual canvas covered three tonner was already waiting in the station forecourt and they hastily threw their kit over the tailgate and scrambled after it. The limited vision available out of the back of the truck showed that they were driving through tree lined country lanes punctuated by darkened villages. Once or twice they caught brief glimpses of pub doorways briefly illuminated by lifted blackout curtains and saw little knots of pedestrians gathered by shops and houses.

Eventually the truck slowed to a stop by a red and white painted knife-rest barrier.

They could see what looked like a perimeter fence and the white outlined silhouette of a guardroom. There was a brief sound of voices, the truck ground into gear again and made a further stop outside a hutted admin. building. They had arrived at Royal Air Force Station Halfpenny Green for the penultimate stage of their operational training.

A white-capped station policeman directed them to their temporary quarters. Allen, Harry Burnside and Stan made their way to a transit billet where they dumped their kit. They would have something a bit more permanent allocated when they completed their arrival procedure in the morning. Les Hough and John Baron had headed off for the officers mess and another temporary billet. They would eat and have a few beers in their respective messes that evening. It would give them a chance to tune in to the station grape-vine and find out what sort of a place they had come to.

The station had one major peculiarity; the perimeter fence didn't extend much beyond the guardroom. The main road ran directly across the airfield and hence in addition to the usual obstacles crews in circuit had to look out for cars, bikes and large red Midland buses crossing the runway. Apart from that it was the sort of place that they had grown used to. Aircraft parked at dispersals, big T10 maintenance hangars, and the usual gunnery butts, bomb dumps, fuel stores, classrooms, parachute section and motor transport yard. Across on the domestic site were mess buildings, a station cinema, station headquarters, a parade ground and still more hutted billets. The billets were much of a muchness for all of the aircrews. They were either hump-backed Nissen huts or shed-like wooden structures all heated by small cast iron stoves usually fuelled with coke. The stoves reeked of fumes, there was never enough coke but wherever you moved in the billet you seemed to find enough of the stuff to crunch under your shoes or lodge in your socks.

In peace-time and decent weather Halfpenny Green could have been rather pleasant. It lay on the fringes of the Welsh Marches and its quaint name would have been reflected by the bucolic charm of the locality. Allen was not aware of much in the way of charm. In April 1944, desperately trying to replenish the casualties suffered during the Battle of Berlin, the OTU was working flat out. With only the briefest of pauses for the formalities of joining the station they were pitched headlong into an intensive flying programme.

The crew flew whenever an aircraft was serviceable and the weather clear enough to leave the ground. Cross-country flying, mainly by night, was the principal task and Allen was under constant pressure to sharpen up on his GEE procedure to the point where he would be able to fix his position every three minutes. The importance of constantly establishing drift was hammered home and he was drilled in the procedure of passing back wind reports which might, on operations, be averaged and re-broadcast to the bomber stream. Constantly harassed by radar-directed flak and night fighters the only way that the night bombers could survive was by flying accurately in tight streams which would punch through the defences in a concentrated mass. Precise navigation was not only a means of finding targets, it was also the principal way by which the defences could be prevented from giving their undivided attention to individual aircraft. Bombers survived in the same way that zebra did when attacked by lions. The stream kept together and the main force escaped while the defences were occupied picking off cripples or stragglers. It was not a cheering metaphor and Allen for one was not cheered. It did however give a powerful incentive to learn as much as possible at OTU. The mark ten Wellingtons that they flew may have been fairly clapped but they were capable of being operated at around eighteen thousand feet. The Hough crew were being initiated into the realities of operating in very high wind velocities and temperatures in which carburettors could be choked and wings and control surfaces so encumbered with ice that the aircraft lost height uncontrollably. The altitude also required the crew to breathe oxygen from on-board supplies in order to remain reasonably alert. It was not a sophisticated system and all of them suffered from some degree of anoxia much of the time. The cold and lack of oxygen made even the simplest of tasks exhausting and the need to maintain a fast and accurate navigational plot was made significantly more difficult.

Quite how difficult these conditions could make things was emphasised on what should have been a relatively easy daylight cross country. They had been briefed for an early morning take off from Halfpenny Green, a climb out on a north westerly heading through the Cheshire Gap which would avoid high ground before they reached a safe altitude, and a high level run to Chicken Rock in the Irish sea , south of the Calf of Man. It was not a good day. The wind strengthened and veered unpredictably with altitude and thick cloud prevented them from establishing a clear ground fix. To add to Allen's difficulties GEE was playing up, the pulses looked all wrong, and he was thrown back largely on dead reckoning. Les, the skipper, was not happy either. At their briefed altitude of 18,000 feet they were still running in and out of cloud and they were beginning to experience trouble with icing. Loud thumps on the fuselage indicated that ice was breaking away from the propellers and leading edges of the wings and impacting on the frail fabric covering. Rising engine temperatures also showed that the lubricating oil in the Hercules engines was coring, forming a thickened mass in the centre of the coolers and not circulating properly.

While Allen battled to persuade GEE to provide some useful information and Les Hough wrestled with the throttles and pitch controls the rest of the crew stared out into the murk and cursed the cold. Allen knew that they were approaching their turning point but below lay virtually unbroken cloud and John Baron in the bomb aimers position could see neither land nor sea.

Suddenly there was a shout from Stan in the rear turret. "Here Chiefie, there's a funny looking kite with two wings climbing towards us. What is it?" Stan did not distinguish himself here. First, he should have addressed his warning to the skipper and prefixed it with an instruction to take some sort of action. Things happened quickly in the air and hesitation frequently ended in disaster. In a perfect world he should have perhaps have known what the strange machine was but in 1944 biplane fighters had vanished from the recognition manuals and only enthusiasts could reasonably be expected to recognise them. It was as a consequence a forgivable lapse. It was however not one to be repeated. His principal role was to look out, identify threats, and call for a fast evasive manoeuvre. A gunner with an inadequate knowledge of aircraft recognition was a fairly doubtful asset. The puny ·303 guns in most RAF turrets were outranged and outweighed by Luftwaffe fighter weapons. The primary escape mechanism for night bombers was not defensive fire but evasion and this needed to start as soon as a potential threat was spotted. It did not do to wait and hold a conference before doing something.

Allen did not hang about. He was into the astrodome in a second. From this position he had a clear look at the mysterious aircraft, which was by now above them, slightly behind and out to the port beam. It was a single engined biplane fighter. He dismissed the idea of an Italian CR42. Italy was basically out of the war and there was no possibility of a lone Fascist operating over the Irish Sea. "Irish Sea", the penny dropped. "It's an Irish Air Corps Gladiator" he said "But I think they're neutral". As he said that the Gladiator swung into a classical curve of pursuit and he saw a couple of winking lights flickering from the port wing and engine cowling. He had seen enough films to know what that meant even without the added clue provided by the tracer ammunition. A surprised sounding Stan said it for him. "The bloody thing's firing at us, what shall I do? Bloody well fire back" yelled the irate skipper. Stan's guns hammered briefly and then stopped. They were iced up, only one had fired at all and then it too had jammed. The Gladiator disappeared into the cloud beneath them and was seen no more. Fortunately it had opened fire when it was way out of range and only two of its four guns appeared to have been working.

Another shout from John Baron drew Allen's attention to a hole in the cloud through which a coastline was visible. They had drastically overshot their turning point and were over the Irish Free State. Allen could see Dublin Bay, Howth and Kingstown, Or Dun Laoghaire as it is now known. He knew exactly where he was and giving the skipper a new course he took them back towards the English mainland. It was not an easy return journey. Cloudbase was at less than a thousand feet and they had to cross the coast low down and skirt the balloons and gun defences of Liverpool, while avoiding the high ground of Wales and the Peak District to the north and south of them. Once within range of the airfield beam approach beacon they were able to home in and there was an audible "Thank Christ" from someone on the intercom when the mainwheels thumped onto the runway. It was a weary and chastened crew that climbed out of the Wimpey and made their way back to the flight office for de-briefing.

When they were not flying there was a good deal of ground training. John would work out on a simulated bombing tutor, Allen was introduced to the new H2S ground surveillance radar, Harry Burnside was initiated into the mysteries of noise jamming on the German fighter control frequencies while the skipper spent hours under the hood of a Link blind flying trainer. Stan alternated between a skeet-shooting range, a turret tutor and much needed aircraft recognition lectures. Incidentally Allen's status had changed shortly after their arrival at Halfpenny Green. He had been so long training in Canada and had already completed a five month signals course, that he had done enough time as a sergeant to be eligible for the next step. He was therefore able to fix a brass crown above his stripes and as a flight sergeant, now answered to the traditional title of Chiefie.

It was also at about this time he was told that if he did well on the course he could be posted directly to the Pathfinders. The thought did not thrill him. Pathfinders did a first tour of forty five operations and as the chances of completing the standard thirty were not good this didn't seem the best of ideas. He decided that an adequate competence would serve them all best. He did not strive to draw attention to himself, thinking that with a bit of luck the crew would avoid having to make any awkward choices.

The pace of the course intensified and their training gained an uncomfortable new realism when they were briefed for their first Nickel. Nickel was originally the code word for a leaflet raid but by this stage in the war had become a general term for any sort of relatively minor warlike activity on which crews in their final stages of training might be despatched. When Allen saw his crew posted on the order of battle his stomach churned uneasily. Now he was about to go on an operation during which serious attempts to kill him were likely to be made.

The role allotted to the Hough crew was simple enough. They were to form part of a diversionary force that would head out towards Terschelling in the Frisian Islands. They would be dropping four-penny bundles of "window", two thousand aluminium foil strips some 30 cm. long by 1.5 cm wide, held together by an elastic band. Once the band was removed and the bundle released into the slipstream it formed a cloud of foil which reflected a signal which looked like that made by a heavy bomber.

This very simple strategem would present the German night fighter controllers with a serious problem. Ten Wellingtons dropping window would present a radar signal which looked like a very significant force of heavies. As they headed in towards the Dutch coast it was possible that this force might be headed towards the North Sea ports of Bremen, Hamburg or Wilhelmshaven or they might turn southwards towards the Ruhr valley. They might even continue on an easterly heading and wind up attacking Berlin. In any case they would be perceived as a significant threat and would distract attention from the Main force attack which would be headed elsewhere.

The obverse side of creating such a problem for the Luftwaffe was that the imaginary threat could attract an only too real response. Flak ships off the Dutch coast commonly mounted radar directed 88mm. guns which could throw an eighteen pound shell up to 20,000 feet and some of the bigger vessels carried 105mm guns that could reach nearly ten thousand feet higher than that. Radar equipped night fighters from coastal airfields could range well out into the North Sea to intercept incoming raiders. As a result the more successful the spoof, the more seriously would the Germans take the threat.

At the specialists briefing that afternoon the crew gave the matter their full attention. They all knew that this time it was, as the Americans say, for real. They might be turning back at the enemy coast but plenty of things could happen to them in spite of that.

At his navigation briefing Allen copied the course details onto his pad before inking the necessary lines onto his chart. He repeated the exercise on the topographical map that John Baron would be given as well as preparing a list of headings for the Skipper. Navigators were not immortal and if he were killed or wounded at least two other people in the crew would have sufficient information to get the survivors home. This was a routine drill, he had been doing something like it ever since his days with the Hampden OTU but this time there was the decidedly uncomfortable feeling that something really might happen to him. He remembered with a clarity that he couldn't erase from his mind, the vision of the medical orderlies at Babbacombe paddling in the surf and collecting, in a biscuit tin, the remains of that FW 190 pilot. He probably thought that he was on a pretty safe operation too. He pushed the thought as far back into his mind as possible and tried to concentrate on the matter in hand.

At the general briefing the crew were given the latest information on the operation. Its purpose, their particular role and the last known positions of convoys or flak ships, while once more the gunners were reminded to keep the hydraulic oil in their turrets warm by traversing them from time to time and to keep their eyes peeled for night fighters.

They weren't due to go out to their aircraft until early evening and at an OTU the machines were so intensively used that another crew would carry out what amounted to the night flying test. All they had to do was to hang around until it was time for their first flying supper. The rest of the afternoon seemed to drag on for ever. Allen tried to read but couldn't concentrate on anything and wound up listening to the American Forces Network on his little portable radio. Then at last to supper. Flying supper was a real bonus. The mess cooks served fried eggs, proper shell eggs, bacon and fried bread, to the crews going on operations. Then, after a final cup of tea they climbed into the trucks that took them down to the crew room to dress in their flying gear and draw parachutes. Les Hough also went and collected a ration of chocolate and chewing gum for them. There wasn't much conversation while they dressed and not much as they boarded the truck that took them out to the dispersal where their Wellington was parked. The truck stopped on the starboard side of the machine where one of the fitters had the door open. Before climbing aboard they indulged in an age old Bomber command ritual, the pee against the tailwheel. After that they slung their kit in and, climbing after it, filed down the narrow catwalk to their crew stations. Stan Lee had the loneliest spot in the rear turret, the rest of them were concentrated in the front of the aircraft.

The inside of the Wimpey was fairly dark and pungent with a reek that Allen grew to recognise as typical of night bombers. It was an odour that combined oil, high octane petrol and Elsan lavatory fluid. He pulled on his soft leather helmet and plugged in his intercom. Despite the overcast it wasn't quite dark outside, as the early March dusk had not yet turned to night, but he switched on the little lamp over his plotting table and arranged the contents of his navigation bag around him. He opened the chart on which he had already inked the course lines and checked the forecast wind. Nothing had changed since briefing and he wrote the first course for the skipper to steer on a slip of paper ready to pass forward. The crew checked in on the intercom and shortly afterwards he heard John Baron and the skipper running through the checks and the engines were started. Once the engines were running and the generator was operating he switched on the GEE to warm up and tuned to the first frequency that he had been given. He settled himself down, took the first of the ready sharpened pencils out of the cigarette tin wedged into the top of his navigation bag and was ready to go. To his surprise he realised vaguely that his apprehension seemed to have largely gone but he was too busy to be introspective enough to wonder why.

The noise level rose as power checks were completed and after a while a gentle jolting told him that they were taxiing out from their dispersal. They stopped at the holding point then he heard Harry Burnside call that they had been given a green. "Turret to port Stan" said the skipper then, "okay mates here we go". The engine noise rose toward the familiar threshold of pain, the jolting turned to a rapid vibration through the entire airframe and then ceased as the wheels lifted from the tarmac runway.

The wheels and flaps were retracted with a perceptible change in trim and they climbed for a while on the runway heading. Allen passed the first course to Les Hough before turning to fiddle with the

GEE box, line up the traces and, peering at the graticule on the chart, pencil in the first position. The Wimpey climbed steadily on an easterly heading towards their intended coasting-out position of Cromer just south of the Wash.

They were climbing through well broken cloud and there was still sufficient light left to see the countryside below them half hidden in a pool of darkness. The blacked out landscape of middle England seemed pretty featureless from altitude and as GEE was working well and not jammed that far west Allen continued to pencil in positions based on his readings from the screen. John was now down in the bomb aimer's position armed with the chart that Allen had marked earlier and after about forty five minutes announced that he could see the edge of the Wash. Allen went forward for a look and positively identified the part of the coastline that runs west to east before swinging a little south to Cromer. They were in luck, and had a positive fix and a good idea of the upper wind before starting the 150 mile run across the North Sea to a position just west of Texel.

By the time that they crossed the coast the light was reduced to little more than a bright rim behind them out to the westward. A relaxed voice from the rear turret said

"kite coming up from behind, it's another Wimpey". Allen briefly abandoned his position and stepped up to the astrodome for a quick look. Stan was right. Another Wellington was closing on them slowly and before the light had completely gone they saw one other.

A voice came on the intercom. It was Les Hough. "Okay Stan" he said " go ahead and test your guns. Testing guns skip" Stan came back and the twin Brownings in the tail made the whole airframe shudder as they fired off a hundred rounds into the empty night sky.

The ten OTU kites seemed to be on course and they would start windowing once they were within comfortable range of the German coastal radar. By now they had been above ten thousand feet for some time and they were all on oxygen. The clumsy masks hampered their movements but without them all of them would have lost their night vision, most would be unconscious within minutes and even the most resistant would be incapable of performing simple intellectual tasks.

Even on oxygen, at eighteen thousand feet mild anoxia was a debilitating factor. It was to become more so as operating altitudes increased. Everything became more difficult and when, about forty minutes out from Cromer, a rather reluctant bomb-aimer started peeling the elastic from bundles of Window and putting them out from the chute, he found the task surprisingly hard.

As they approached the West Frisian Islands Allen uttered a phrase that was to become charged with meaning. At the time it was a simple statement of fact. "Enemy coast ahead" he said and for the first time ventured into a new, alien and hostile darkness.

At first there was no evidence of that hostility although the constant gentle yawing of the Wimpey showed that Stan was traversing his turret, keeping the hydraulic oil running freely and searching the sky behind for signs of night fighters. The front turret was unoccupied. John, cursing as he fumbled with the bundles, was busy windowing and at that height in the dark it was virtually useless as a defensive position. A fighter approaching from ahead would close so rapidly that neither aircraft would make visual contact in time to fire.

Then he heard the skipper on the intercom. "There's flak bursting to port and starboard at about our height. I'm going to weave a bit but stay on heading to maintain our track. How far to our turning point Allen?" Allen's last GEE fix had looked good but he moved forward to have a look. He could see the line of the Frisian Islands clearly through a gap in the cloud, with the northern shore of Texel almost directly below them. He returned to his bench, glanced at the chart again and plugged in his helmet. "Turn to port now Skip," he said "the Main Force kites are coasting out over Southwold and we'll be moving well away from the stream". He could see a bit of bursting flak through the cellon windows but it seemed scattered and as they turned north and then westward he lost sight of it. The window cloud was probably masking the Wurzburg gun control radars and the battery commanders seemed uncertain of their height and heading.

As they headed away from the coast again the skipper came back on the intercom.

"I'm going to lose height and gain some speed. Never mind the briefed airspeed we'll go to two sixty five and if the buggers want to chase us we'll make it hard for them". Then to John and Stan, "Keep your eyes open blokes, night fighters often follow the stream and now we're not windowing we'll show up on RDF like a silver dollar on a sweeps arse".

Fifty minutes later John reported the Wash ahead and the Wimpey, still losing altitude slowly, flew on over the darkened Midlands until they came within range of their own control frequency. They received an immediate clearance to land and just over four hours after take-off taxied to their dispersal and switched off engines. It had been a long four hours! De-briefing was a bit anti-climactic. Apart from scattered flak bursts they had seen no sign of opposition and had very little to say. They did however qualify for a mug of tea and a very large tot of overproof rum which sent them of to bed feeling a sense of cheerful achievement.

The next day they were stood down and so, after a late start and an early lunch, the entire crew caught the bus to Stourbridge and assembled in the Woodman which, as so often happened, had for some mysterious reason become the chosen pub of the local aircrews. After several pints the tension of the previous day finally unwound and they talked about their first trip. The generally expressed opinion was that it hadn't been too bad and they hadn't done too badly. A few more pints later they decided that they were hungry and set off for another of their frequent ports of call, a local fish and chip shop.

Like most young men they were permanently ravenous and one of the first things that a crew did on posting was to identify any available eating places. Restaurants were few and far between and in any case usually beyond their means. Even in a period of strict rationing however, fish and chip shops and pie shops continued to offer their wares. Fish and chips, apart from the doubtful provenance of the fat in which they were fried, were usually edible enough. Pies were much more suspect. God knows what they contained. The chalked blackboards on which they were advertised proclaimed beef, chicken, mutton or rabbit but horse, pidgeon or worse were more likely fillings. Chips, vinegar, ketchup and hunger were effective appetisers and they were in no mood to ask awkward questions. This time it was fish and chips and, cheerfully disregarding the injunction against eating in the street they opened the greasy newspaper-wrapped parcels and ate it on the way to the cinema. At that stage in the day they had no difficulty in getting seats and, with frequent breaks to empty beer filled bladders, they spent three and a half happy hours at the pictures. After that they returned to the Woodman again for more beer before catching the last bus shortly after the call of "time gentlemen please"!

The next day it was back to work. A long cross-country including a "bullseye" exercise in which they carried out a dummy bombing run over an infra-red camera which recorded their simulated bomb release point. After that it was two more nickels, each one almost a carbon copy of the first and then, at the end of May, the end of the course.

With week-end passes for forty eight hours at each end and a week's leave in the middle they had a full ten days to look forward to. Allen and four of the crew went home. Les Hough went to London where he teamed up with some other Aussie pilots. Allen had invited him to come back to Darlington but it wasn't home to Les and he preferred the metaphorical bright lights of the capital. In their pockets they all had railway warrants to Bury St Edmunds the railway station for RAF Wratting Common where they were to start the final stage of their training at a Heavy Conversion Unit.

14. Heavy Conversion

Leave felt pretty good after the hard graft of OTU. It was nice to get up late. It was nice to have access to a bathroom where there was a fighting chance of some hot water and which he only shared with his parents and little brother. It was also a pleasant change to be able to moon about a bit and take life slowly for a day or three. Although most of his old mates were by now in the services there was usually someone he knew around and time passed agreeably between home, pub and the odd dance.

There was another girl around now, Rita, a lass he had first met at a church social before the war. He had liked her from the start, they got on well, but they now had something else in common. Rita had been called-up, conscripted into the Auxiliary Territorial Service, the ATS; effectively into the army. She was in fact acting as a shorthand-typist but the army needed these too. Such was the shortage of "manpower" that every able bodied person was being drafted into service of some kind and despite having an invalid mother she was required to serve where she was directed. She had started out by being posted to Feltham in west London and from there, as her mother's condition worsened, to York. The only concession that the army had been prepared to make was to post her near enough to home to be able to continue to visit her Mum a bit more frequently but in the Spring of 1944 her mother died.

In the social climate of the time the notion of her father coping alone was inconceivable and as a consequence she was posted to Darlington where she could be a private in the ATS from eight until five and then her father's housekeeper for the rest of the time. The notion of an active able-bodied man requiring a housekeeper seems ludicrous from the viewpoint of the 21st Century but at the time it seemed perfectly reasonable. Society did not think that a single man in his fifties with a full-time job could possibly cook, clean or wash for himself. The fact that large numbers of women were managing to combine these functions was blithely ignored. The up side of this ludicrous situation was completely unintentional - it was possible for Allen to see her regularly when he was on leave.

The unexpected bonus of a girl-friend and meeting old friends was great but the shine was sometimes knocked off it a bit as more and more of his mates from the ATC and the Model Aircraft Club seemed to vanish, posted missing or killed. To a man they had joined the RAF, most had volunteered for aircrew and few had survived into the Spring of 1944. It had been a hard war for flyers.

But in the meantime it was Spring. Darlington was close enough to the Durham countryside to make some decent walking country accessible and there was a pretty girl to take dancing. Dancing of course meant ballroom dancing - waltzes, quicksteps and foxtrots - and the dance was an important part of popular culture. The ability to dance at least the basic steps was as common among young people as the ability to kick a football was to most schoolboys. Dances were held everywhere from mess huts to parish halls and most towns would have their local Palais de Dance, a big commercial ballroom employing a professional dance-band. The protocols were curiously formal. You wore your best suit or best uniform, the girls wore long dresses and matching shoes and you would usually approach a partner and politely ask her to dance with you. Dance halls were good places to meet girls and good places to entertain them. You could forget the war for a while and concentrate on the girl you were holding and the problem of making your feet go where the music seemed to demand.

It was a happy leave but the music had to stop sometime and ten days later Allen found himself dragging his kit into another Nissen hut at RAF Wratting Common. Stan and Harry were already there, kit strewn about their bedspaces and Allen soon added his gear to the disorder in the room. Later on they elected to wander down to tea in the sergeant's mess and take a look at the flight line on the way. The billets were scattered away from the field and they hadn't yet managed a good look at the aircraft they were going to fly. As they made their way along the cinder path they heard the roar of four big radial engines and a Stirling on final approach came into view. It wasn't the first they had seen but it was the closest look that they had managed. Even in the air it looked large. The path curved round towards the perimeter track and as they paused on the edge of the airfield the machine that had just landed taxied to a nearby dispersal, cleared its engines with bursts of throttle and, one by one, switched them off.

There was a brief silence and then Stan spoke. "Bloody Hell!" he said, "I know they call it a heavy conversion unit but I didn't know they meant that heavy". The others saw his point. The nose of the Stirling seemed to stand above the ground like a barn roof, the main-wheels were man high and the undercarriage members towered ten feet above them. Even from a distance it looked enormous. "The skipper will cope" said Harry and with that they strolled on towards the mess hut and tea.

The following day they assembled with the chief ground instructor and the other new crews on the course. They learned that they would pick up another gunner, for the RAF heavies had a mid-upper turret as well as one in the tail, in addition to the little used bomb-aimer's turret in the nose. They would also be joined by a flight-engineer. With four engines and all the associated tanks, pumps, fuel cocks and ancillary equipment one pilot simply didn't have enough hands. The Americans solved this problem by putting two pilots in their heavy bombers but neither available manpower nor training facilities gave the RAF the ability to do that. It was also true that the Americans were flying big aircraft in daylight and close formation. With unpowered control systems the constant labour of keeping station would have been too much for one man to manage. The loose stream formation maintained by the RAF night bombers did not demand the same precise station keeping and one pilot could manage it alone.

They also learned that initially at least, they would have relatively little to do. Les would have two weeks of intensive ground school to do before he started to fly and most of them would not join him until he was cleared to fly the big machine solo. The skipper duly disappeared into the classrooms to be initiated into the mysteries of operating four engined aircraft while the others pursued a fairly sketchy revision programme. A few days later they were joined by another gunner, Geordie Lawson, a 21 year old ex-miner from Hetton le Hole, County Durham, and shortly after that by their flight-engineer, a slight pleasant lad from the Republic of Ireland who was inevitably christened Paddy by the crew. Paddy soon went off to the classrooms to join Les with whom he would have to work very closely. It would be his job to manage the engines, operate the fuel systems and give the pilot as much help as possible with the mechanics of the operation. The more time that a skipper could devote to actually flying the machine the better. Everyone was likely to live longer that way!

By the end of the second week the flying programme started. Les went off with a screened pilot and after watching a couple of circuits flown by his instructor, moved into the left hand seat and took the controls. Allen and John, who were watching discreetly from the lee of a dispersal hut, saw the Stirling taxi out, complete the power checks and take off. It re-appeared in circuit, made an approach, touched down and once securely on the runway the throttles were opened and it overshot and climbed away again. The procedure was repeated uneventfully several times more until an about an hour later the machine braked to a halt at the end of the landing run and taxied off back to its dispersal point. Over the next couple of days Les flew several times with his instructor until after some four hours his log was endorsed "fit to fly solo in daylight".

At the time Allen didn't realise quite what his skipper had achieved. The Stirling really was a giant, with the top of the canopy nearly twenty three feet from the ground, as high as the ridge tiles of a house. With a high stalky undercarriage intended to give the wings a high enough angle of attack and a relatively low-set fin it lacked rudder authority and was prone to develop a truly hideous swing on take off. Each of the Hercules radials developed fourteen hundred horse power and on full take off power the torque was ferocious. Les appeared to have taken this all in his stride and none of them was ever aware that he had needed to tame this particular monster.

At this point Paddy and Allen joined him in the air. Allen had to keep track of their position and bring them back to base and Paddy had to deal with all those tasks that Les lacked hands or time to attend to. Allen's job was fairly easy, it was basically map reading at low and medium altitude in broad daylight and good weather. Paddy's was an entirely different matter. Until then he had been operating in the relatively stress free environment of a classroom or a parked aircraft. He had no previous flying experience and was totally unprepared for the reality of carrying out his tasks at high speed in the reeling cockpit of a Stirling.

After their first flight together the following day it was clear that he had not enjoyed the experience. When they left the aircraft he was so pale as to be verging on green and was sweating freely. Normally a pleasant and sociable soul he became very quiet and answered in monosyllables when spoken to. It was fairly clear where the trouble lay, he was suffering from air sickness. This was by no means uncommon with new flight engineers. Hastily trained, they had little or no air experience to speak of and were required to carry out tasks that required them to read dials with their heads down and bend and stretch into the interior of the cockpit. It was not surprising that they experienced a degree of nausea.

The next hurdle was night flying. Once again Les was joined by their instructor but this time Allen was in the navigator's position keeping an eye on where they were, Harry was manning the wireless operator's bench and both gunners were in the turrets. By this stage in the war daylight attacks by Luftwaffe fighters were almost unheard of, but night intruder operations were a different matter. It was not a good idea to fly at night with the turrets unmanned and Stan and Geordie were in position with guns loaded and ready for action. Paddy stayed on the ground, not because he was unwilling to fly but because with a screened pilot aboard the flight deck would have been uncomfortably congested. After just over three hours dual instruction, spread over two nights, Les was declared competent to fly the Stirling in the dark and the complete crew could at last fly together as an entity in all conditions.

They started off on an easy one, a low-level daylight cross country. Take off was at ten thirty in the morning. It was a perfect late Spring day. A cold front had just passed through and the air was crystal clear. They took off in perfect visibility and the Stirling climbed like a homesick angel in the cold dense airmass. The first two legs went like a dream. Navigation was little more than a map reading exercise and they ran as if on rails until the sun began to warm the ground up and they encountered the first thermals of the day. Little cumulus clouds began to form in streets that ran across the sky and as the big machine ran underneath them it began to pitch and roll in the rising air. Up until that point Paddy had obviously been enjoying himself but the effect of the disturbed air was almost immediate. His colour faded to a transparent white, he began to sweat profusely and suddenly he started to throw up violently. Within minutes he was almost prostrate and what is worse the smell and the example began to affect the others. Les and John began to feel queasy until in sheer desperation Les asked Allen to come forward and take Paddy back to the rest bed in the rear fuselage.

From then on every trip led to the same consequences. In daylight the slightest turbulence, at night the need to concentrate on engine instruments as the machine rolled and tilted, would lead to a deathly pallor followed by sweating and uncontrollable vomiting. Poor Paddy was subject to chronic motion sickness and there seemed no realistic prospect of his condition improving. Les, always protective of his crew, gave it as long as possible but in the end he gave in to the inevitable. A chronically airsick flight engineer would be a permanent liability. In the interests of crew safety Paddy had to go. In the event it almost certainly saved his life but he was heartbroken at the time and they all regretted his departure.

It is worth remembering that he, like many other volunteers from the Republic of Ireland, was willing to put his life on the line to fight Fascism. Nobody can do more than that and it wasn't his fault that he had to give up when he did. As an aircrew volunteer he was not compelled to transfer to a ground trade and he was honourably discharged and returned home to Ireland.

Paddy's disability rapidly became a major problem for the Hough crew. Here they were, almost at the end of their time at HCU and without a flight-engineer. They did a few flights with any spare bod that happened to be available and then Jack Tales volunteered to join them. Jack was 26 years old, already a warrant officer and had completed a full tour of operations before being screened and rested by posting him to HCU as an instructor. Allen tried to talk him out of it. He had survived one tour and with a bit of luck the war might end before he was called upon to do another, Why should he push his luck?

Jack could see the sense of this as well as anyone but his wife had been killed in the Sheffield blitz, he had no ties and his whole life was wrapped up in the Air Force. A close knit crew was not unlike a family and he probably found that comradeship comforting enough to compensate for the risk. It was to be an expensive decision for him, but a fortunate one for the crew. After Jack joined them they really did have a hard core of competence. Les was a better than average pilot, Allen was unusually well trained as a result of his change of role and Jack, about to start his second tour, had a very good idea of how the job should be done.

The course ploughed on. They flew on three engines, simulated fire in the air and practiced every conceivable emergency drill. They also learned a lot about the Stirling.

It had acquired an unfortunate reputation. Its colossal undercarriage with its curious double folding action was famously vulnerable to side loads and its equally famous tendency to swing on take-off made those side loads only too likely to occur. Despite the formidable power of its four Hercules engines it could only carry a full bomb load up to twelve or thirteen thousand feet which put it at something approaching point blank range for the German heavy flak units.

These problems were caused by basic and relatively easily corrected design faults.

The first of the four engined heavies, the Stirling was preceded by a half sized prototype powered by four Pobjoy Niagra engines. When they came to scale it up they realised that the take-off performance was seriously affected by the low angle of incidence at which the wing was set. It wasn't tilted far enough back at the root to generate adequate lift at low speeds. The proper solution would have been to re-design the wing attachment to increase the angle of incidence but the Air Ministry deemed this too costly and time-consuming. A quick fix was achieved by simply lengthening the undercarriage legs. This improved the angle of attack but only at the cost of blanketing the fin and rudder, which made swing correction very difficult until the tail was up. It also resulted in a stalky, complex and heavyweight undercarriage that was inevitably badly adapted to cope with any kind of severe lateral loading. The poor ceiling of the aircraft was the direct consequence of an even more stupid decision. The standard hangar doors on peacetime RAF fields were only wide enough to admit aircraft with a maximum wing span of one hundred feet. As a consequence the Stirling wing was built down to those dimensions and the resultant high wing loading crippled its altitude performance.

So much for the bad news. The good news was that once off the ground and within its achievable height band the Stirling was tough, manoeuvrable and very pleasant to fly. The standard of construction was high, rather like that of a quality saloon car. Doors shut with a satisfying clunk, fittings were robust and although the forward fuselage was well braced inside the after fuselage was clear, unobstructed and big enough to walk down in comfort.

An apocryphal story was told of a pilot who could not trim his machine on a cross country exercise. The tail kept dropping, then, when he trimmed forward to maintain airspeed, it built up until he trimmed back, whereupon the tail would drop and the whole process begin again. The poor skipper became more and more frustrated as he porpoised across the sky until eventually he sent the flight-engineer back to investigate. The flight-engineer came back grinning all over his face. The problem was caused by the mid-upper and rear gunners playing darts. Every time they walked forward to the board slung under the mid-upper turret the weight shift changed the trim. It probably wasn't true but given the size of the rear fuselage it was at least plausible.

What was true was that the Stirling was tough enough to throw about. Evasive action was a great deal more violent than anything that they had tried in a Wimpey.

Les, flying once more with a screened pilot was shown how to perform a proper corkscrew. The first time they tried it was at relatively low altitude. "You don't want to be wearing oxygen masks when you first do this," said the screen but didn't enlarge on the advice.

Once they reached eight thousand feet they were advised to hang on and they heard their instructor's voice on the intercom. "Fighter, fighter corkscrewing port!" As he said that the control column was pushed hard forward and the aircraft bunted into a steep dive. At the same time the wheel was racked firmly to the left and they almost half-rolled to port. Allen's charts, instruments, equipment and even heavy oxygen bottles floated up around his ears under the negative-g only to plummet back down as his head was jammed into his shoulders as the turn was violently reversed and the nose pulled up. The Stirling rolled back in the opposite direction and as it went into an equally steep climb the speed decayed until it seemed just off the stall. Suddenly the nose went down again and the whole process was repeated.

The interior of the machine was a shambles. Charts, torches, fire-extinguishers, pencils, rulers, parachutes and loose flying gear was strewn all over the place. Both gunners had been sick, happily not into oxygen masks, and the elsan toilet at the back had shed its lid. Even more happily the elsan, with the aircraft equipped only for a training flight, had not been used or charged with fluid.

There was a brief interlude while some order was restored and the crew breathed again. Their relief was a bit too premature however as this time they heard the skipper's voice on the intercom saying "Fighter, fighter corkscrewing starboard!" and the whole performance was repeated. This time they went on for three or four turns before trying a banking search and then returning to base for a de-briefing.

Once parked with the engines stopped it was a pretty sorry looking crew that climbed out and lay on the damp grass. All of them except Les and Jack looked fairly green. The gunners bore obvious evidence of their predicament and Harry had a livid bruise developing on his cheek where a walk-around oxygen bottle had caught him a glancing blow.

"Okay," said the screen "that's what you have to do. It's no good doing it gently, the fighter will just stay with you squirting cannon shells up your arse. You have to lose him on the first diving turn and if he tries to follow you on that, he'll overshoot as you climb back on to your heading!" He took a cigarette out of his top pocket and lit up. "You don't have to worry about breaking the kite. You might pull the wings off a Wimpey, you might spin a Halifax but a Stirling or a Lancaster will cope". He took a couple of meditative drags. "The big problem is exhaustion. You get pretty tired throwing one of these things about so if you are rough enough to lose him on the first pass you stand the best chance".

Stan said that he had been so busy hanging on and throwing up that he hadn't even thought about firing his guns. Geordie nodded in agreement and obviously regretted the abrupt head movement. "Forget it"" said the screen. "If you see the bastard coming don't piss about with those pop guns but tell the skipper which way to corkscrew. If you get a clear shot as he overtakes give him a squirt by all means but those bastards carry so much armour you will need to hit the canopy to do much good. Keep your bloody eyes open and evade. That's the way to stay alive"!

That night the crew were stood down and caught a bus that was laid on to take them into Cambridge. Once there they headed for the Eagle, a pub much frequented by aircrews from both Bomber Command and the Eighth US Army Air Force. The evening was quite warm and so they bought their drinks and sat around in the courtyard outside.

Les took a long pull at his pint "I reckon we got some good advice today" he said.

"He scared the shit outa me with that first bunt mind you"! "Scared the shit out of you" said Stan. "What about us?" Geordie chipped in "Some Lancs carry a pair of fifties in the tail now, just like the Yanks. I reckon they'd give a fighter a run for its money"!

"Never mind that" said Les "duck first and fight if you have to, lets not have any bloody heroes in this crew. You know the drill, fighter, fighter and tell me which way to go"!

There was a rumble of mutual agreement and then the subject was changed to food. They decided that after another couple of pints they would go in search of some fish and chips.

They spent six weeks at Wratting Common with Les spending thirty hours or so in the air and the rest of them a varying proportion of that time. They had flown by night and by day, had practiced every drill in the book and were beginning to function as a competent and well knit crew. They were just about ready to go to war and Allen felt reasonably confident that they might give a pretty fair account of themselves.

15. Bren Guns, Paint Pots and Death

At the end of the course they were given the usual leave. Aircrew did very well for time off and they all looked forward to it, especially as the May weather promised a bit of welcome sunshine, but the gilt was slightly knocked off the gingerbread by the news of their next posting. This was not to an operational squadron as they had expected but to a battle school at Methwold, an airfield not far from their HCU. "What the bloody hell" said the skipper when he heard the news, "is a battle school?" A week later they found out.

When they reached Methwold they went through the familiar arrival drill but this time they were steered well away from the flight line, assembled in crews and issued with boots, steel helmets, denim overalls and web equipment. The webbing baffled some of them but Allen, drawing on his vaguely remembered experience as a Home Guard lance-corporal soon figured out how to piece it together. It's as well that he did for it needed to ride comfortably. Soon it was festooned with ammunition pouches, gas capes, packs, spare bren barrels, hand grenades and water bottles. For the next two weeks they dragged this impedimenta around while they played at soldiers, spending their time learning, or in many cases re-learning, how to use standard infantry small arms: rifles, sten guns, bren guns, mortars and grenades. They scrambled over obstacles, plunged through assault courses and discharged all of their weapons with varying degrees of danger to life and limb. When they were not doing that they changed into PT kit and exercised furiously. They also bitched furiously. They had spent all those years training as aircrew and here they were, apparently being trained as infantry. It didn't seem to make very much sense and nobody really explained why the hell they were doing it.

Eventually the course more or less petered out until on the 5th June they found themselves lounging around on the airfield, sheltering under the wing of a 149 Squadron Stirling. Allen was chatting to a fellow navigator, a bloke of about his own age, a Lancastrian called

Bob Hart, known as Hawker after the famous light bomber of the early thirties. It was a curious conversation based on an exotic sphere of knowledge. Hawker had been an organ builder before he volunteered for the RAF and he was identifying the home towns of the little circle of idlers by the organs that their parish churches possessed. He knew each church by the organ installed and could identify both the manufacturer of the instrument and the quality of the sound that it produced.

Suddenly this pleasantly frivolous conversation was interrupted by an unwelcome intruder, an administrative squadron leader seeking a couple of volunteers for a job. His request was met with a marked lack of enthusiasm and a deafening silence. Every one of the group had been in the RAF for a minimum of two years and had long ago learned never to volunteer for anything. The officer became more insistent. Someone had to do it. It was a very simple job. Would he have to detail someone? All the usual moral blackmail was deployed without actually telling anyone what the job was. In the end the amiable Hawker yielded, climbed to his feet and followed the importunate one off in the direction of the flight office. He glanced over his shoulder and smiled wryly before breaking into a trot to catch up. "See you later blokes" he said, but he never did!

The little group broke up an hour later when they were told to go off and get their tea before reporting back to the flight line for a special job. When they got back they found a truck had dumped long handled brushes and cans of whitewash at the dispersals. A rigger chalked lines on the underside of the wings of the parked aircraft and they were told to paint broad stripes of white between the lines. In the best tradition of the Royal Air Force nobody actually told them why they were so messily engaged. They didn't know it but they were painting special invasion markings on every machine that might venture over the Channel or into the area of the beachheads. Anything that flew was liable to be shot at on sight if it did not carry these identification marks. By the time it was full dark all of the aircraft had been painted but they had not made an elegant job of it. Only the underside of the wings had been coloured and whitewash was unlikely to prove very durable. It was only in the coming weeks that more permanent markings extending over both top and bottom surfaces of the wings were provided but by then their rushed efforts had largely served their purpose. Given the number of machines in the air at the time, relatively few aircraft were engaged by their own side and air force casualties caused by friendly fire were surprisingly low during the invasion period.

Eventually they staggered off to bed but sleep was made difficult by the amount of activity that seemed to be going on. Not only were the station aircraft operating but the night sky was full of the sound of aero engines. When they got up in the morning and Allen turned on his little portable radio they heard the news. Four years after being so rapidly and ignominiously bundled out of France by the Wehrmacht, the Allies were returning. The long awaited Second Front had been opened and allied troops were storming the Normandy beaches.

News was at a premium and any crew that had flown over the invasion area was at the centre of a little knot of fascinated bystanders trying to find out what was going on. BBC radio bulletins were listened to in something approaching silence and members of the station intelligence section found themselves unusually popular. With the benefit of hindsight we tend to think of the invasion as an inevitable victory but at the time, when the bloody repulse of the Dieppe raid a couple of years before was still fresh in their minds, Allen and his mates did not see it that way. They were optimistic about the outcome but far from certain. They certainly were not expecting any sort of walk-over and indeed the Normandy campaign never became one.

The first absolutely hard news they heard was both saddening and maddening. 149 Squadron, one of the two Stirling squadrons based at Methwold, had lost two aircraft on the night of the assault. Seconded to special duties, they had been dropping pyrotechnics and dummy parachutists in the Pas De Calais to divert attention away from the real invasion area. The unspecified job that Hawker Hart had "volunteered" for was despatching these decoys through the side door and bomb bay of a Stirling. Stooging around over occupied Europe at low speed and low altitude they were highly vulnerable to flak. Deprived of the cover provided by a bomber stream they were also obvious targets for prowling night fighters. Nobody knows what got them because none of them survived. There were nine on board, the usual crew of seven plus Hawker, and a sergeant called Bellamy, another pressed man from the battle school.

They also discovered that their two gunners, Stan and Geordie, had been rather more brusquely ordered to fly with 218 squadron aircraft and had spent the night shoving bundles of window out of Stirlings which flew in slow overlapping orbits over the Channel to simulate the advance of a fleet invading the Pas de Calais.

They weren't particularly shocked at the end met by Hawker and poor Bellamy. Most of them were destined to go the same way in the next few months. Casualties were just a fact of life to them, but they were deeply offended by the way that some wingless administrator had conned their mates into a job without even being warned that it was likely to be pretty hazardous. Les Hough was almost incandescent with rage and went so far as to express his views to the Australian High Commission. "It was" he said "bloody stupid to waste highly trained aircrew like that. Did the silly bastard realise for instance, that he had deprived a new crew of the navigator that they had just settled down with?" Needless to say nothing came of his protest but over fifty years after the event Allen still remembers it with untypical bitterness.

The battle school was largely over but still no postings came through and they were given a series of make work jobs. After all the urgency of the last six months and the desperate panic to get them ready to replace operational losses, the RAF seemed to lose interest. Then in mid June the long awaited operational postings arrived. They were to go to 218 Squadron which, like 149, was flying Stirlings out of Methwold.

Allen was a bit taken aback. The Stirling, although the first of the four engined heavy bombers to go into service with the RAF, was already obsolescent. "I don't bloody believe it" he said in the pub that night. "I've gone from Hampdens to Wellingtons to Stirlings and now we're starting on ops we're getting fucking Stirlings again. I've navigated every bloody antique on the inventory of the Royal Air Force"! Les advised him to dry his eyes. He had been making a few enquiries, keeping his ear close to the ground and had a rather different slant on things. First and most obviously, they liked Methwold, largely because it was conveniently close to Cambridge which they found a very agreeable town. Second, because the Stirling had been suffering unacceptable casualties as a night bomber with the Main Force, 218 had been seconded from Bomber Command as a Special Duties squadron. Special Duties in military parlance is usually a euphemism for dangerous but this did not seem to have been the case recently. The special duties concerned mainly involved dropping supplies to the Maquis, the French Resistance, and despite the recent experience of 149 these were not usually very hazardous operations. Not, that is, compared with night bombing raids on Berlin or the Ruhr valley. The bush telegraph rumoured that 218 had gone for weeks without losing a crew or an aircraft.

Lying awake that night Allen wondered what it was going to be like. His training was finished at last. The long journey from his clerk's desk at Catterick Bridge station, through the converted boarding houses of Babbacombe, the bullshit of Cranwell, the adventure of Canada and finally back to England, was over. He knew that operational flying was going to be dangerous and suddenly felt frighteningly vulnerable, now he was at last about to do it. Paradoxically though, he also felt curiously confident. He knew that he could do his job and that he was part of an above average crew. Plenty of people did survive a tour of thirty operations, why not them? Anyway, he would worry about it all in the morning. At least he knew where he was going next and something about the unit that he would be flying with.

It was, as it happened, the easiest posting that Allen had ever experienced. As they were already on the station they were spared the business of binding around the various sections obtaining signatures, all they had to do was shift their kit into a different billet. The following morning they reported to their new squadron orderly room and with a minimum of fuss were absorbed into the squadron.

It was, to put it mildly, anti-climactic. He had become used to the makeshift, shabby, humdrum character of training organisations, but perhaps irrationally he thought that things would be different on a squadron. He knew that it was ridiculous, but he half expected some sort of a formal welcome to the brotherhood. At very least he thought that a new crew might get a handshake and a few solemn words from the Squadron commander. Somehow, when about to be invited to charge the guns at Balaklava you expect to hear at least an echo of distant trumpets. What they actually encountered was a corporal with a clip board allocating them to a hut.

16. Finishing School

Les and John were in one billet and Allen and the other NCOs were in another but apart from the latter group having a bit less space there was very little real distinction between them. In both cases the huts were simple wooden buildings, little more than oversized garden sheds, heated by cast-iron tortoise stoves and furnished with metal framed beds and sheet steel lockers. Allen's hut was already half occupied by an all-NCO crew whose possessions were strewn chaotically about the place. As they walked into the shadowy interior they were met by the familiar smell of damp wool and soot and the equally familiar feeling of spilled coke crunching under their feet. Once their kit, according to inclination, was either dumped or put away they went back to the orderly room and met up with Les and John again.

A harassed-looking flight sergeant dug into a filing tray, consulted a list and told them that they had been allocated to C flight. An LAC clerk took them outside and pointed them in the right direction and so they made their way to the flight office. Once there they kicked their heels in the crew room while Les was interviewed by the flight commander. He emerged twenty minutes later and told them to hang about while he went for a check-ride with a screened pilot. Operational squadrons liked to form their own views of a new pilot's ability before he started to lead his crew against enemy targets and this was the first part of the process.

The crew wandered down to the flight line, with the unspoken intention of offering a bit of moral support, and watched while their skipper started up, taxied to the end of the runway in use and took off. Quite irrationally, given the difficulties involved in coping with the beast, they weren't actually very concerned. Les had flown Stirlings before, and after their experiences at OTU and HCU they had a well justified faith in his competence. Sure enough their skipper satisfied the screen. He handled all the minor emergencies that were thrown at him and, when the big machine returned to the field, did a few circuits and bumps before taxiing to a dispersal pan and switching off. A small Hillman van brought both pilots back to the flight-commander's office from which Les emerged smiling broadly a quarter of an hour later.

The crew then assembled in a sunny corner outside the crew room while Les briefed them. The news was once again a bit anti-climactic. The Stirlings had been largely off main force operations since sustaining heavy losses the previous winter. Since then they had principally been used to drop supplies to the French Resistance or to attack relatively lightly defended short range targets. The invasion of France meant that their supply dropping role was drastically curtailed and so 218 Squadron were being withdrawn for further training before being re-equipped with Lancasters in the near future. There was a mutter of discontent from the crew which could be summed up as "not more bloody training" but it was fairly half hearted. At least they were likely to stay alive a little longer.

Allen's first meeting with the navigation leader was mildly comical. By that stage in the war navigators were awarded a half-wing brevet with an N embroidered on it. Allen, originally trained as a Coastal command observer-WT, had been given the far older-established winged O brevet and the navigation leader, confused by this, addressed his first enquiries to John Baron the bomb aimer who also wore a winged O. As navigators were generally considered the brains of the crew he had assumed that the commissioned observer was likely to be the navigator. His confusion was forgivable. Aircrew were essentially identified by brevet and in the hectic pace of the air war the O was a survival from the bronze age of Blenheims, Wimpeys and Hampdens. Allen was promptly told to sew an N on his working battledress tunic and reserve his original badge for his best blue.

Once the identification problem was solved Allen started a programme of ground instruction in preparation for a considerable programme of intensive flying training. This was to prove a good deal more than a formality. Bomber Command had undergone a quiet revolution in navigational technique during the winter of 1943. Despite the fact that the savage attrition of the night offensive meant that the burden was borne by a constant stream of newly trained crews, a whole range of new technology was transforming the capabilities of the survivors.

The Stirlings operated by 218 Squadron had the same engines and airframes as those which they had flown at Heavy Conversion Unit but their navigational equipment was considerably more sophisticated. The Hough crew had already encountered GEE and discovered how, so long as it was not being jammed by the Luftwaffe, its lattices of radio signals could be read off from a cathode ray tube mounted in a console in the navigator's station and plotted onto a special chart to give extremely accurate position fixes. New to Allen was an even more sophisticated bit of kit known as GH. It appeared to be very similar to GEE but could give positions which were so accurate that it could be used as a blind bombing aid. It was clearly very precise, as to his surprise Allen found that he had a bomb release mechanism installed in the navigation compartment. On GH raids the bomb aimer was bypassed completely and the navigator talked the pilot along the release track and toggled the bombload himself. What neither Allen nor the rest of the crew knew was that GH incorporated a transmitter and complementary ground repeater in order to steer the aircraft along a measured arc of a circle. This knowledge would have made them decidedly uneasy, as when Allen was been introduced to H2S, a ground scanning radar device which, under ideal conditions produced an image of the terrain below on a similar cathode ray tube, he was warned that night fighters could home in on these transmissions from a very considerable range. As the kind of ideal conditions demanded to make H2S useful required that the electronic equipment be well maintained and behaving, the rotating scanner beneath the fuselage functioned properly and that the searching signal beam encounter clearly defined ground features, they rarely occurred. The contrast between coastal waters and cliffs might be clear. The presence of ships or islands on large expanses of water could be determined but once inland, the distinction between ground features was usually hard to see. The situation was not improved by the fact that the technology was so new and the necessary skills to tune and maintain it adequately were very much in their infancy. Ground scanning radar probably had enormous potential but in mid 1944 it was so unreliable that 218 Squadron's navigators rarely used it. Once they discovered that it acted as a beacon to night fighters, rarely became never. They simply left the sets switched off. Had they known that the infinitely more accurate GH included a transmitter that could be tracked by fighters they may well have treated it with equal caution.

There were however other goodies that were in a more advanced stage, had no known snags and did work with considerable reliability. The P14 compass fitted to all RAF aircraft at the time was a good dependable instrument of its kind, but it was subject to all the usual ills that ordinary compasses suffer from. It could be interfered with by metal equipment in the cockpit area or the various bits of electrical gadgetry found in the front end of the aircraft. Worst of all it took a relatively long time to stabilise after a turn and during violent manoeuvres. During evasive action for instance, it was seriously affected. The distant reading compass was a brilliant solution to most of these problems. It was a magnetic compass slung in gimbals towards the rear of the aircraft and well away from most sources of potential interference. The magnetic compass was inter-connected with a gyroscopic compass which would of course continue pointing in a straight line in the direction set until progress around the curve of the Earth caused it to precess or lose track. The magnetic compass would automatically correct this error and the gyro would, in turn, stabilise the direction indicator. Both the navigator and the pilot had DR repeaters on their panels and the pilot's P14 was merely a back-up instrument. Nor was this all ; the DR compass and the air speed indicator were connected to a further piece of wizardry known as the air position indicator. This was essentially a primitive computer which recorded every change of course and speed and gave a continuous read-out in latitude and longitude. This position was based on the assumption that the aircraft was flying in still air and did not compensate for wind speed, but the difference between the API reading and an accurate GEE, GH or visible ground fix would enable the wind to be calculated with considerable precision. The DR compass and the air position indicator turned out to be robust and very reliable instruments. By mid 1944 Bomber Command navigators no longer needed to rely on dead reckoning, astronavigation or hazardous radio fixes. All of them had the means and most of them had the skills to fix their positions with some accuracy and so the loss of the dubious assistance of H2S was a fairly minor handicap. Given all this it is curious that Bomber Command was still committed to a policy of night area bombing raids on cities, at a time when their navigators could find most medium range precision targets in the dark and with the aid of GH stand a very fair chance of hitting them in almost any weather.

And so, while they waited for the arrival of their new Lancasters, the Hough crew trained and trained and then trained some more. Day and night cross countries, simulated bombing, real bombing with nine pound practice bombs delivered into the Wash, fighter affiliation exercises and ditching drills. Both the fighter affiliation exercises and the ditching drills were illuminating. Climbing into a dinghy in the cold water of the camp static water tank (A large circular cement-rendered brick tank intended to provide water for the camp's fire service.) was difficult enough. The prospect of surviving the impact of ditching, escaping from a sinking fuselage through inadequate escape hatches and then boarding the dinghy in any sort of a sea, was intimidating in the extreme.

Ditching drills were essentially depressing, they just hoped that they would never have to do it, but simulated fighter attacks were a very different matter. They learned a great deal from these. They discovered once more, for instance, that a corkscrewing bomber was a very difficult target to hit. As the evading aircraft lost and gained height by three or four hundred feet, lurched violently from side to side by much the same amount and varied its airspeed from nearly three hundred knots in the dive to less than a hundred in the climb, few fighter pilots could keep it in their gunsights. By the same token few if any gunners could fire back effectively. The task they faced was very like that of accurate clay pigeon shooting while riding on a roller coaster. Similarly, the only real chance that an intercepting fighter had was to attack before it was seen and so the primary task of the gunners was to act as lookouts. At night, unless they were operating in bright moonlight, they knew that the Luftwaffe night fighters relied on radar to intercept the bomber stream and visual contact to attack individual aircraft. Unless, as was all too often the case, it was approaching from the big blind area below they could see the fighter as soon as the fighter crew could see them. The outcome would depend on who reacted first.

Experience had soon showed that if a fighter missed on the first pass it would probably lose its target in the dark and would simply go on to search for another. Providing that one of the gunners spotted the attacking fighter and yelled out the vital instruction to corkscrew it was likely that attacking fighters would miss. As it was all but impossible to direct accurate return fire from the reeling gun platform provided by a corkscrewing bomber there was little point in making the attempt. Denied the beacon provided by a stream of tracer ammunition the attacker would almost certainly lose the target and hence the best policy was to lie low and not return fire. The lesson first learned at Heavy Conversion Unit was rammed home. If the gunners confined their attention to acting as look-outs and simply directed evasive action they were more effective than they would have been making feeble attempts at shooting back with rifle calibre machine guns. Even in daylight the corkscrew was a very effective evasive manoeuvre providing that the gunners saw attacking fighters before they came within range.

Hindsight suggests that even arming RAF bombers with heavy calibre machine guns would have made very little difference to their chances of survival. It was evasion that was their primary means of defence and hence completely removing the turrets and substituting streamlined lookout positions would have added fifty knots to their airspeed and made them all but impossible for most Luftwaffe night fighters to intercept. The JU88 and Me110 fighters had a very modest speed advantage, another fifty knots on the target speed would have virtually eliminated it.

The other thing that came out of the endless training was that the crew became progressively more efficient. They also became a cohesive group with many of the characteristics of a family about them. Like a family there were elements of friction about their relationship but also like a family even if they didn't actually like each other very much they would tolerate each other's idiosyncrasies and form a solid front against outsiders.

Theirs was a peculiar two dimensional relationship born of the peculiar highly technical war that they found themselves fighting. It was rooted entirely in the immediate present and they rarely discussed their pre-war life, their families or anything about their past. To this day Allen has only a very vague idea of what any of them were doing before the war or even before they joined the crew. Les for instance trained in Australia and had been a journalist before he enlisted. He was an extremely competent pilot but whether this competence resulted from experience as a staff pilot on a training establishment somewhere or whether it was just a natural talent was something that Allen never knew. It was the same with the others. He knew very little about their pre-RAF existence because they never discussed it. They all lived in a constantly moving present in which the immediate concerns filled their whole being and left no room for the past or the future. The immediate reality was the hazards that they faced, the demands of flying highly complex aircraft and the looming prospect of operational flying. If they were stood down then their attention was directed to finding a good pub, a place to eat or what was on at the local cinema. The past was largely irrelevant and the future so hazardous and survival so precarious that they did not care to think about it too much. The entire focus of their attention was concentrated on the instant with event horizons that could not lie much beyond the next exercise or the next operation.

Over fifty years after their brief hectic career they remain in Allen's memory as something approaching caricatures. They live essentially as a simply sketched outline with a few distinctive features. Added to that is a vivid memory of shared experience and very little else.

Les Hough, the Australian from Adelaide, seemed several sizes larger than life. Away from home he was determined to live up to his perception of a fair dinkum Aussie and personified the role of Crocodile Dundee nearly fifty years before it appeared on the screen. He had little regard for rank or authority, told the tallest of tall stories and was fiercely protective of his crew. As a mature and experienced twenty six year old he was significantly older than the two gunners. Exuding confidence and having travelled half way around the world to be there he was to be something of a father figure to them. The gunners, Stan Lee and Geordie Lawson, had each been in the service less than three months when they joined the crew. Young and more than a little naive, they had been enthused by the glamour of a flying badge and were to find the dawning reality of operational flying increasingly frightening. With the benefit of hindsight we now know that it was the youngest and oldest members of aircrews that found the business most difficult to cope with. Those under twenty-one and those over thirty were worst affected by the stress of combat flying. The younger ones lacked the confidence that comes with a little more maturity and the older ones usually had too many emotional ties outside the service. Stan, the rear gunner, was a small, fresh faced, rather diffident working class lad from Bristol. Geordie Lawson in the the mid-upper turret, at about five feet five inches tall, was equally small. A slight, dark, undernourished lad with bad teeth, he came from a County Durham pit village and had an accent so impenetrable that Allen had to act as an interpreter with the rest of the crew. Both boys found the reality in which they found themselves increasingly bewildering. It was the custom at Methwold to watch the station aircraft depart and return from operations. As a consequence everyone was all too well aware of their losses which, even when they were confined to attacking easier targets, were not inconsiderable. 149 Squadron had continued to operate their Stirlings from Methwold and had lost five during the period between June and July. Several more had returned with battle damage and dead or injured men on board and a number of damaged aircraft had crashed or force-landed in the immediate vicinity. It was very obvious to the spectators that the glamour of the flying badge came with a substantial price tag attached. All things considered, given their youth and inexperience the boys coped a great deal better than anyone could reasonably expect them to.

The others members of the crew had all been in the air force for a great deal longer and apart from their greater maturity had been psychologically toughened up by their experience. Despite this or perhaps because of it they seemed either unaware of the problems confronted by these raw lads or unwilling to involve themselves. It was Les and Allen that jollied them along, pulled their legs in the pub and guided them as they learned their trade. Dad and Uncle Allen, it seemed funny given that Allen was all of twenty-one himself, but it seemed to work. The lads became reliable members of the crew and Stan in particular blossomed as a character. Les, not normally a man to suffer fools gladly, was endlessly patient with them and only ever lost his good humour when Geordie became excited and shouted on the intercom.

"Calm down you daft pommie bastard" he would yell. "I can't understand a fucking word you're saying. Speak clearly for Christ's sake" Once back on the ground he would point out with considerable force that if he didn't understand a command to corkscrew they would all be dead. Geordie did his best and would get that one vital command out intelligibly but any more complex conversations continued to require Allen's services as an interpreter.

Harry Burnside the radio operator came from a respectable working class family in east London and, as Les once pointed out, "stuck out like a silver dollar on a sweep's arse" among the Hough crew. It wasn't the fact that he was a great reader, so was Allen. It wasn't even his rather reserved manner, Jack and John were equally quiet. What made him stand out in the crowd was his immaculate appearance. He was always well dressed. His uniform was clean and pressed, his shirts and collars were spotless and even his shoes and buttons were regularly shined. His slight air of prissiness didn't extend to sobriety however and he enjoyed an evening in the pub as much as any of them. He was also extremely good at his job. His logs were always correct and up to date, he could pluck bearings from the worst of inference, he kept the intercom working efficiently and he wasn't a bad air gunner if called upon. Harry was a distinct asset to the crew.

Jack Tales the flight engineer was a little, red faced, sandy haired man in his mid twenties. He came from Sheffield and proved to be the quietest man in the crew. The others, even Les, were a little shy of him as his reserve came from an obvious deep unhappiness. His family had been killed in the Sheffield blitz and he really had nothing that he cared about to go back to. He clearly valued being part of the crew and enjoyed being with them but much of the life had gone out of him and he was relatively silent in company. Allen had originally tried to talk him out of volunteering for a second tour of operations when he suggested that he might take Pat's place. His failure to do so was a tragedy at one level but Jack was superbly competent and with a little more luck, might have made that little extra that would have got them through safely. Certainly he knew exactly what he was doing. He balanced the fuel system perfectly, watched the gauges, helped with the throttles and coped with minor in-flight emergencies. Above all things he was a fount of operational wisdom. He taught Les to run in to the target a little above the briefed height, turn that height into speed over the target area, level out long enough to get a decent aiming point photograph and then go like hell in a descending turn onto the course out. He emphasised the need for the gunners to call for a corkscrew if they as much as suspected the presence of a fighter. "The only way to be really sure" he said, "is to wait until it opens fire". "The problem with that" he added, " is that by then the tanks are on fire, the bombload's gone up and we're all fucking dead"! Jack was another substantial asset and in the event he kept his presence of mind right up to the last.

John Baron the bomb aimer, like Jack, was relatively quiet in company but his reserve was probably rooted in an inability to cross the barrier of social class with any real degree of ease. He was tall, slim, fair-haired and urbane with an accent that betrayed his Home Counties and public school background. Why Les disliked him quite so much remains something of a mystery to Allen. His best guess is the one floated earlier. John appeared to be an almost stereotypical English toff and he raised every egalitarian hackle in Les's aggressively Aussie nature. In fact he was a pleasant enough bloke, was competent at his job and it was just unfortunate that visual bomb aiming, in Three Group at least, was a relatively infrequently used technique by that stage in the war. Les however didn't like him and was quite open in saying so to Allen. It wasn't a deep rift in the crew but it was always a bit of a niggle just below the surface.

On the credit side, despite a bit of low level friction the Hough crew worked well together and despite this personality clash, to the outside they presented a solid front. Nobody messed with Les's crew.

The crew were well bedded down in the squadron when, in mid July, the tempo changed abruptly. They were summoned to a general squadron briefing, itself something of a novelty when not operating, and addressed by the CO. "The good news is that the Lanc. Threes are coming" he said. "The bad news is that we're going back on main force. We are all off to Feltwell to Lancaster Finishing School the week after next, and after that we shall be operating regularly again"!

They travelled light on the short journey to Feltwell, leaving most of their kit in their billets and the process of conversion was swift and surprisingly painless. Despite looking decidedly utilitarian and rather crudely finished after the essentially pre-war refinement of the Stirling, the Lancaster was entirely functional. For most of the crew the differences were minimal. For the gunners one hydraulically powered turret is very much like another. Similarly for the wireless operator and the navigator their crew stations were fairly similar and equipped with much the same kit. The flight-engineer's was a bit different, he had a folding rumble seat to the right of the skipper's instead of the redundant second pilot's seat that he had occupied in the Stirling. The bomb-aimer's compartment however, was an enormous improvement. It was a bit snug, and crawling under the flight-engineer's position getting in and out was difficult, but once in the view was perfect. The entire lower nose section was glazed, with a perspex bubble incorporating an optically flat section for the bomb-sight and a blister which permitted a view both downward and to the rear. It was possible to man the front turret by simply standing up but as it was almost never used this was usually of purely academic interest.

It was for the pilot that the Lancaster was such a vast improvement. His seat was on the left as was usual with excellent visibility through the glazing all around him. The controls were conveniently grouped with throttle and pitch control levers lying comfortably close under the right hand and the trimmers in easy reach. Even more importantly the handling characteristics were superb. It was another big aircraft with unpowered controls which had to be manipulated with brute muscle power but they were much better harmonised and therefore seemed lighter. It climbed well and with a shorter and more robust undercarriage the landings were a great deal less eventful than those experienced in the Stirling.

Les did the first few flights with a screened pilot sitting beside him on Jack's folding seat while Jack observed over his shoulder. In the pub after their first days flying he enthused about their new machines. "They were beauts" he said, and the crew were content.

There were snags of course. The fuselage was a good deal more cramped than the Stirling's had been and the main spar protruded waist high, so far from the floor that it had to be crawled over to get forward into the front crew compartment. The escape hatches left something to be desired as well. Only the rear gunner, who could simply rotate his turret and roll out backwards through the rear doors, and the bomb-aimer, who lay prone on the closed forward hatch, had a relatively easy escape route. The rest of them had to make their way down the dark interior of the fuselage and exit either through the rear door, a tiny hatch forward of the astrodome or crawl under the flight-engineers position and jump through the forward hatch. There was another small hatch in the glazed cockpit roof for the pilot.

Nor of course could parachutes be worn all the time. Some pilots sat on a seat type parachute but these were pretty uncomfortable and so most of them wore observer type harnesses like the rest of the crew. In an emergency it was necessary to retrieve the actual canopy packs from wherever they had been stowed and clip them on to the harness before they could attempt to bale out. In the dark the reeling interior of a disabled Lancaster would be difficult to leave. It wasn't a nice thing to think about and they responded in the only way possible. They didn't think about it!

After a hectic week of day and night flying, lectures and emergency drills they were deemed operational. They packed their skeleton kit and returned to Methwold to find the first of their new Lancasters waiting for them. By 10th August 1944, 218 Squadron were nearly ready to wage war again.

17. First Blood

Operations did not start immediately as it was about ten days before the last of the new machines was delivered and the whole squadron needed time to settle down with their aircraft. Airframe fitters needed to find their way around an entirely different structure and engine fitters had to cope with radically different power plants - liquid cooled, in-line Rolls Royce Merlins instead of air cooled Bristol Hercules radials. For the radio and instrument mechanics not much had changed but even the armourers had to learn different techniques for stowing the much heavier bomb-loads that the Lancasters carried.

They were all very pleased with their brand new Canadian built mounts. After the battered hacks of OTU and HCU and the hard used Stirlings that they had flown when they joined 218, despite their utilitarian build they seemed pristine beyond belief. They even smelled new like new cars, and everything worked. The Packard built Merlins with which they were powered came with lavishly equipped tool kits to supplement the inadequate poor-quality implements usually provided by the RAF, and so the fitters and riggers were equally happy with them.

The aircrews spent their time in familiarisation and day formation exercises while the pilots in particular did all they could to test the limits of performance of their new machines. The squadron's new commanding officer, known as The Vicar since he took to addressing them at briefings from a specially constructed pulpit-like podium, was unwise enough to tell them that the DR compasses, with which the Lancasters were also fitted, could not be toppled. He announced that the Lanc could not be banked beyond ninety degrees and that the gyros could cope with that easily. This was not a wise thing to say to Les. On their next flight he called for some practice evasive action. During the subsequent wild corkscrews the big machine rolled well past ninety degrees and Allen, who had been clinging to his bench for dear life, observed that the DR compass had indeed been toppled and was swinging wildly. Needless to say Les did not keep this information to himself. Every other pilot in the squadron had to try the same trick and within days there was not a crew that failed to return from an air test or an exercise without a job for the unfortunate instrument bashers. It was fairly crazy stuff. Contemporary flyers would certainly think that subjecting big aircraft to such hideous stress levels was asking for trouble. Given the probability of fighter attack that these relatively inexperienced pilots faced however, the added confidence in their ability to throw their machines about given by this apparent lunacy was probably a factor in extending their lives.

Two weeks after their return to Methwold Les was told off for a 'second dickie' trip. He was to fly an operation with an experienced crew to be shown the ropes. These second dickie ops were not popular with crews. An existing crew didn't much like having a stranger on board, cluttering up the flight deck and getting in the engineer's way. The new pilot, in an aircraft with no dual controls fitted, had to sit uselessly on the engineer's rumble seat with no real job to do. The new man's crew were equally unhappy. It was not unknown for pilots to go missing on these trips and the remaining headless crew , as it was known, had to start all over again with an unfamiliar pilot.

It was to be a night raid and Les was called for a briefing about mid morning. Only John shared the officers mess with him and so none of the rest of the crew saw him before he went down. Allen however, casually wandered over to the cinder path leading from the briefing room before lunch and hung around until Les came out. They fell into step together and walked towards the flight line. Les answered the unspoken question. "Could be worse" he said. "It's Russelsheim, taking off about ten."

Late that evening the rest of the crew were assembled at the threshold of the runway in use to watch the heavily laden Lancasters lumber into the sky. Happily it was an uneventful departure. There were no taxiing accidents, nobody lost an engine on take-off and as the navigation lights marked where the aircraft were climbing on track into the night sky, they turned away en-route for the George in

Methwold village for the last half hour or so before closing time was called. Their conversation in the seedy little bar was a bit forced. Everyone was wondering how Les was getting on but nobody wanted to talk about it. The fag-end of the evening seemed to drag on. The usual faintly resentful locals played darts, cribbage or nine-men's-morris but the equally usual noisy groups of aircrew were largely absent. Most of the crews were otherwise engaged that night. "Time gentlemen please!" the landlord called, and they rose to their feet and walked slowly back to camp. John split off and headed for the officer's mess while the rest of them made their way to the billet.

The other crew were absent and the shadowed interior of the hut was empty. Allen tuned his little portable radio to AFN and then lay on his bed trying to read. None of them undressed but some of them dozed on their beds until some time between two and three in the morning they heard the grumble of aero engines in the circuit and, pulling boots and tunics on, made their way towards the watch office. By the time they reached the flight line the first two aircraft were down and taxiing towards their dispersals. Within thirty minutes or so the last of the squadron's machines had landed and the runway lights were extinguished. They had only counted eleven back, but whether the twelfth had diverted elsewhere and more importantly, which machine it was, they didn't know. They could have waited for the crew buses to return for de-briefing but there was a quicker way. They walked over to the watch office, as the control tower was known at the time, and had a quick word with one of the duty ops-clerks. "It's D Dog that's missing" she said, "Pilot Officer Humphrey's crew"! They were sorry about Humphrey, Like Les he was an Australian and like Les also, a good natured soul but their regrets were tempered by simple relief that at least their skipper was OK. They had what they came for and somewhat sobered but content, they went off back to their billets and to bed.

Les appeared again just before lunch the following day and in a quiet corner by one of the bomb shelters down near the flight line they sat on the grass while he told them about the trip. He hadn't enjoyed it very much. The overwhelming impression was one of confusion, with the host crew using the verbal short cuts of familiarity while talking to each other on the intercom, with a bewildered Les largely out of the loop. Nor was he particularly impressed by their competence.

"Oh fuck it," he said. "One down, one to go, then we can get stuck in together!"

"It's all right for you skip," said Harry. "You'll have done two before we start and we'll wind up doing our last ops as spare bods!"

"No bloody fear!" Les retorted "All the Aussie pilots in this squadron, and that's most of us, are on to that one. The Dominion government has ruled that we finish on thirty … and when we finish, you finish!" God knows whether they could have made it stick with the RAF. As it happened they never got the chance to find out but it was very heartening to hear him say it with such conviction.

In the mean time Les had to do another second dickie trip, but with the rapid progress of the allied armies that followed the breakout from the Normandy beach heads, army support operations were continually scheduled and cancelled as plans were overshadowed by events on the ground. It was nearly the end of August before Les went again and he had another equally unpleasant experience on a night operation to Kiel. Seventeen Lancasters went down that night, mainly to fighters and Les returned sobered by the sight of some of them blowing up on the approach to the target. Ever the good skipper, he didn't want to shake the younger members of his crew but he felt free to talk to Allen and Jack. "We need to be pretty sharp" he said. "Those jokers aren't pissing about"!

Now that Les had done his second dickie trips they knew that they were going to begin in earnest but August came to an end before they at last started their tour. On 4th September the entire crew saw their names on the battle order for the first time.

The briefing was scheduled for early the next morning. After the traditional pre-operational bacon and eggs Allen was summoned to the earlier navigators briefing and discovered to his mild surprise that his first proper operational flight was going to be carried out in daylight. The squadron was to be part of a force of nearly three hundred and fifty Bomber Command aircraft flying a tactical support mission for the invading allied armies.

Once the navigators had pencilled in the courses and turning-points on their charts the rest of the crews entered the briefing room and the various specialist leaders did their stuff. The bombing leader gave details of loads and fusings. The gunnery leader exhorted his men to keep their eyes open and make sure that their targets bore crosses on their wings. The signals leader passed out details of frequencies and emergency procedures. The meteorological officer gave current weather information and the station intelligence officer gave them details of their objectives and possible hazards en route or over the target.

The target was Le Havre, still held by the Wehrmacht but cut off by the eastward advance of British and Canadian forces. Their task was to soften up the defences of the town. They were to smash fixed fortifications like bunkers and pill boxes and to destroy as much of the defending anti-tank artillery as possible.

They expected heavy flak defences. The ports had been protected by hundreds of light and heavy anti-aircraft guns in the constant struggle to keep the U-Boats based there operating in the face of constant air attacks. They could expect gun defences manned by the Kriegsmarine, the Wehrmacht, The Waffen SS and the Luftwaffe and most of the defending gunners had been given a great deal of recent practice both by day and by night. It looked as if they were going to make their debut the hard way.

They were told that their bomb-load would be made up of a mixture of five hundred and one thousand pound general purpose bombs. They were to run in to the target at twelve thousand feet, heading almost due south and approaching from the seaward side. Once they had bombed they were to make a gradual turn to starboard and clear the target towards the Baie de la Seine before turning northwards for base. They were slightly cheered by the fact that most of the surrounding areas were now in the hands of the allies and if they were forced down or baled out they were likely to fall into the hands of friends. The down side was that they were about to attack one of the most heavily defended ports in Europe in daylight and at medium altitude.

There wasn't much waiting. The aircraft had been air tested the day before and were already fuelled and bombed-up. Allen had just enough time to finish inking in the courses on his chart and the simpler topographical maps carried by Les and John before it was time to get ready. With the rest of them he went down to the crew room where they dressed in their flying kit and collected their parachutes. Allen, cumbered with bulky green navigation bag as well as his parachute pack and harness was sweating freely as he walked out to the crew bus. John was also lugging a navigation bag and all of them were carrying 'chutes and harnesses as well as their various bundles. Les had already collected the chocolate and escape kits while Jack and Harry had picked up the thermos flasks and sandwiches. Thus laden they left the crew room and a few minutes later they boarded the wagon and were driven out to their dispersal.

Les had a quick walk round the Lancaster and they all had a final pee before boarding the aircraft through the rear door. Les, Jack and John went in first, closely followed by Allen, then Harry and finally Stan and Geordie the two gunners.

Allen was particularly aware of the pungent smell of fuel, oil and Elsan fluid as he pulled himself in and then groped his way forward in the semi-darkness of the fuselage. He could hear the others grunting and cursing as they stowed their parachutes and wriggled into their stations. He crawled over the main spar and settled onto his bench before slinging his parachute under the end and laying out his tin of pencils, rulers, protractors and his Dalton computer. He pulled his helmet on and plugged in the oxygen tube and microphone jack and then pinned his first chart firmly down to the softwood bench top.

Soon the intercom became live and Les called for a crew check. Allen busied himself, pausing only to announce that he was listening in on the net and was conscious of the usual pre take-off activity. He heard Les and Jack chanting their litany: "Number two tanks on, booster coil on, pulsometer pumps on, master cock on, ignition on, contact starboard inner"

The Merlin crackled into life to be followed by the other three shortly afterwards.

Even with a leather helmet and headphones on the noise level was deafening. Allen was only separated from the engines by a thin dural skin and as Les and Jack carried out their power checks the sound approached the threshold of pain. Once the engine-driven hydraulic pumps were functioning the gunners checked their turrets for elevation and traverse while Harry completed his radio checks. Now it was time for Allen to start work. He would be continually occupied from then until the time they joined circuit over Methwold at the end of the operations. Now that the generators were running he switched on his GEE set and gave it a chance to warm up before tuning. He set his altimeter repeater and noted the vibration of the air speed indicator repeater needle which suggested that it was free and hopefully functioning. Then, the basic housekeeping done, he toggled his microphone switch and said "Nine minutes to take-off Skip", before passing him the runway in use, the direction and strength of the surface wind and the barometric pressure setting for the altimeter.

Soon they were given a green light by the runway caravan and he heard Les and Jack talking as they taxied towards the runway in use. They paused at the threshold and he heard Les say "Turret to port Stan". The engines surged briefly to full power, throttled back and then opened up as they pulled forward to the runway centre line. They slowed, turned into wind, the brakes hissed and then with a tremendous racket they started to accelerate down the runway.

This should have been a fairly heart stopping moment, it certainly became one subsequently. With three quarter full tanks and a fourteen thousand pound bomb load Les had never flown an aircraft so heavily loaded before. If they lost an engine or developed a bad swing they were probably all dead. As it happened the whole thing was too novel. Allen was so busy and so concerned that he didn't make a fool of himself that he didn't have time to think about it. The high speed vibration of the wheels stopped as they became airborne and Allen made a note in his log and opened his mike. "Airborne at 0915 Skip" he said, and once this was acknowledged went back to his chart. He heard the wheels and then the flaps retracting before the Lanc banked and climbed in a steady turn over base. He heard Jack and the gunners calling the positions of nearby aircraft before opening the mike again and giving Les his first course for the target.

The deafening noise of the engines seemed to fade as he became used to it and he settled into a steady routine of obtaining a GEE fix every six minutes. Although they were flying in the broad daylight of a late summer morning the ground was obscured by industrial haze. Until they were south of London accurate navigation was much easier with the aid of GEE than attempting to pinpoint ground features in the murk below, afterwards it was merely simpler.

The bomber stream was more of a loose gaggle than a formation. They had been briefed to stay tight enough to prevent individual bombers being picked out by predicted flak but they didn't attempt the tight groupings favoured by the American Eighth Air Force. Even so the crew felt the Lanc shudder from time to time as it hit the slipstream of other machines ahead of them. Allen heard the gunners keeping Les informed and John passing him position reports from his vantage point in the nose of the aircraft. They dog-legged round the London gun defended area climbing all the while and coasted out over Eastbourne at around ten thousand feet.

As Beachy Head came into view from the rear turret Les's voice came on the intercom. "Oxygen on fellas, we're at ten thousand". Everyone acknowledged and Allen announced that they were exactly on track and on time. He had sneaked a look to confirm their position on coasting out and a hasty comparison between that, the GEE plot and the air position indicator had given him a very accurate idea of the wind at their height.

He passed a course correction forward. "About sixty miles to the target Skip" he announced. "Level out at twelve thousand feet". He heard Stan and Geordie seek permission to test their guns and on Les's "okay" the airframe vibrated and the noise of the bursts was clear over the background roar of engines. Even John's guns were loaded for a daylight operation and after he had fired those he was given permission to fuse his bombs. Les's voice on the intercom again a bit later. "Keep your eyes peeled gunners. Only twenty miles to go now and the Jerries have still got fighters whatever the bloody intelligence officer said about air superiority".

Twenty miles. Allen's belly knotted briefly and then he settled back to work and after the next GEE fix, calculated their course out of the target and wrote it on a slip of paper. At almost the same instant he heard John say "I can see the target. Its in sight now, ahead and below at twelve o' clock".

"Are you sure?" came back Les.

Jack answered that one. "Well it's a big port and judging by the fucking flak it's not on our side! Come and have a look Nav".

Allen studied his last fix, stood up and looked over Jack's shoulder. The ground haze that had plagued them until they were well south of London had completely cleared and the sun shimmered off the sea below.

"That's it right enough" he said, "and we're still bang on track. Just maintain this heading".

With near perfect visibility and in broad daylight he had nothing else to do until they were through the target. John was occupied pushing out bundles of window to confuse the flak control radar and would soon be busy with the business of the bombing run. At this point Harry would take over the chore of windowing by pushing more bundles out of the flare chute. Allen passed Les the chit on which he had written his course out of the target area and indicated that he would stay forward to provide another pair of eyes. He could see other Lancasters in the stream, and escorting fighters at their height but well out on the flanks. High above them he could see vapour trails and the glint of sun on wings and hoped that these also came from their fighter cover.

A few minutes later John called for bomb doors open and the fuselage was racked by howling draughts and an increased noise level. In front of them and at their height the sky was full of the smoke of bursting flak. Clouds of tracer from light flak was coming up and falling well below the stream but the heavy stuff looked almost solid. Intercom conversation became curiously quiet and clipped. Les told the gunners to continue to keep their eyes open for fighters and not to concentrate on the flak. They acknowledged briefly and Allen was aware of the fact that both of the turrets were swinging methodically. John started the patter of a visual bomb run: "Left… left… steady… steady…" and Allen realised that he could actually hear the explosions of the shells coming up. Every few seconds the fuselage rang with a great coughing sound that could only be rendered as CRRUMP!

He noted to his surprise that he was curiously not frightened. He felt an odd detachment as if it weren't happening to him. He heard Jack speaking to Les who, with a set face, was trying to fly as accurately as possible through the turbulence of the barrage.

Then John again on the intercom: "Right, steady, steady"" then with a degree of elation "Bombs gone, jettison bars across, close bomb doors. Let's get out of here"! They briefly maintained their heading to clear the target area and from their altitude the docks and the buildings of the town were clearly visible. John reported that their bombs seemed to have exploded in a defended area but it was hard to separate them from the detonations caused by the other aircraft in the stream.

Allen sneaked a quick look downwards saw the smoke from bursting bombs and was puzzled for a second by the dotted yellow lines that seemed to surround the town. Then he realised what he could see were the dayglo yellow scarves and identification panels put down by the encircling allied forces of Crerar's First Canadian Army. Every tank and truck bore a panel and scarves were even laid out in front of infantry and artillery positions.

By then they were through the target and Les had already set the course out on his compass. He lowered the nose in a shallow diving turn away from the target, out to sea maintaining the turn until they were on course back towards the English coast. Allen had one more quick look round, concentrating up sun and above them, before settling down on his bench and resuming plotting GEE fixes. He was aware of John coming back to check the bomb bay for hang-ups and also, with some relief, of him reporting that all their load was away without any problems. They crossed the coast again to the west of Beachy Head and once again, dog legging around the London area, set course for Methwold slowly losing altitude en route. By now the sun was behind them and, as is usual in hazy conditions, visibility was much better looking down sun. Allen continued to rely on GEE however, largely as a matter of routine but also as experience had shown that it was more reliable inland than trying to identify landmarks with any degree of accuracy.

After about ninety minutes John confirmed their position when he reported Cambridge out to port. Les called "Roughedge" for Methwold control and the familiar landing drill started. Harry had to wind in his trailing aerial while Les and Jack chanted the litany and responses: "Auto pilot out, M gear, brake pressure, carb heat to cold". Roughedge came up with landing instructions; "Join circuit at 2,000, you are number three to land, runway 090, QFE (surface barometric pressure) 1016, wind 250 at 15". Les acknowledged and Allen busied himself tidying up his plot until he heard the whine of flap and undercarriage gear and heard Les call "funnels". Then shortly after "Engineer full flap. Airspeeds nav!" At that Allen looked up at his ASI repeater and read off the speeds: "120,120, 115,115, 112,112, 112, 110, 110, 110, fence, 100, 98, cut" and with a thump and a slight shimmy they were down. They rolled along the runway to an intersection and then taxied off, joined the perimeter track, and made the way to their dispersal, where the ground crew were waiting for them. With a squeal of brakes Les pivoted the big machine on the pan and, some three hours or so after take off, switched off the engines. The Hough crew had completed their first operation.

Allen peeled off his sweaty helmet and was conscious of his hair sticking to his scalp. He unplugged his intercom jack and oxygen tube, collected his gear and, burdened with his nav bag and parachute pack, crawled back over the main spar, shuffled down the fuselage and joined the rest of the crew on the grass by the rear door. The air smelled very good.

Once outside they divested themselves of harnesses and flying clothes and enjoyed the luxury of an unencumbered pee. Cigarettes were lit by most of them while Allen lit his pipe and puffed contentedly for a few minutes. Now they could talk. In the air there had been little said. Intercom conversations had been brief and business-like. Les discouraged casual chatter. As he said when they first crewed up "I don't want to miss a shout to corkscrew or a collision warning just because some silly bugger feels lonely". Now they were on the ground it was different and there was a buzz of conversation. Allen, who was supposed to log such things asked the first question.

"Did anyone see any of our kites go down - I certainly didn't?" To his surprise, given the apparent volume of flak they had encountered, nobody had. Neither had anybody seen any hostile fighters. At this point the ground crew, who had anxiously waited for them to return from their first operation, wandered across and the conversation became significantly more frivolous. Then the crew bus came and they went back to the briefing room for interrogation.

They didn't have long to wait for their session with an intelligence officer and were quite surprised to be offered a tot of over-proof rum so early in the afternoon. Nobody complained however and they sat there sipping the fiery stuff as the IO completed the de-briefing form. They didn't have much to say. Visibility had been very good. They had no difficulty in identifying their target and John was reasonably satisfied that his bombs had been delivered to the right place. There had been no enemy fighters but plenty of flak and they had seen nobody go down. So far as they were aware no bombs had fallen out of the target area.

The business over they arranged to meet up in the George that evening and went off back to their billets to dump their gear before walking down to their respective messes for an early tea. After that they all got their heads down for a couple of hours. Despite the fact that it was only a three hour trip they had been up since five that morning and they were all dead tired.

Sitting together in the George that night they went over the events of their first op. Les was the first to speak: "I reckon that was an easy one" he said and Jack, who had experienced a few hard ones, nodded agreement. "That bloody flak was bad though" said Geordie. "That was naan so bloody easy". Jack chimed in. "It wasn't quite so bad as it looked. In the dark all you can see of flak is the flash of the heavy stuff bursting and the light tracer coming up. In daylight the smoke from the bursts hangs around and it always looks thicker than it is. It was heavy enough though, you've all got your feet wet"!

"It wasn't me bleeding feet that was wet" chirped Stan. "It was nearly me trousers. Some of those bursts rattled my turret like a bloody tambourine". There was a general guffaw of laughter. Then someone from another crew said that "daylights were easy", only to be sharply contradicted by a reminder that that Flight Lieutenant Haggis and his crew had gone down on one the week before. They had been hit by flak over St Omer, were seen losing height, and had gone into the sea near Felixtowe on the way back. None of them survived.

Allen and Harry went for another round. When they were all settled down with drinks again Les spoke. "I'm right yer know, Jack agrees and he's done this all before. It wasn't too bad and we've had an easy start. Let's hope we get a few more like that to settle down on".

The following day they heard that it had indeed been an easy one. There had been no losses inflicted on the bombers. This was a marked contrast to a night raid on Stettin five days earlier when 23 Lancasters went down.

Their good fairy must have been listening to Les because four days later they were briefed for another daylight on Le Havre. 149 Squadron who shared the field at Methwold were also operating and four of their Stirlings were in the stream that day, the last time that the type was used on a Bomber Command operation.

This time however it wasn't so easy and they took off into a sky chequered with great masses of cloud. They climbed through it, pitching and rolling in the turbulence and intermittently bumping in the slipstream of nearby aircraft.

They coasted out over Beachy Head, going on to oxygen at ten thousand feet, but as this time the sky in front of them was darkening with a steadily descending cloud base, Allen stayed in his position maintaining a careful GEE plot. He gave Les his final course to the target and told him to level off at twelve thousand feet.

"I'll try nav" said Les "but we're nearly into the murk. If we go much higher John won't be able to see the ground".

They pressed on towards the target but were unable to climb much more than a few hundred feet. Les told the gunners to keep their eyes peeled. "We ain't very likely to see any fighters in this clag," he said, "but we won't see other kites in the stream 'til they're nearly on top of us". A quarter of an hour later Allen heard John ask if he could arm his bombs and pass over the business of windowing to Harry. Briefly his belly griped and he experienced a sudden acute awareness of fear. It was him sitting there and in a few minutes they were about to start their second opposed bombing run over a fairly hot target. Once again he discovered that he could take refuge in work. He was simply too busy to give it more than a brief thought and he settled back to his chart.

He heard John start to give course corrections on the run in and again heard the terrifying noise of heavy flak bursting too close for comfort. John spoke on the intercom, calm but sounding frustrated.

"This broken cloud is obscuring the bloody ground. I'll have to identify a target of opportunity. You won't get much notice!"

"You do that mate," said Les. "Just don't do any dummy runs in this stuff!"

Allen pencilled the course out of the target on a slip of paper, stood up, passed it to Les and had a good look around. There was stratus not far above them with thick broken stuff not far below. The skipper was right enough, there wasn't much fear of fighter attack in this but the sky at their height was dotted with bursting flak. A larger than usual gap opened below them giving a clear sight of the town below and he heard John give two quick course corrections and then call "bombs gone". At that Les initiated a shallow diving turn to starboard just as one of the gunners called "Kite going down to port".

They headed northwards, more or less re-tracing the course they had followed on the earlier raid, and the visibility improved as they flew back towards base. The landing was uneventful but this had seemed a significantly dicier trip.

In the mess that night they heard that only a hundred or so, of the over three hundred aircraft on the raid, had bombed. The rest of them had been forced to abort and even so two Lancasters had been shot down by flak.

Two days later they were called for another early morning briefing tasked with the same target. This time it was going to be a big one. The briefing was much more precise than before. There were two British divisions going in to support the Canadians and an assault on the town was planned for the following day – 11th September. Pathfinders were going to mark eight individual German strong points and accurate bombing would be required if they were to help the tanks and infantry attempting to storm the defences of the town.

The business of assembling over five hundred Lancasters, more than four hundred Halifaxes and forty five Mosquitoes took a good deal longer and the 218 Squadron contingent climbed for height over base before joining the stream. Visibility was good and the sky was clearer than the last time and dotted with cumulus clouds. It was humid however and the met officer had spoken of scattered thunderstorms building to the south.

Allen, beavering away at his plot, heard the odd exchange between Jack and the skipper and the gunners reporting the proximity of other aircraft in the stream. John passed him a pin point on Beachy Head again and he checked it against his GEE plot to calculate the wind. Again he heard Stan and Geordie seek permission to test fire their guns and the subsequent brief bursts from the turrets. His last calculation completed he passed Les a course correction and an estimated time of arrival at the target. Ten minutes later he heard John report the target in clear sight and request permission to fuse his bombs and stop pushing out window. Les gave him the Okay and Harry came up to say that he had started windowing in turn. A few seconds later John asked for the bomb doors to be opened and the noise and draught level in the fuselage increased considerably.

Allen sneaked a quick look out for a position check, pencilled in the course out of the target on a chit of paper and stood up to pass it to Les. He noticed that the cloud in front of them was towering up in great cauliflower mass but as it was well clear of the target and it didn't seem to present any problems. There were still plenty of wide clear gaps in the cloud from which fighters might emerge and so he stopped where he was to act as an extra lookout and a fire controller if necessary. The stream was fairly concentrated by this stage. Nobody wanted to be singled out by the AA gunners and the risk of collision seemed less than that of being shot down. He could see the smoke of bursting flak ahead and at their level and noticed escorting fighters way out to the flanks and high above them. He didn't really blame them for giving the flak a wide berth, but as the fuselage began to shake with the by now familiar CRUUMPs he certainly envied them.

John was on the bombing run now and had identified their particular target. "Left, left, steady—I can see our markers bursting, the green ones—right, steady". Then "Bombs gone, jettison bars across, close bomb doors". He went silent waiting to see the explosion of their load while Les after maintaining the heading for a few seconds racked into a descending turn to starboard. Allen noticed that the big cloud in front of them was a great deal closer than he had thought. They were certainly going to clip the edge of it as they turned out of the target. Les realised that too and before it happened had lowered his seat and concentrated on the blind flying panel. He wasn't worried. At least the flak had stopped and they would be out of cloud and flying visually in a minute or so.

As they entered cloud all Hell let loose. Suddenly they were flying through the mass of turbulent descending air that was spilling down the sides of a big cumulonimbus. The Lancaster dropped like a stone and the super-cooled droplets in the cloud iced up the airframe in seconds. Ice was being slung from the prop blades and hammering on the sides of the fuselage, the canopy and turrets were being obscured and Jack, who had been slung from his seat, was struggling to engage hot air to warm the carburettor intakes.

Every loose article in the aircraft was being thrown about with parachute packs, oxygen bottles, instruments, charts and coffee flasks being slung everywhere. Horrified, Allen watched the altimeter unwind seven thousand feet in what seemed like seconds but was probably more than a minute, until suddenly they broke out into the sunlight and Les regained control. They were now below three thousand feet and heading out into the Baie de la Seine and they had all suffered a considerable shaking. Stan in the tail probably had the worst of it. Without warning he had been rattled about in his reeling turret and plunged into darkness, without even being aware of the fact that they were going into cloud.

Even after this the crew maintained a remarkable calm. There was no babble on the intercom. Just a strangled "Christ" from someone who obviously had left his mike open. Les's voice broke the silence. "That was a bit bloody dicey! Check in please fellers."

They checked-in in turn and Les told the gunners to stay in their turrets, Allen and Harry to carry on, while John and Jack restored some sort of order in the front of the aircraft. Allen gathered up his scattered charts and instruments and resumed his interrupted GEE plot. His first instruction was to increase revs and climb up to join the bottom of the stream. They didn't want to be crossing any convoys at low level. Both Royal and Merchant Navy gunners tended to fire at any aircraft they saw and American vessels were equally trigger happy.

The rest of the flight was completely uneventful however and after de-briefing back at Methwold the consensus was that it had been a good prang and so far as anyone knew there had been no losses to flak or fighters. Just to gild the lily they were stood down that night with trucks laid on to take them into Cambridge.

Early that evening, seated in the bar of the University Arms, Les took a pull at his pint and looked at Allen. "Bloody hell nav, did you know that a thundercloud could do that to a kite like a Lanc?" Allen said that he hadn't but he suggested that they "give the bloody things a bit more room in the future. Of course", he mused out loud, "we won't be able to see 'em in the dark but you don't get too many big uns at night". With that the subject was changed to a much more cheerful one. They had completed their first three ops now and were beginning to know what they were doing. Nor had Bomber Command lost too many aircraft on these daylight raids on France. Maybe Jerry was beginning to give up a bit?

Two days later they were reminded that he was not. The squadron went on a night raid to Frankfurt and lost three crews. As it happened the Hough crew were not on the battle order that night and had gone to the pictures in Cambridge. At breakfast the next morning they heard the bad news. Flying Officer Corlis, an Aussie with an RAF crew had gone down, as had Flying Officer Smith and all RAF crew. More worrying, one of the few RAF pilots, Flight Lieutenant Sellar, with an Australian Flying Officer doings a second dickie trip and a highly experienced crew that included an Aussie rear gunner and a Canadian radio operator had also failed to return. If blokes like that were getting the chop it didn't do to take anything for granted.

They got a bit of a breather however. The news from France and Belgium had been fairly good up to now. The allied armies were advancing rapidly and the first American troops had reached the German frontier on 10th September - the day of their last raid on Le Havre. On the 15th Allied forces entered Holland but then came the bloody fiasco of Arnhem and tactical operations to support the ground forces were planned and cancelled as they were again and again overtaken by events. As it happened it was to be another ten days before the crew operated again.

They were still in fairly good shape. Despite their shaking over Le Havre and the news of the squadron's awful night of the 12/13th. of September, they had enjoyed a relatively easy ride so far. When they were briefed for another daylight on Calais on 20th September they couldn't believe their luck. It was a short range trip in good visibility. Allen kept them bang on track. John did a faultless visual run and put the bombs down accurately, and of the nearly six hundred and fifty Bomber Command aircraft despatched only one was lost.

Five days later they went to Calais again. As a raid it wasn't a great success. The command despatched eight hundred and seventy two aircraft but cloud cover meant that only two hundred and eighty seven of them were able to bomb through breaks in the cloud. So far as the Hough crew were concerned it was a good trip. No aircraft were lost and John managed to get his bombs away through a conveniently placed gap in the cover.

Two days later they went again on a cloudy overcast day. it was a smaller force this time - two hundred odd Lancasters, eighty plus Halifaxes and thirty five Mosquitoes.

As they ran into the target at twelve thousand feet it was completely covered with cloud. John declared that he couldn't see a thing and it looked as if they would have to abort. Allen, probably followed by the rest of the crew, groaned quietly. An aborted trip didn't count towards a tour and they weren't all going to be short easy trips to French targets.

Before anyone could comment the Master bomber came on the air with an instruction to lose height and bomb from below cloud. By now they had ceased expecting fighter opposition over France but the thought of facing the flak at low level in a heavy bomber was frightening. Agile fighter bombers like Typhoons or Thunderbolts were suffering heavy losses on ground attack missions and the thought of mixing it with the light flak in a Lancaster made Allen's stomach churn.

He didn't have too much time to worry. As they ran in he completed his final calculation for the course out and moved forward to pass the chit to the skipper. Les grinned at him and pointed to the flak bursts but the heavy stuff seemed to be having trouble tracking them at their height and much of the light stuff seemed to be below them. John put their bombs down accurately on a battery position and they turned away unscathed to head back out to sea.

The journey back was uneventful and they landed at Methwold after a three hour trip with the prospect of a weeks leave to look forward to. After de-briefing, tea and a couple of hours kip Allen had arranged to meet Les and walk down to the George. The others had gone off, heading for an earlier train, but there was no connection to

Darlington for Allen and Les was due to meet up with some Aussie mates in London the next day.

They met by the camp gate, ambled down to the pub and while Allen got the first round in Les chi-iked with another Aussie pilot while he found a couple of chairs.

"Cheers mate," said Les as he took his pint. "The spy says that we only lost one today, despite going in at that height. They can't all be that easy though!"

"Maybe the buggers are giving up," said Allen, but he knew they weren't.

18. Nights are Different

Just like the last time home leave seemed pretty good to Allen. The sheer ordinariness of it pulled around him like a comfort blanket. It was good to have Mum busying herself about the house and to take Dad down to the local for a pint at lunch time. It was good to sleep in his own bed and hear his little brother thundering about the house doing whatever little brothers do. Looking around at the aeromodelling journals, pulp magazines and books about flying that still filled his room he was amazed at his innocent younger self. He hadn't thought in those days that the price of achieving his ambition to fly might be large numbers of people making serious efforts to kill him. It seemed almost incredible that for the last few weeks a lot of flak gunners had been doing just that. Had it really happened to him?

He was at home now however and he pushed all thoughts about operations to the back of his mind. Even the food was better at home. Civilians didn't normally eat as well as aircrew but the combination of Dad's vegetable garden, a bit of barter and Mum's cooking made the Clifford household rather different. His only real problem was continuing to convince his parents that he was still involved in training. His mother seemed to swallow the story uncritically but he was fairly certain that his father had tumbled to the fact that his operational career had started.

Thanks to the emergency daylight saving regulations Double Summertime meant that there was still a good bit of light in the evenings and Rita was fairly free once she was off duty. As a result the pair of them were able to behave very much like any other young couple. Daylight and weather permitting they could take a walk, go to the cinema or enjoy a dance.

In contrast with Allen's other life, pubs didn't feature very much in their shared time. In the north-east in the nineteen forties, women were not expected to enter pubs. There was no formal barrier but in the attitudes of the regulars, the bar staff and the landlord, it was made patently obvious that they were not welcome Tea shops however still abounded and so there was always somewhere warm where they could take refuge if they needed to.

On leave at least the war was becoming a little bit less obtrusive. Although the Arnhem attack had failed and the south east of England was still under attack from rockets, a few flying bombs and the odd nuisance raid, there were signs about that suggested that the war wasn't going to last for ever. The most noticeable of these was a gradual easing of the blackout regulations. Unless there was an air raid alert in force a few shaded street lights were now permitted. Vehicle headlights were still masked but they emitted sufficient light to make cars and lorries less of a hazard than they had been. The total blackout that had made the streets so dangerous had ended, or at least was becoming a bit more endurable. In spite of this tolerance was wearing thin, the war had been going on for far too long and everyone was tired, shabby and fed up with it.

His time at home seemed to pass all too quickly and it was soon over. Soon he was humping his kit through the darkened streets on his way to the railway station and the war. When Allen walked back into the billet after the usual tedious journey he was greeted by Harry, who told him that they were on the battle order for the next day. It was going to be another daylight op, which meant a hideously early start, so he had a quick wash and shave and turned-in early. He was wakened in the small hours by the orderly corporal and signed the list on his clip board as evidence that he had been roused.

It was still pitch dark when he went down for the pilots and navigators briefing the next morning and the backs of his eyes ached as he struggled to shake off the muzziness of a short and disturbed night. Les was there of course but the others were snatching an extra hours sleep before joining them for the general briefing later on. The first thing they checked was the target, was it a bad one, Solingen for instance? The tape on the wall map stretched from a rendezvous point over Southwold to the mouth of the Schelde. A Dutch coastal target, it could be worse. The navigation leader gave details of courses, airspeeds, heights and turning points and Allen scribbled furiously to get the details down. While he transferred the details from the summary sheet and pencilled-in his chart the CO continued to brief the pilots as he outlined the purpose of the raid. This time they were to attack the sea wall that surrounded the island of Walcheren and it was to be a fairly complex operation. Target marking was to be provided by Oboe[5] equipped Mosquitoes and Pathfinder Lancasters and the main attackers were to make up eight groups of thirty main Force Lancasters.

When the rest of the crews joined them the bombing leader took over and gave his men details of bomb loads and fusing. Accuracy was to be crucial. The sea wall was a long, thin linear target and any bombs that missed would be merely blast a shallow hole. If they were to stand any chance of damaging the embankment they would have to put down their loads directly on to it.

The 218 Squadron machines, like most of the others, were carrying a mixture of four thousand pound thin case cookies, as well as one thousand and five hundred pound general purpose bombs. It was hoped that the relatively cheap blast bombs would breach the sea wall but Bomber Command were not certain that they could do it. Unknown to the Main Force crews, just in case this didn't work the last wave of Lancasters was made up of 617 Squadron machines carrying twelve thousand pound Tallboy, deep penetration Earthquake weapons.

The intelligence officer, explaining the purpose of the raid at the end of the briefing, told them that the allies had liberated the port of Antwerp and found the docks reasonably intact. Their lines of supply from Normandy were desperately over-stretched and they badly needed a major port closer to the front lines as they advanced eastward. Unfortunately the approaches to Antwerp were dominated by

[5] Oboe was a very accurate electronic target location device. It required paired ground stations to transmit guidance signals to the attacking aircraft and as each pair could only handle one aircraft at a time its capacity was limited.

German held pockets. Until something could be done about that, the docks were unusable.

Walcheren, lying directly across the estuary, was a major obstacle. The island was held by the Wehrmacht and their artillery completely blocked access to the port. The intention, in bombing the sea wall, was to create breaches big enough to inundate the island.

Most of the polders, the reclaimed fields, on Walcheren were below sea level and as the intelligence officer rather ponderously said "it was thought that localised flooding would seriously hamper the defence". The Hough crew, whose navigator could read contour lines, thought that the defenders would be adequately protected from the likely depth of water by serviceable wellies but they were not consulted on the issue. They were going to Walcheren like it or not and they were going in at very low level, five thousand feet or less.

They didn't have long to worry about it. Allen just about had time to ink in his charts and pack his navigation bag before they went down to the mess hall for the usual bacon and eggs. From there it was down to the crew room and the frantic business of drawing parachutes, Mae Wests, chocolate and escape kits. Navigators also had to collect and carry a sextant although few of them ever used one. No sooner was this done than the crew buses arrived and they were on their way to the dispersals. There was just time for a quick last minute pee before boarding their machine and getting themselves ready for take-off.

As he stowed sextant and parachute, set out his equipment, plugged in intercom and oxygen connections and pulled on his helmet, he was aware of an increasingly familiar sensation in his belly. The combination of a 3am start, a greasy fried breakfast and the awareness that they were about to face the flak at low level made his stomach knot in a brief spasm. He tried to ignore it and as the intercom came alive and he heard the others go through their checks he began to busy himself pinning his first chart to the bench top.

He heard Jack slide back the starboard side window of the cockpit and shout to the ground crew, then the starboard inner started with the usual racket shortly followed by the other three. He tightened his helmet strap to minimise the noise and, now that the generators were running, switched on the GEE console to allow it to warm up. He checked his figures again, first from the form and then from the chart, before writing the first course on a chit ready to hand up to Les. He heard pilot and engineer running methodically through their drills and after power checks on all four engines, he toggled the intercom and passed the pre take-off details - departure time, runway in use, barometric pressure, wind strength and direction. As they bumped and weaved their way around the perimeter track he remembered the details of their bomb load. For the first time they were carrying a cookie and if anything went radically wrong on take-off the impact would almost certainly detonate it, fused or not. "Ah well, best not to think about it!" The next thing he heard was Les say "Turret to port Stan" before swinging into wind and opening all four throttles to take-off power. The heavily laden Lancaster accelerated slowly. The jolting of the undercarriage became faster and faster, then changed to a rapid vibration which ceased as they left the runway. Allen waited until the undercarriage and flaps were up before reporting their take-off time. A minute or so later, as he heard the skipper ask for reduced climbing power, he opened his microphone and called for their first heading. At the same time he passed a chit forward to confirm the course and then turned to commence his GEE plot.

From now on he was simply too busy to worry about anything. The business of taking a fix every few minutes absorbed his entire attention. About the only other details that registered were a couple of visual fixes coming back from John in the Bomb-Aimers position and even those demanded a cross reference to his plot and a hasty wind calculation. He was vaguely aware of John seeking permission to fuse his bombs and the odd clipped report from the gunners. Even the vibration down the fuselage of test firing failed to disturb his fierce concentration. There were some thirty aircraft in their wave, flying in a loose gaggle but close enough for them to be jolted by slipstream fairly frequently. They were heading for the most westerly part of the island, Westkapelle, and at their altitude they wouldn't see it until they were very close.

He was pretty confident that they were bang on course. GEE was working well, his last ground fix on coasting out had given him a fair idea of the wind at their height and they were tucked well into the gaggle. Their planned approach was intended to take them along a straight section of the sea wall so that as long as their bombs were lined up accurately they should have a fair chance of hitting it. Lateral error of course would completely defeat them. Left or right and they would either kill fish or make a big hole in a field. It was essential that they get their approach exactly right.

He heard Les warn the gunners to keep their eyes open. They had been briefed to expect fighter opposition and he could feel the Lanc yawing when the turrets rotated as Geordie and Stan meticulously scanned the sky. He called ten miles to target and heard John ask for the bomb doors to be opened. Les asked Jack for climbing power and sneaked a few hundred extra feet of height. When they went through the target he would trade that height for speed and cross the zone of thickest flak like a bat out of Hell.

He heard John call target in sight, wrote down the homeward course on a slip of paper and stood up. As it was a daylight raid the curtains around his compartment had not been drawn and looking forward between Les and Jack he could see the line of the sea wall precisely on their track. There was a good deal of light and heavy flak coming up and the lingering smoke from the bursting heavy shells made it seem very dense over the target.

Les was still yawing their machine, ensuring that it skidded through the sky and rarely actually flew in the direction that it was pointing. The ground gunners were obviously taken by surprise by their low altitude and the 88 mm. batteries seemed to be having difficulty in tracking them. There was plenty of light flak coming up not just from the ground but also from ships in the estuary and the sky seemed to be full of coloured tracer. The light stuff was fused to self-destruct and air burst if it failed to hit anything. Small fragments of light shell were falling from above and rattling on wings and fuselage as they closed on the target. So far however, so good, and as Les straightened up for the bombing run the light stuff was still missing them and although they had heard the CRUMPP of heavy shells boom down the fuselage nothing had come too close.

They could see the detonation of bombs put down by the previous four waves, the ground was cratered and the sea was being churned up by explosions. Les levelled the aircraft momentarily and as John called "Bombs gone" held on briefly for the photoflash and then banked away seaward. Allen, who had been looking out for fighters, glanced down in time to see a cluster of bomb bursts, a section of the sea wall collapse, and the sea begin to flood through the breach. They didn't linger to see it but the following two waves demolished further sections and the services of 617 Squadron were not needed. All their crews had to do was return home and pull off a safe landing with a twelve thousand pound bomb still on board.

Apart from John inspecting the bomb bay and declaring it clear, nothing was said for some while. The gunners were still swinging their turrets in the search for fighters and Les was rolling the aircraft into a banking search to ensure that nothing sneaked in from beneath them. Allen went back to his bench and resumed the GEE plot and apart from a couple of minor course corrections worked in silence. About a quarter of an hour out the intercom came alive. "Skipper here. I think the bastards were having an off day, did anyone see any of ours go down?" Nobody reported seeing anything and the intercom went quiet again. Soon John reported that the English coast was in sight and Les came up again. "Gunners keep your eyes open for other kites in the stream. OK to smoke now".

The rest of the flight was uneventful but they were given a late turn to land and by the time they had taxied back to their dispersal, shut down and given the battle damage report to the ground crew they were feeling fairly weary. When they went in for de-briefing they were told that not only had the target been successfully attacked but none of the raiders had been shot down. The next item of news was even more welcome. They were stood down for twenty four hours.

"Good Oh!" said Les "Get your heads down for a few hours after lunch and we'll go into Cambridge tonight. One of me mates has fixed me up with the loan of a jeep. All pissed tonight fellas. Adolf can wait until another day!"

By the time that they had eaten and had a few hours sleep the late afternoon light was fading. Good as his word, Les was seated at the wheel of a jeep waiting down near the MT yard. They all piled in and at that point Les let in the clutch with a thump and they hurtled off through the lanes on the thirty mile journey to Cambridge. They left the jeep near the Eagle but not until Jack had rooted under the bonnet and removed the rotor arm from the distributor. Jeeps were regarded as fair game by both RAF and USAAF crews and if they weren't immobilised they were likely to be "borrowed".

Several pints of bitter were drunk. An interval was taken while they ventured out for fish and chips and then a couple more rounds were consumed. They had all taken the precaution of bringing a pint beer mug to the pub with them. By that stage in the war pub glasses were in short supply and the only way to ensure that you would be served, always assuming that the pub had any beer, was to bring your own glass. Needless to say, everyone had filched one and they had become something approaching a standard part of aircrew equipment.

Les, somewhat carried away by the events of the day, ordered a large whisky, but of course, as the rest of the crew had expected, none was to be had. Whisky was in remarkably short supply and in Cambridge, a city frequented by crews from both air forces, it verged on the unobtainable. Muttering profanely he settled for another round of bitter but he was obviously irritated by his failure and it cropped up in conversation for the rest of the evening.

Far too soon for them time was called and they weaved their way gently out of the pub. Groping their way back through the darkened streets they located the jeep and Jack put the rotor arm back. On their way back to Methwold Les was still contemplating the whisky supply problem. It was a longish journey in the dark and they nattered sleepily to the driver over the noise of the engine. Suddenly the jeep lurched as he turned his head to the crew in triumph. He had solved the problem. "We need to go to one of those pubs where the posh Poms eat" he announced "those jokers all like their grog and they don't drink beer"! There was a chorus of agreement, which resulted as much from a desire that he keep his eyes on the road as anything else, and shortly after that point they arrived at the guard-room. Once the jeep was parked up in the MT yard they made their way back to their respective billets. They were all exhausted. Despite the couple of hours that they had snatched that afternoon they were chronically short of sleep and a long night and a long lie-in seemed called for.

Late the next morning, after a leisurely wash and shave, they made their way down to the flight office. A glance at the battle order showed that they were posted for ops the morning after next. It was going to be another 3 am. start for Les and Allen with the others joining them again an hour later. They decided to make the best of the stand-down the following day and get back in time for a reasonably early bed. They had been punch-drunk with fatigue at the beginning of the Walcheren op and they wanted to start a bit fresher this time. Without a vehicle it would take too long to get to Cambridge and so they decided to catch a local bus and go to the pictures in Downham Market.

Later that day they sat in the stuffy darkness of the cinema, companionably enjoying the film, then afterwards called in to a pub for a few drinks before catching the bus back to camp. It was as they stood among the little crowd of late shoppers and homecoming workers that Allen was suddenly seized again with the incongruous nature of his situation. Yesterday he had been over Walcheren being shot at, tomorrow he would be over another hostile target being shot at again and here he was, standing in a rural bus queue while people around him gossiped about shopping and allotment gardening. Somehow the whole situation seemed surreal.

It seemed worse at 3.30 the following morning as he clumsily signed the list on the clip board proffered by a sleepy orderly corporal. He dragged himself out of bed, pulled on his battle dress and after a perfunctory splashing of the face with cold water, made his way down to the briefing room.

Les joined him at the door and as they went in together their eyes were drawn irresistibly to the wall map. The tape plotted a route that went an awfully long way south and terminated at Saarbrucken.

"Fuck me," said Les after a pregnant silence. "Our first trip to the Third and bloody last Reich. I hope the fighter cover's good because we're going to be in Adolf's home paddock". Then the briefing began and soon they were both scribbling furiously. This was to be an army support operation, an attempt to cut the road and rail links that were keeping alive the German opposition to the American Third Army. Accurate bombing was essential as the Americans were very close to the city and they were briefed to pay close attention to the instructions of the Master Bomber. Should their targets change they would be re-marked by the Pathfinders, green target indicator bombs to mark, and red TIs to cancel. If Bomber Command decided that the Americans were too close, or were seriously worried about their ability to hit the correct spots, the order to abort the operation and bring their bombs home would be given by the code word "marmalade" transmitted on the Master Bomber's frequency.

By the time Allen started to pencil in the charts the rest of the crew had joined them for the main briefing. They were told details of their bomb load, how much fighter cover they could expect and where the worst flak could be expected. John was also required to mark his topographical map with American free fire zones. These could not be crossed at low level without attracting heavy AA fire from batteries protecting the American forces from fighter bomber attacks.

After briefing they went off for an early breakfast before going down to the crew room to get ready. They drew their usual ration of sweets and chocolate and collected their kit before the buses took them down to the dispersals and their waiting aircraft. These were already air tested, fuelled and bombed up so Les and Jack did the walk-round in the early morning light while the rest of them climbed aboard and started their checks. There was still no order to start up and after a while they vacated the aircraft and started a desultory kick-about on tarmac of the dispersal pan. An hour or so dragged by, until a bit later a little Hillman van appeared. The flight commander's head poked out of the window and he beckoned Les towards him. There was a brief exchange of words before he drove off and afterwards Les turned towards them. He did not look happy. "There's been a bloody cock up" he said. "Take-off's been postponed for four hours. We're to go down for an early lunch and re-board for a twelve thirty take off".

At twelve thirty they were back again but before they had a chance to do anything another four hour delay was announced. Shortly after that they were told to stand down for the afternoon and report back to the briefing room for further instructions at half past six that evening. By now most of them had been awake for over ten hours and some tried to snatch a little sleep. The situation did not lend itself to relaxation however and the best that any of them could manage was a fitful doze.

They returned to the briefing room to find their instructions largely unchanged. The only real difference was that it was to be a standard Bomber Command night attack and any air opposition would come from Luftwaffe night-fighters. It was not cheering news to receive. Whatever fighter superiority the Allies might enjoy over Germany by day, at night things were different. The night sky over the Reich was still an extremely dangerous place to be.

Flying supper, usually noisy with nervous conversation, was unusually subdued. It was nearly fourteen hours since they were roused for their initial briefing and the series of delays had kept tension high. Nobody was admitting to feeling the strain but all of them were feeling pretty weary by then. The two young gunners were not of an age to cope well with sleep deprivation and, pale and hollow eyed, they were visibly showing signs of exhaustion.

Most of their kit was still in their aircraft and so, pausing only to collect flasks of coffee and packets of sandwiches from the crew room, they boarded the buses and went back out to their dispersals.

They stopped by their machine HA-C, known as Charlie, and the glimmers from darkened flashlights showed where the ground crew were waiting for them. The rear door was opened and they climbed in. It was like going into a narrow cellar. The interior of the fuselage was pitch dark as they didn't want to impair their night vision by using torches or switching on any interior lights. They groped their way to their stations, dumped their gear and checked their equipment. Allen drew the curtains around his position. He would need his little angle poise lamp switched on in order to see his charts and it was important that the light should not leak out to blind the others at the front of the aircraft. He settled down, plugged in his intercom and oxygen leads again and busied himself pinning down charts and rearranging his gear. His stomach felt queasy after yet another fried meal and he was thoroughly uncomfortable. He was dressed for a night high altitude operation with a khaki shirt, heavy dark blue knitted roll neck sweater and a battle dress jacket. The Mae West worn under his parachute harness rode up and chafed his neck and his helmet was already feeling tight against his head. The earphones were making his ears sore and he knew that the oxygen mask would soon be rubbing on the bridge of his nose. He was also feeling more than a little scared. A degree of apprehension before an operation was to be expected but there was something about the darkness that made it worse. Human beings do not, in general, function well at night even if they are well rested and few of the men in the 218 Squadron crews had seen their beds for eighteen hours.

He forced himself to concentrate on the job and wrote the take-off information on a slip of paper ready to pass to Les. This was going to be a hard one. It was a cloudy night and there was going to be very little chance of seeing the ground well enough to establish their position. With reasonable luck however, GEE would be functioning for most of the way. Jamming shouldn't be much of a problem until they were very close to the German frontier and they should be almost in sight of the target by then. If GEE failed then they were back to dead reckoning or astro and he didn't fancy that very much. Dead reckoning was only reliable if you got the winds exactly right and astro required a protracted period of flying straight and level, not a healthy pastime over Germany at night.

"Concentrate, concentrate", he told himself, then he was vaguely aware of the start-up drill followed by the clamour of the engines. Once the GEE was switched on to warm up he had nothing to do for a few minutes. He passed the usual take-off information to Les and then, after what seemed an interminable wait, came the careful creep round the perimeter track, the power checks and the take-off into the darkness.

It was here that the old joss began to work. He settled into the collar and forgot everything in concentrating on his plot. He heard the revs come back to climbing power and Charlie climbed steadily on track. He knew that Les would have lowered his seat and would be concentrating on his instrument panel. He would be methodically scanning through DR compass, artificial horizon, air speed indicator, turn and slip indicator and altimeter. Forward look-out would be largely left to John while the gunners kept a sharp eye below and on the rearward 270 degrees. Apart from Les, they had little else to do but sit there and try to keep awake but he was plotting a GEE fix every three minutes and passing new courses and corrections to keep Charlie in the stream.

It grew steadily colder and at ten thousand feet Les told Harry to open the main oxygen cock and then gave the order "Oxygen on everybody!" John came up on the intercom reporting them as over the Thames Estuary and identifying Margate just out to starboard. Allen checked his plot against the air position indicator and did a quick calculation. The forecast winds at this height seemed to be about right. They continued the long climb out over The Straits of Dover. Broken cloud largely obscured the French coast and John couldn't establish a visual fix as they coasted in.

It was getting bloody cold. Les asked Harry to turn the heat up and Allen warmed his fingers at the little hot air trunk directed down at his bench. Chilled hands made him clumsy with pencil and ruler but even then the casing of his Dalton computer struck cold against his fingers.

The intercom again and Les's voice. "Oxygen check everybody," and one by one the crew checked in. The turret mechanisms vibrated down the airframe as the gunners swung them and scanned the sky. Harry came up on the intercom with a broadcast wind which seemed roughly in line with the one indicated by their last positive fix. By now they were up to their briefed altitude of twenty thousand feet and were throttled back to cruising power. The sound of the four Merlins was now almost a white noise fading into the background and only noticeable when they drifted out of synchronisation and Jack fiddled with the throttles to bring them back again.

He was tired, but he was used to that, and the constant demand of the plot kept him going. He was cold too, with sweat clammy on his body, feet chilled and fingers stiff and fumbling. He tried to wear his silk inner gloves but soon abandoned them. He found that he couldn't grip his drawing instruments and the smooth fabric slipped on the dial controls of the GEE box. His oxygen mask was dripping his condensed breath on the chart, smudging the lines and blurring the calculations.

Suddenly Stan's voice on the intercom sounding high pitched but clear, "Fighter, fighter, corkscrew starboard!" Les reacted instantly with the nose pitching down at the first word before rolling steeply into a steep starboard bank. Loaded with seven tons of bombs and more than two thirds of their fuel the big machine accelerated downhill like a lift with a broken suspension wire. Allen, who had no means of strapping himself down to his bench, clung on for dear life. With only a little pool of light from his angle-poise lamp he couldn't see much but he noticed his instruments float past his nose under the negative G and over the noise of the engines he heard the walk-around oxygen cylinder stowed by his bench hit the top of the bulkhead Suddenly they rolled out to port and the nose came up steeply. Allen's chin was jammed down into the collar of his tunic and the blood drained from his head. The deceleration was equally spectacular as they soared upwards and the speed bled off almost to the point of the stall. Just as he was congratulating himself on the fact that he had not thrown up and that the tail still seemed to be attached to the fuselage, the nose pitched down again and they repeated the manoeuvre.

This time they settled down more or less on track and when Les's voice spoke on the intercom, he was obviously breathing hard with the exertion of throwing the laden Lancaster about. "Where is he gunners, can you see him?" Stan replied. "I think you lost him on the first one Skip. It was a twin engined kite and he went straight over the top of us".

There were Mosquitos in the stream and it could have been one of them but the gunners' disciplined reaction had been faultless. Stan had made the sighting and called for evasive action. He had resisted the temptation to blaze away in the dark and had neither shot at a friendly machine nor revealed their position to a hostile one. Geordie, who had seen nothing, had similarly kept his cool and resisted the urge to let fly at anything.

Les again, "Skipper to gunners, I'm going to do a banking search, keep your eyes peeled." They saw nothing, neither did John who was looking out below and Les, assuming that the strange machine was either an overtaking Pathfinder Mosquito or night fighter that they had shaken off, returned to their original heading and calling for more power, started to climb again.

A quick check established that everyone was OK and that nobody had vomited into their oxygen mask. This last problem was not merely a matter of comfort. At twenty thousand feet a mask blocked with the frozen contents of the stomach could produce unconsciousness in minutes.

Jack, Harry and John were moving about trying to reduce the interior of Charlie to some semblance of order while Allen retrieved his scattered kit and settled down to re-establishing his GEE plot. It had seemed like half an hour since Stan had called "fighter" but a glance at his watch showed that it had in fact been less than five minutes. Two minutes later he drew the next cross on the chart and settled down into the routine again. After the sudden shot of adrenaline his fatigue had vanished and he was surprisingly awake and relatively unflustered.

Les on the intercom again, "Where are we nav? I haven't seen any other kites and there are supposed to be over five hundred of us in the stream". Allen gave their position as sixty miles short of the target and still on track.

Les's concern was understandable. He hadn't seen another machine since the last of the navigation lights was turned out as they cleared base. Being squarely in the stream was important. Like the gazelle of the African plains, their principal means of defence was evasion and their ability to blend in with the rest of the attackers prevented them from being singled out and picked off by flak or fighters. If they were seriously out of position they were going to be dangerously vulnerable. As it happened they were well tucked in. They couldn't see any other Lancasters in the darkness of the night sky but the little rumbles of turbulence that they encountered from time to time were caused by the slipstreams of machines flying in front of them. They should have recognised them after their daylight experiences but they were further apart and less violent, and anyway, things seemed different in the dark. It was all part of the learning experience.

Allen glanced up at the repeater panel and noted that they were climbing. Les was doing his usual trick of gaining enough height to give them a fast downhill run through the target. He fixed the last GEE position, noted that they were still on track, and factored in the expected airspeed before calculating the course out of the target area. He wrote it down on the usual chit and put it in the clip ready to pass forward. He heard John turn over the task of pushing out window to Harry in preparation for the bombing run.

John on the intercom. "Bomb aimer to nav, I still can't see the target?"

They had to be close and Allen switched off his light, pushed back the curtains and stood up. At first he could see nothing but darkness but he toggled his mike and said "Target should be about twenty five miles dead ahead, about three minutes" and as he said that, the first green TIs went down and the flak opened up. It was terrifyingly impressive, as the sky ahead changed from darkness to a bubbling mass of bursting shells just below their altitude and a carpet of interweaving light flak tracer far below them.

"It's there" he said but he didn't bother to switch on his mike. He thought that Les and John had probably noticed.

He nudged Jack's shoulder and motioned him to give Les the chit with the next course on it. Les, in turn, glanced at it, nodded, and concentrated on his flying

He heard the call for bomb doors to be opened and John started his patter......

"Left… left… right…. Left…. Left… (left was always repeated so that any correction given twice was clearly a left one) … steady…" and they were flying faster, diving gently, directly towards a carpet of bursting green target indicators. The Master Bomber came up on the RT, "Don't creep back, bomb on the greens, bomb on the greens". John's patter sounded confident and as the range was foreshortened by their great height they seemed very close to the target.

More TIs exploded on the ground in front of them with great splashes of green fire then suddenly they heard another voice on the Master Bomber's frequency. "Marmalade, marmalade!" the order to abort the bombing run and take the load home. Then again the first voice "bomb on the greens, bomb on the greens!" Then the second voice sounded again more urgently, "Marmalade, marmalade!" For what seemed like ages but must only have been a matter of seconds the two voices repeated their contradictory orders with increasing urgency.

John on the intercom sounding flustered "It was the abort code, close bomb doors and we'll have to take 'em home".

Les, insistently, "Skipper to Bomb Aimer. Bomb on the greens. There aren't two bloody Master bombers. Let the bastards go on the greens!" Charlie levelled out momentarily.

There was a hesitant silence and then "OK Skipper" and shortly after that "bombs gone, jettison bars across, close bomb doors".

The bursting flak continued to echo down the fuselage and they could hear the impact of fragments on the decking. Soon the descending arc of their turn took them clear of the target and Allen returned to his bench. As he closed the curtains he was aware of John coming back to check the bomb bay for hang-ups. He was concentrating on keeping his footing as he scrambled back over the main spar and he didn't look at Allen as he passed.

A few seconds later he reported back. "No hang ups but I can see fires on the ground through holes in the bomb doors. We got a bit peppered back here". Les acknowledged and then, after reminding the gunners to keep a good look out and not stare at the target, the intercom clicked off and there was a long period of silence.

Allen was busy as ever lining up the GEE pulses and plotting the fixes. The intense cold continued to bother him but what he found particularly irritating was his apparent difficulty in doing basic calculations. He was finding simple multiplication sums hard to manage and was resorting to writing down little strings of figures, or clusters of dots, and adding them up. He soldiered on however, cursing himself for stupidity when he fumbled with his Dalton computer, and as the line of plotted points marched north and west he continued to pass Les new headings and course and speed corrections.

Slowly Charlie lost altitude until Les's voice on the intercom told them that it was OK to remove their oxygen masks and smoke if they wanted to. Smoking was of course officially forbidden in the air. An alloy structure laden with volatile high octane fuel, oxygen bottles and pyrotechnics was something of a fire hazard. However in the hierarchy of risk faced by the young men of Bomber Command accidental fire in the air did not seem to rank very high. As a result most of them smoked once they were below oxygen height and relatively free of the danger of fighter interception. Allen, who was beginning to feel more alert, filled his pipe and gratefully puffed away.

John got a visual fix as they crossed the English coast again and they found themselves squarely on track. The rest of the flight was uneventful, they were given an early turn to land and after the usual fag of taxiing and shutting down the aircraft they climbed wearily out of the rear door. On his way back down the fuselage Allen had noticed a fairly unpleasant reek and a glistening oily substance streaked in a spiral round and round the interior. Geordie, who had just climbed down from the mid-upper turret, was in front of him and he noticed that his overall was smeared and stained with the same stuff.

"Christ!" he said, "is that blood?"

"Naah..." said Geordie, "Ah think it's shit. The lid came off the fookin' Elsan when we went into that corkscrew and stoof went all oover the place!"

As it happened Geordie was wrong. All that the Elsan toilet contained was evil-smelling disinfectant fluid, happily nobody had used it for its primary purpose.

Once out of the aircraft they gave their snag and battle damage report as succinctly as they could before boarding the bus back to interrogation.

They were all fairly subdued as they gave their account of the raid. It had seemed fairly shambolic to them and they were by no means certain that they had even bombed the correct target. About the only positive thing that they could report was that they had seen no other Lancasters go down. Allen was intercepted by the Navigation Leader as they left the table who stretched out his hand and said "Let's have a look at your chart son." He handed it over rather reluctantly. Untidy, covered with ineptly done calculations and smeared with dribbled condensation from his oxygen mask, it looked a thorough going mess. He dreaded what comments this effort would attract. As it happened the leader took a quick glance grunted and tucked it under his arm. "Go and get some sleep lad and come back in the morning. We'll talk about it then!"

The next morning, rested, washed, shaved and breakfasted, Allen felt a very much better man. He walked down to the navigation office and braced himself for a bit of a bollocking. To his surprise the Navigation Leader gave him a chair, spread out the chart in front of him and smiled amiably. "Bit of a mess isn't it?" he said. Allen nodded, embarrassed by the condition of it. "Actually it isn't too bad. The turning points were OK, you got in on time, you got out on time and the winds were OK. I've seen a lot worse."

Allen gestured to the chart "But it is a mess," he said "and I didn't seem able to do the simplest thing without an effort". The leader raised an eyebrow. "Was that your first trip high and at night?" Allen nodded agreement. "It will get a bit better when you're used to it but it's always pretty well like that. You're cold and Anoxic and at best your system is working at about half throttle. We're all like that The only consolation is that the Gerry crews are in the same state. It levels it down a bit."

Vastly cheered, Allen went off to find the rest of the crew. They too were looking remarkably cheerful. It might have seemed like one continuous cock up but intelligence were reporting a highly successful raid.

A photo-recce Spitfire had taken pictures showing that the railway junction and marshalling yards had been almost destroyed and the main roads were heavily cratered and unusable. The American Third Army, who were pushing up to the Siegfreid Line, were absolutely delighted. Prisoners were saying that their lines of communication had been effectively cut off. Even better, only three attacking Lancasters had gone down, about one half per cent of the force. It had seemed a bloody awful night but at that rate they might even get through their tour in one piece.

19. I Knew You Started Scared

Les, who had been down to the flight office, gave them the good news. "We're on again tonight blokes! Briefing at six!" There was a gentle groan. "Dry yer eyes! We've only just had breakfast and there'll be night flying supper tonight. Let's all piss off down to the George!" There was a mass exodus in the direction of the village and once a couple of pints were down the memory of the previous night didn't seem so bad. They got their heads down again for a couple of hours in the afternoon and after an early tea Les and Allen went in for briefing.

The target for that night was Dortmund; the beginning of what became known as the second battle of the Ruhr and with over five hundred aircraft tasked it was going to be a biggish raid. The others came in about an hour later and winced a bit when they saw the target. The Ruhr flak was famous and if night fighters got into the stream it would seem like a long way home. The knowledge didn't seem to spoil any appetites and they all got stuck into their bacon and eggs after briefing.

The journey out was in clear skies but they still didn't see any other aircraft once their navigation lights were extinguished. This time however they recognised the little patches of turbulence they kept striking and were comforted by their frequency at the turning points. They knew that this meant that they were tucked well into the stream. There was a bit of flak visible from defended areas on either side of track but they didn't see much until they were in sight of the target. They were flying at over twenty thousand feet in good visibility and hence saw the first TIs go down from a long way off. Les, as usual, was well up on the step and they went through the target at considerably more than the briefed airspeed. The sky was the same bubbling cauldron that they had seen over Saarbrucken and the sound of the shell bursts and rattle of fragments on the fuselage was equally noisy, but again their luck was in; they came to no harm and were soon turning away from Dortmund and on course for home. The rest of trip was uneventful; they saw a little more flak but observed no air to air fighting.

They wondered quite what was going on when they got back. Ground crew were out in force and instead of the usual small reception committee of sleepy fitters and riggers waiting to take snag and damage reports the dispersals seemed to be crawling with people. As the crew bus took them back to interrogation they saw bomb dollies and big Matador refuelling tankers going the other way. It looked ominous!

As they drank their rum at de-briefing they were told that Bomber Command had mounted another major raid on Bremen and a number of diversionary ops. that night. It looked as if they had thoroughly confused the defences and given the Dortmund raiders a relatively easy ride. Any euphoria that this might have inspired was dissipated by one of the earlier crews who were on their way out by now. They had been right to be concerned about all that activity. "Don't get too happy cocker" their pilot said to Les, "We're on again in the morning. Another bloody daylight".

He was only too right. Briefing was to be at seven thirty, breakfast at nine and take-off was scheduled for around eleven. They made off back to their billets, undressed and after a token wash, crawled into bed. It was going to be busy tomorrow and they needed some sleep.

Briefing revealed that their target was to be Kleve on the Dutch German frontier.

With the failure of Operation Market Garden, the 1st.Airborne Division's assault at Arnhem, the allies were occupying an exposed salient. The operation was aimed at the road and rail communications that might threaten their flanks. They were briefed to expect fighter opposition and were told that a strong escort of RAF Spitfires and USAAF Mustangs would be protecting them.

There was very little cloud about and visibility was good all the way to the target.

Their guns were loaded with maximum range daylight tracer ammunition for this operation and Les's instructions to the gunners were radically different to their usual brief. "Keep your eyes peeled and if you see a fighter coming in belt away at it. Don't piss about making sure that it's in range. We want to frighten the bugger off, not earn a DFM for shooting him down. Make sure there's plenty of tracer going his way and he'll likely turn it in!"

In the end it was a bit anti-climactic. There was plenty of flak over the target but the only fighters they saw were their own escorts. The 218 Squadron gaggle dropped their loads in clear conditions and they saw bombs bursting all over the target area. They saw no other Lancs in the stream go down and the trip back was also without incident. They even got an early turn to land and as a consequence were among the first in interrogation.

Once the de-briefing was over they arranged to meet up in the George that night and then made their way back to the billet to dump their gear. Allen shed his kit, had a quick wash, and left the hut on his way to the mess for tea. He was surprised to see Les waiting to intercept him. He was grinning all over his face. "I've just seen the flight commander" he said "We're off ops all next week. We're going to do some intensive training on GH. Fuck your luck nav, but the rest of us are gunna have an easy week!"

They celebrated the news of their brief break from ops by abandoning the seedy pleasures of the George and heading off to Cambridge in a borrowed jeep late that afternoon. Les was driving again for the simple reason that he was the only one among them that knew how to. They parked up near the Eagle and made their way into the bar through a heaving mass of aircrew drawn from just about every allied nationality. They produced their glasses, ordered pints and proceeded to down them as quickly as possible before demanding an immediate refill. After about the fourth drink the world was beginning to look a much more cheerful place and the small world of the bar was suffused with laughter and conversation. The talk was all of old friends and what had happened to who. Like Betty's Bar in York, the Eagle was one of those places where aircrew gathered to exchange gossip. If you really wanted to know what was going on in your corner of the war this was the place to find out. The air was full of tobacco smoke and the bar was loud with jokes, singing and improbable stories and the crew were very happy. They spilled out into the night when Time was called and made their way to a fish and chip shop. As their fingers extracted the hot, salty, vinegary fragments from the greasy newspaper-wrapped bundles they made their way back to the jeep and the long lanes that led to Methwold. After all it hadn't been a bad day.

Les had not been far wrong. The GH training started the next day and Allen spent most of the first part of it in the classroom while the rest of the crew happily did nothing very much. He was not technically minded and hence much of the why it worked failed to register very well. What he did remember was how it worked and what he had to do to make it function.

Essentially the traces on his cathode ray tube provided a position index. Unknown to him these were the result of pulses from ground stations triggered by the transmitter in the aircraft. Two powerful ground transmitters radiated signals like ripples in a pool and when they intersected, at a position that could be marked by an electronic marker set on his display, the aircraft would turn down one of the arcs which ran through the target.

At a pre-determined warning point a clockwork mechanism would be started which, providing that the speed of the aircraft over the ground could be calculated accurately and the time taken by the bombs to strike after release was known, should drop the bomb-load at precisely the right moment. It required Allen to calculate winds, temperature and altitude precisely and Les to maintain exactly the right altitude, speed and headings. It also, incidentally, provided the predictors of the radar directed flak batteries with an undeviating target that made no attempt to evade.

After three days or so of hard graft in the classroom they started the airborne part of the course. This involved making runs over a ground target with a camera recording release and impact points. At this stage Les rather regretted his ribaldry because he too started to earn his corn with a vengeance while the rest of the crew did little more than watch admiringly. Hour after hour they flew to invisible signposts in the sky from which Les had to fly with absolute precision. Allen, having completed his calculations by the time they reached the marker point, would press the bomb release at the side of his bench and start the clock. Les would maintain height, speed, and heading until the pointers coincided and the camera took its last picture to show the notional point of impact.

After three more days of this they were bored rigid but Allen could operate the gear and do the sums and Les could fly with the required degree of precision. They were a trained GH crew.

This was to mean of course, that every time they mounted a GH raid Allen was bomb aimer as well as navigator. Not surprisingly John suffered some merciless ribbing as a result.

"Only useful for shoving out window" and "well, bomb aimers never were a great deal of bloody use" came fairly well up the list, but John endured it with good grace and, in the event, did his fair share of visual bomb aiming into the bargain.

Their stand-down ended abruptly on 14th September when they were involved in Operation Hurricane. This was to be a deliberate attempt at impressing the German leadership and the German population with the absolutely overwhelming strength of the allied air forces. The plan was to hit the same city three times in less than twenty four hours. It resulted in a raid by over a thousand RAF bombers in the early morning, a raid by over a thousand USAF bombers during the day and a further thousand bomber night raid made by the RAF. In a very real sense it was an overt effort at terrifying the Germans into submission but knowing what we know now about the degree of control exercised by the Nazis it was an impossible objective.

The Hough crew however knew little and cared less about the grand plan when they saw their names on the battle order. All they knew at that stage was that briefing was to start at 3.30 am. for the first raid and they were very probably going back again at nightfall.

Their target was Duisburg and they took off in their usual C Charlie shortly after six. Allen was, as usual, seated at his bench busily engaged in maintaining his plot and passing speeds and headings to

Les. They were well towards the front of the stream and as the heavily loaded Charlie clawed for height he heard the gunners reporting the proximity of other bombers. Most of the outward flight was over territory now occupied by the allies and they were not joined by their fighter escort until they were east of Brussels. From his position he saw nothing, of course, except his GEE console, the repeater instruments and his charts, but he heard John's voice identifying visual pinpoints and the odd brief report from the gunners. It was cold at twenty thousand feet but they were briefed to stay high. The Ruhr flak was ferocious and they weren't going to make it any easier for the gunners than they had to.

Suddenly he heard Stan's voice on the intercom. "Fighter, fighter, corkscrew port!" and almost simultaneously the clatter and vibration of the guns firing from both turrets.

By then the nose had pitched down, they were rolling steeply to the left and the stuff on the bench was floating past his ears as he hung on for grim death. The fuselage filled with the reek of cordite and the guns continued to fire in long bursts as they rolled right and started to climb. Geordie this time, "It's OK skip. He overshot and dived away. I don't think we hit him!" Allen prepared to offer a translation but Les had obviously understood as he levelled Charlie out and resumed their course immediately. He came up on the intercom. "Good show gunners, can you see any more of the bastards?" Stan's rich Bristolian burr this time, "No skip, all I can see are Spits above us. There was only the one Jerry and he pissed off down when he missed us!"

They were beyond the battle lines now and while Jack and Harry restored a bit of order to the interior Allen was busily working out the heading for their run in to the target. They knew that the Wurzburg flak direction radars would be feeling for them ready to feed range, bearing and azimuth to the gun predictors and John was shoving out bundles of window as fast as he could. The flak over Saarbrucken and Kleve had been bad enough, this was going to be a lot worse. He pressed his intercom switch. "Nine minutes to target, final course zero nine five." He passed the confirmatory chit forward. By now Harry had taken over the job of pushing out the window for, as this was going to be a visual attack, John was readying himself for the bomb run. He glanced up at the airspeed indicator and altimeter to check that Les was grabbing his customary few hundred feet, then finalised his calculation for the outward heading, wrote it down and stood up. He passed the chit to Les and then looked towards the target.

Shit! the flak was intense. The sky ahead was filling with the black smoke puffs left by earlier shell bursts. In among them were constant clusters of flame-centred black smoke as more shells burst in salvoes. He saw one of the other aircraft ahead of them in the stream trail smoke and flame from a wing before dissolving in a great gout of fire and oily smoke. Far below clouds of tracer were climbing upwards and just ahead the first bombs were beginning to explode, the shock waves rippling outwards.

Already they were gaining speed in a shallow dive and John's voice was calling the corrections on the bombing run. The fuselage was constantly rocked by the familiar great echoing CCRRUMMP of heavy shells, and fragments were rattling like hailstones on the skin of the aircraft. He scanned the sky intently. There was no fighter opposition and their own escorts were high above them. Allen didn't blame them; he too would have been high above them given half a chance.

They levelled out momentarily. He heard John say "bombs gone" then after a brief pause for the aiming point picture they resumed their dive, rolled out to the left and turned on to their return course. The flak continued to harass them and he could not only hear it but smell it, as the pungent smell of explosive filled the fuselage and seeped under his oxygen mask. Relieved of the bomb load and a good deal of fuel Charlie was a good deal easier to manoeuvre at that height. Les took advantage of this, kicking the rudder pedals to make her yaw so that they were rarely flying in the direction they were pointing. Eventually they flew out of the flak and John and the gunners reported that it seemed to be thinning out a bit over the target. The whole area seemed carpeted with the shock waves of explosions and it looked as if many of the batteries had been hit. For a short time at least the defences appeared to have been almost overwhelmed. In spite of this the gunners had seen at least two more attackers shot down over the target and the first wave at least had a hard time.

Allen couldn't spare any more time and, as the risk of fighter attack seemed small, he dived back into his usual position and resumed the plot. The return journey was uneventful and they were back at their dispersal soon after eleven o clock.

Once again Charlie had sustained nothing worse than superficial scars from small flak fragments and the worst task confronting the fitters was the need to wash Elsan fluid from the inside of the fuselage. The armourers were busying themselves cleaning and re-loading the guns and the bomb trailers were waiting until the oil and coolant had been topped up and the Matador tankers had transferred their loads to the fuel tanks.

Les and Jack had their usual word with the crew chief and then the buses came to take them to interrogation. The de-brief was cut fairly short. They sipped their rum as the intelligence officer filled in his report and at the finish were told that they had to return for a further briefing at ten that evening. American Flying Fortresses were also on their way to Duisburg that morning and the RAF were going back again after dark.

The crews streamed out of the room and made their way back to the billet to dump their gear before going into lunch. Most of them got their heads down for a few hours before tea in the late afternoon. The raid was the main topic of conversation in the sergeants' mess after tea. The BBC had announced the loss of fourteen of the attacking force which, given the pasting received by the early wave on the way in, suggested that the flak had been temporarily suppressed. Fourteen out of over a thousand was pretty good by their standards, although it is worth bearing in mind that it still entailed the death of nearly a hundred young men.

The second briefing of the day was not an elaborate affair. 218 was to be in the first of two waves of attackers and would be carrying a mixed bomb load, a 4,000 lb. cookie, five hundred pound GP bombs and two small bomb containers loaded with incendiaries. The latest reconnaissance flights had shown a fiercely burning target and marking was not considered necessary.

They went into supper at ten forty five, enjoyed their bacon and eggs and within the hour were boarding their aircraft. Take-off was just after midnight and as the heavily loaded Lancaster climbed slowly up to its operational height Allen settled down to his plot.

He was once again sitting alone in a very small, dimly lit, curtained compartment. He was on the frightened side of apprehensive, very cold, breathing oxygen through a dripping mask and completing a long series of intricate calculations. His kind of flying had long ceased to be an adventure. It was now a highly skilled, very dangerous, quasi-industrial task and he didn't like it very much.

He kept passing speeds and headings forward and every now and again John would come up on the intercom with a visual fix or Harry would come up with a broadcast wind. Allen would factor them into his calculations and amend the plot. Lancaster H-AC, known as 'C Charlie' was being guided accurately towards the still burning city of Duisburg.

They could see the target from forty miles out but Allen was too busy to look until after he had finished his calculations for the last inward heading and the first homeward leg. They were not a chatty crew. The intercom was strictly reserved for essential communication and casual conversation was not encouraged. The atmosphere in the front of the aircraft was always more like a drawing office than a combat aircraft but Duisburg was an exception to the rule. The burning target was so spectacular that one by one, those of the crew that could see it felt moved to comment. The usually taciturn John was the first. "Bloody hell Skipper" he said "look at that!" Allen eventually finished his task and, drawing his curtain, stood up and looked forward. At first, his eyes still accustomed to the relative brilliance of his working light, he couldn't see very much but as they adjusted he realised that he was looking at a vast area of flame engulfing the battered city. He also realised that the flak had managed a degree of reorganisation and was putting up a considerable barrage ahead of them. Suddenly the sky to port was illuminated by a great gout of fire as a bomber blew up. Fuel, oil, bomb load and pyrotechnics combined to create an enormous pyre in the sky.

Les came up on the intercom. "Gunners don't stare at the kite going down. Keep searching the sky. It might have been a night-fighter that got them!" Stan and Geordie acknowledged.

John came up on the intercom on the bomb-run, chanting his course corrections and eventually announcing a relieved "Bombs gone, jettison bars across, close bomb doors" before coming back to check for hang ups. They swung out of their high speed run over the target and settled down on the first leg of their homeward journey. Charlie dropped below oxygen height over western Belgium and once they were over the channel coffee and sandwiches were passed around and the smokers lit up.

They were fortunate in being given an early turn to land and by three in the morning were sitting in the interrogation room being debriefed. An hour later they were in bed, sleeping like logs after a very long day. In the mess next day they were passing round a copy of a newspaper, it was the Express or the Mail. One of the staff reporters had been on the raid and the headline above his account was "I saw Duisburg die."

"Don't you fucking believe it," said a New Zealand air gunner. "The bastards'll be shooting back tomorrow!"

Apart from air tests and a bit of training there was no flying for the next three days. The double trip to Duisburg had worked both crews and aircraft fairly hard and some overdue maintenance needed attending to. The crew managed a spot of maintenance too. There was a bit of a party in the sergeants' mess, a decent film on at the station cinema as well as a trip to Cambridge to take in another film and a visit to the Eagle. They didn't leave their return too late as they knew they were on the battle order for the next day, the 18th, and briefing was to be at five am.

The tape on the big wall map led to Bonn and once the basic information was written down and the charts were pencilled in, the navigators of GH equipped aircraft were given an additional briefing. The raid was going to be entirely GH marked and so all of the bomb aiming would rest on them. Their machines were identified by two horizontal yellow bars painted on the tail fins. They would climb over East Anglia until they were clear of cloud and then orbit at an agreed position. Two other aircraft which were not equipped with the aid would formate on them, follow them to the target and release their loads when they saw their leader bomb. It sounded a bit hit and miss but it was simple and simple techniques often work well.

They were flying Charlie again and took off at about half past eight. They climbed through thick cloud and Les, his seat lowered right down, concentrated on his instruments. Allen was sweating freely despite the intensifying cold. He had to keep his plot going without the aid of visual fixes and be prepared to turn the aircraft down the defined arc of sky once the traces intersected on his set.

After a while they broke cloud and flew on in wide circles over the featureless cloudscape. They could see other GH equipped machines orbiting at their height, also waiting for their followers to pick them up. A little later two other Lancasters formated on them and Stan and Geordie amused themselves by making rude gestures at the other crews until they got bored with the new game. The scattered vics of Lancasters set course and the gathering stream headed out over the North Sea. As they crossed Belgium they could see their fighter escort high above them and the gunners constantly swung their turrets, searching for possible attackers. They crossed the battle lines and then the German frontier, but apart from a few reports of flak bursts above the cloud as they came within range of defended areas and a couple of broadcast winds relayed by Harry, the intercom was silent.

They droned on at twenty thousand feet while John and Harry alternated at shoving out bundles of window and Allen passed a continual stream of speeds and headings forward to Les. Armed with the most up to date estimates of wind and temperature he also calculated the speed and direction of the falling bombs and fed the information into the GH gear. Then, when the traces were cut by the marker, they turned onto the final short arc that would take them over the target. They knew that it couldn't be far away as a positive barrage of heavy flak was bursting at about their height. All the usual sounds were present but they could see no sign of the batteries that were engaging them. All they could see below them was cloud but as the next marker blip appeared on the screen, Allen pressed the bomb release and started the clockwork mechanism. While all this was happening Les was flying as precisely as he could until he heard the bomb releases trip and the load fall away. Then and only then, he was allowed to vary his height, speed or heading and indulge in a little evasive action. This last became a fast diving turn once the following a aircraft had opened up to a reasonably safe separation.

The series of gaggles that made up the stream stayed together on the return journey but there was no sign of fighters and nobody saw what happened to the 115 Squadron aircraft that was to be their only loss. They were landed and de-briefed in time for lunch after an operation that appeared to have run like clockwork.

The next day the intelligence section told the crews that the raid had been highly effective. The 120 odd aircraft of 3 Group, led by GH equipped Lancasters had bombed Beethoven's militarily unimportant birthplace to test the effect of the new technique on an otherwise relatively harmless and lightly attacked target. The old town had been very heavily damaged and the experiment had been deemed a success.

The next three days were uneventful as 3 Group's GH equipped Lancasters were being largely reserved for leading daylight blind bombing raids. Only about a third of their aircraft carried the device but providing the cloud tops were below about 18,000 feet their Lancasters had sufficient margin of performance to maintain the required close vics of three.

Three quiet days seemed like a good idea to the Hough crew. It also gave them the chance to try Les's whisky finding formula. His notion had been that they needed to patronise "one of the pubs where the posh Poms eat".

Allen duly booked a table at the University Arms and on the evening of the 20th the crew ambled into the hotel bar. They were, it is fair to admit, not entirely sober and they also had a disreputable looking dog in tow that they had managed to pick up from somewhere. Somehow they did not feel entirely welcome. Indeed Allen remembers feeling as if frost was slowly forming on his eyebrows. Les however, never the most sensitive of mortals, rose above this and opened the negotiations by testing his theory and ordering a large scotch. The barman denied that they had any scotch despite the fact that a number of well dressed civilians appeared to be drinking from whisky glasses. Les was not disposed to take his word for it and shortly afterwards, following a brief exchange of views, they were invited to leave. As they stumbled dinnerless down the front steps a loud South Australian voice announced that he had been "thrown out of far better pubs than that in the bloody outback." They were however, much too hungry to waste time in further recrimination and they headed off in search of fish and chips.

On 22nd October a hundred 3 Group Lancasters raided the Ruhr town of Neuss in daylight. The Hough crew flew their usual C Charlie on the operation but Allen saw even less than usual. Because they were over solid cloud all the way there and back he was never able to emerge from his compartment From take off almost to touch down he worked solidly at his plot, pausing only to guide Charlie down the arc of the GH signal on the bombing run.

When they swung into position on their dispersal pan and switched off the engines, he finished shutting down his electronics, pulled off his sweaty helmet, rubbed his eyes and stood up. What he saw outside was not encouraging. Once again the dispersals and the perimeter track were swarming with people. Tankers and bomb trains were queuing up and a host of fitters and armourers were waiting for them. Les grinned wearily back at him. "Looks like we might be having a bloody busy night again mate!" he said bleakly.

Happily he was wrong. Whatever plans Bomber Command may have entertained for them that night, in the event they were stood down that afternoon. The worst that happened was that they drank rather more than was good for them and they spent the night peacefully in their beds.

The evening after was not so good. They had known they were on the battle order from first thing in the morning. They also knew that they were all carrying 1,200 gallons of petrol and that bomb loads were almost entirely made up of high explosive. This suggested a frequently bombed Ruhr target. They drew this inference because they knew how much fuel was demanded to reach the Ruhr and also knew that Bomber Command planners had decided that most inflammable structures in these intensively hit areas had already been burned. By this devious process of deduction they were led to expect a trip over the Happy Valley.

They were correct. Briefing was shortly after a very early lunch and when they entered the room the big wall map confirmed their opinion. The ribbon led to Essen and they were once more to try conclusions with the Ruhr defences. The target was to be marked by Pathfinders and bombed visually. It was to be a conventional area attack directed by a Master Bomber and with over a thousand bombers tasked, it was going to be a big one.

Start-up was to be just after four thirty in the afternoon and, as usual, there was a lot to do before they had their flying supper an hour beforehand. By the time they boarded their aircraft it was raining, and a low cloud base made the late October afternoon more than usually gloomy. The pre take-off checks seemed to take forever and once they started the long process of taxiing two squadrons of Lancasters from their dispersals to the end of the single runway someone managed to put a wheel on the grass and had to be towed off. By the time they reached the runway threshold the entire machine reeked of over-heated brake linings and they were sweating with nervous frustration. In contrast the actual take-off was almost anti-climactic despite their heavy load

Les had his seat lowered and his eyes glued to the panel as they climbed out into the low overcast and Allen, intent on maintaining his plot, was constantly thrown about as the big machine bucked and rolled in the turbulent air. They eventually broke cloud high over northern France when Les lifted his eyes and wound his seat up but there was no sign of the ground and they were entirely dependent on GEE for plotting fixes.

Allen sat in his dimly lit compartment, sliding along the bench and reaching forward from time to time to tune his set and then hunching over his chart to pencil a cross on his latest calculated position. They levelled out at twenty thousand feet, the battering roar of the engines moderated and he noted the change in airspeed. Harry passed him the latest broadcast wind which seemed to confirm his own estimate made by comparing the GEE fixes with the readings from from the air position indicator. He was cold, especially his hands and feet, and was uncomfortably conscious of the fact that condensation from his oxygen mask was dripping on to the chart.

Les exchanged the odd word with the gunners, partly to check that their oxygen systems were working and partly to ensure that they were awake. Apart from those brief exchanges they flew without speaking until Allen announced that they were now fifteen minutes away from the target. Harry took over the chore of pushing out window while John checked his bombs and warmed up the bomb sight.

Seven minutes out, settled onto their final heading, Les and John saw the first target indicators exploding on the ground. Heavy flak was bursting around and above them and fragments were impacting on the upper fuselage decking with a sound like a violent hailstorm. The cloud was slightly broken by then and when John eventually pressed his bomb release he could actually see a cluster of TIs burning, as well as a more general glow below the cloud.

Allen was on his feet now, curtains back and looking down at the target. Even when his eyes became used to the dark he couldn't see much and so, passing the next course to Les before he did so, he dived back into his hole and resumed the plot.

They were in cloud for much of the way back and the final stages of the trip were fairly hairy. The Lanc was continually rocked by turbulence. Usually it was the violent motion of the air mass in cloud but sometimes it was the characteristic cobblestone rumble of another aircraft's slipstream. By the time they arrived back at Methwold Les had been flying virtually blind for over an hour and they did not catch sight of the ground until they were at an uncomfortably low altitude. The Bomber Command war diaries admit to the loss of eight aircraft that night as a result of enemy action. A slightly closer look at the table of losses shows another ten were written off in collisions or accidents. Given the conditions it is surprising that they managed to do as well.

It was a very weary crew that filed out of interrogation at a little after midnight but it was also a fairly cheerful one. Nobody had dared mention it until the operation was finished but they were due for leave the following day.

The next morning they drew their passes and travel warrants before boarding a truck for the station. and their various destinations. Most of them were going home but Les, as usual, had arranged to meet up with some fellow Aussies in London. Allen of course was heading for Darlington, and by mid afternoon he was shouldering his kit bag out of the station and tramping off towards the familiar front door of home, at 2 Pierremont Terrace. As always, it was a good leave, but despite having survived seventeen operations he was aware of a faint but persistent thought at the back of his mind. How long can I last?

He spun out the final day as long as possible but the last train that could get him back to base left mid evening and as darkness fell he found himself humping his kit back to the railway station. As he made his way through the streets he was aware of everyday life going on all around him. Light spilled through carelessly blacked out doors, he could smell the familiar sooty odour of coal smoke from domestic fires and snatches of conversation constantly reminded him of the sheer ordinariness of things. All around him people were going home, starting the night shift or greeting friends in the gathering darkness and he was going back to the flak and the fighters. Suddenly he was aware that tears were streaming down his face. Not the breathy tears of fear or despair but the quiet welling of emotion that comes with sadness, or perhaps with the moment of empathy that comes when reading a book or seated in the cinema. He realised what was disturbing him. This was humdrum, comfortable, safe real life. This was what most people did and yet he was going back to an alien world in which all this could be taken away and he might never see home again. He wondered once more quite why he had worked so hard to get himself into such a situation.

The moment soon passed. Once inside the station he made his way to the buffet and had a couple of drinks and after the second pint cheered up a bit. He fell into casual conversation with some other servicemen on the train and by the time he was back to the rural squalor of Methwold he had changed worlds again. Once more he was living in the continuous present that most aircrew elected to inhabit.

He wandered into his billet to find the other crew with which they shared it bickering noisily. This was not unusual. They were a shambolic collection, the navigator was always getting them lost, they seemed to spend most of their spare time squabbling and yet, against all the odds, they continued to survive. "Hey! Watcha think of this Cliffie," one of the gunners said as he caught sight of him but he never discovered what he was supposed to think about. Before he could be drawn into the argument Jack appeared in the hut doorway.

"I've just seen Les," he said. "We're on the battle order for tomorrow. Briefing's after lunch".

The following morning was taken up with the routine business of preparing for a raid. They air tested Charlie before handing her over to the ground crews for refuelling and bombing up. Jack remained to have a word with the crew chief while Stan and Geordie stayed behind to load and fiddle with their guns. John and Harry went off to their various sections to catch up after a week away while Allen and Les ambled over to the intelligence section. They wanted to have a look at the latest known flak and searchlight concentrations and see what was happening to the allied battle lines before going in for briefing.

Coming out of the mess after lunch they saw a "snowdrop", a white-capped station policeman, chaining up one of the camp telephone boxes. Once the crews were briefed for a raid the camp was sealed off until the survivors returned. The sight of the boxes being chained was a fairly sure sign that the operation hadn't been cancelled or postponed. "No chance of a scrub then" said an anonymous voice behind him as Allen made his way to the briefing room.

The tape trace made a couple of dog legs to confuse the defences and finished up at Cologne. It was to be a big raid, nearly a thousand aircraft were involved and the target was to be marked by Oboe-guided Mosquito bombers. In all respects it was going to be a classical area raid. Bomb aiming would be visual and a Master Bomber would exercise tactical control over the target. All Allen had to do was get them there on time.

They climbed through thick cloud again after take-off, and although the base was a good deal higher, they could see little of the ground through the murk and their navigation again relied entirely on GEE. They flew on through the darkness without seeing another aircraft, changing course at their invisible turning points. At each turn they were aware of flying in the slipstream of other aircraft in the stream and were comforted by the knowledge that they were probably on track.

Ten minutes out from the target they started to prepare for the bombing run but John saw nothing until, almost exactly on time, they saw parachute sky marker flares bursting over the cloud a few miles in front of them. John started to call the corrections, and Les put Charlie into a shallow dive towards the target. As usual, Allen stood up and looked out as he passed the first course of the homeward journey to the skipper. He could see little, other than bursting sky markers and a glow beneath the clouds but a great deal of flak was exploding at their height and there was the usual cacophony of sound that he had come to associate with it. The Cologne defences had a fearsome reputation and the flak was intense but it was scattered rather than predicted and he saw nobody hit.

He heard John call "bombs gone", felt Charlie leap upwards when relieved of the load and once the photoflash was gone they turned away from the target. The homeward flight was uneventful, there was a reasonable cloudbase when they started the let-down to Methwold and they were sipping their rum in interrogation not long after midnight on October the thirtieth.

They were stood down for twenty four hours after the Cologne raid and Les managed to borrow a jeep again the following afternoon. He and Allen arrived at the motor transport yard a bit before the others and sat on the bonnet smoking companionably. Les looked faintly embarrassed, not a common expression for him, and announced rather diffidently that he was probably going to be the next flight commander. This would mean flying rather less frequently and thus taking a bit longer to finish the tour.

"Whaddya think?" he said, "Will the boys go for it?"

"They'll be OK," said Allen. "If we spread this one out a bit we probably won't be copped for another. With a bit of luck the fucking war will be over by then!"

The conversation stopped there because the rest of the crew arrived in a noisy group and they piled in and set off for Cambridge. For once in that remarkably wet autumn it wasn't raining and so they queued for the cinema that afternoon without getting soaked. Afterwards they headed off to the Eagle for a few pints and joined the noisy crowd in the saloon bar. They stood in a little knot, the two young gunners flushed and laughing and the others egging them on. Les, ever the good skipper, joshed them along and did his best to take their minds off the anxiety that grew as the tour progressed. He told them the most improbable stories. He claimed to be a film producer at one stage and promised to get the youngsters jobs in the cinema after the war. It was of course the purest bullshit but as a means of distraction highly effective. The other older members of the crew he deemed able to cope and he was probably right. It was the under twenties and over thirties that found the tension least bearable.

They got back to Methwold just before midnight to be greeted with the news that they were on the battle order for a daylight raid the next day. Pilots and Navigators briefing was to be at half past five and so they headed off for their respective billets to get some sleep. Tomorrow was going to be a busy day. The following morning, 2nd November, was gloomy and overcast and at five thirty it was still pitch dark.

Allen and Les, both huddled in greatcoats, made their way towards the briefing room and blinked, dazzled by the fluorescent lighting as they entered the blacked out hut. The red tape of the track zigzagged across the wall map and ended at Homburg on the west bank of the Rhine opposite Duisburg. It seemed an obscure small town until the intelligence officer started his briefing. Homburg was the site of the Meerbeck refinery, one of the last synthetic oil plants in Germany. If they were knocked out then the Third Reich would be totally devoid of fuel and the war must end. As a result they were likely to be heavily defended. The day was going to be cloudy throughout and hence 3 Group's GH equipped Lancasters were the only main force aircraft capable of finding and hitting such a small target.

"The Yanks have already had a go and failed, he said. "Now it's up to us to do the job properly." This last remark was nonsense of course, an attempt to capitalise on inter allied rivalry. In reality these plants were usually repairable in the short run and needed repeated attacks to keep them out of action. Whatever happened they were likely to need several return visits.

The early part of the morning was occupied with the usual preparations and the inevitable pre-operational meal and they took off at about eleven. It was another long cloud climb over East Anglia, on instruments all the way, until they finally topped out at just over eighteen thousand feet. They were soon joined by two other non-GH equipped Lancasters and flew on eastwards in a reasonably tight vic. There were still a few isolated cloud masses at their height and they laboured to get above them. The heavily loaded Lancasters were not easy to handle at nearly twenty thousand feet and formation keeping was difficult. Les was sweating like a pig despite the biting cold, trying to fly as smoothly as possible in the thin turbulent air and Jack was trying to juggle the throttles to minimise the load on his pilot. Les wasn't the only skipper to find the conditions difficult; a couple of 15 Squadron Lancasters in the stream flown by very experienced crews collided three hours into the flight at twenty thousand feet over Holland. Everyone in F/L Earley's all RAF crew was killed and only the wireless operator and rear gunner survived from F/O Hoggard's mixed Australian, Canadian and RAF crew.

Allen saw nothing of what was going on outside his compartment. He was completely occupied in maintaining his plot with no external references, and was doing his best to give the skipper as few corrections as possible and as much warning of course changes as he could. Just after eleven thirty they reached the GH marker and turned onto the final course for the target. Now they were flying down a short arc of sky maintaining a set speed and altitude with as much exactness as possible. It was at this time that the desultory flak that had pecked at the stream became an intense barrage. Allen could see nothing but he could hear the great clanging crashes that echoed down the fuselage and the constant rattle of fragments that impacted on the skin of the aircraft. John and Harry had been busily shoving out window in an attempt to confuse the radar predictors of the flak batteries below but their absolutely undeviating course gave the gunners a near sitting duck to shoot at.

After a particularly deafening succession of crashes a voice on the intercom said "Fuck me, look at that!" but Allen had no idea what it was talking about and simply lacked the time to worry about it. After what seemed like forever he they passed the next marker and he pressed the bomb release. After another eternity they felt the whole aircraft leap as the load was shed and after a brief pause to let their followers drop and break clear, Les racked into a steep turn onto their approximate homeward course. While he did this, Allen, at last free of the GH plot, worked furiously to calculate their exact next heading. As soon as this was done he toggled his microphone and passed it to Les then, writing it in large figures on a slip of paper, stood up and passed it forward over Jack's shoulder. Then, and only then, he took the opportunity to look out and back at the target. Through a gap in the cloud he could see fires and a great column of black smoke but most of his attention was directed to the flak. He had never seen anything quite like it before. The sky was filled with the smoke of recent shellbursts and predicted fire was putting up long lanes of flame-cored bursts on either beam.

At first he couldn't understand how they could possibly have escaped being hit but after a second or two he noticed that most of it was remaining slightly above and to either side of the stream.

Then Les's voice on the intercom: "Don't look at the fucking flak gunners. Look out up sun for fighters. Once we clear this shit they might have a go at us".

They didn't; there was no sign of fighters other than their own escort far out on the flanks and high above them.

Once they were clear of the battle lines their followers sheered off and they started the long descent through cloud. It thinned and broke up as they approached the North Sea and John managed a visual fix on the Stour estuary as they were coasting in. They were among the last to land this trip and were very surprised to see that all the squadron aircraft seemed to have returned. The flak had seemed so bad that they had expected to lose a few, but luck seemed to have been with 3 Group this trip. In fact, apart from the two aircraft that collided on the way in, only three other Lancasters were lost on this operation, less than three per cent of the attacking force.

After interrogation they discovered that they weren't on the order of battle for the following day and arranged to meet up in the George that evening. The George admittedly was a fairly squalid little pub but it was nearby, usually had beer and was somewhere a mixed officer and NCO crew could meet if they couldn't get into Cambridge. Les and Allen met up near the camp gate and made their way down to the village, to find all of the others except John already in the bar. They were a bit subdued at first, they were dog-tired and the Homburg flak had shaken them a bit, but after the second pint the world seemed a bit rosier. Jack was the first to talk about it.

"I reckon," he said, "that the window we were putting out buggered up their flak direction radar. Did you notice that their height was wrong and most of the time their salvoes were bursting out to the side of the stream. They couldn't see us most of the time because of the cloud, so they couldn't hit us".

Geordie, who had enjoyed an uncomfortably clear sight of the proceedings from the mid-upper turret gazed owlishly over his pint.

"If those foockers ever do get a good look at us aah for one doant waant t' be there. Aah shit a brick today!" At that point John came in, another round was called for, and the subject was changed.

They didn't operate on the third and fourth of November. On the third Les managed to borrow a jeep again and they went to the pictures in Cambridge and on the fourth there was a party in the Sergeants Mess. Despite the party the crew drank little or nothing and turned in relatively early. They were tired, they were on the battle order for the following day and briefing was at seven thirty.

They were not happy when they left the briefing. Their target was Solingen, the Sheffield of the Ruhr and the Solingen flak enjoyed an awesome reputation.

As they started their take-off run Allen was feeling decidedly "windy" but soon they were climbing through ten tenths cloud again and he was again far too busy to have much room in his mind for anything but maintaining his plot.

It was to be a GH raid and once they topped out of the murk at about eighteen thousand feet they went into a wide turn waiting for their followers. It wasn't long before he heard Stan report that two other Lancs were about to formate on them and they headed out over the North Sea. They were above a solid undercast somewhere over Holland when Geordie, in the mid-upper turret, reported seeing their fighter escort several thousand feet higher. They pressed on for another hour or so, the intercom silent except for oxygen checks, until Allen saw the traces come up on his GH screen and he started talking the skipper into the target.

Eventually they started down the final short arc of the bombing run and Allen pressed the release button at the marker. Now it was down to Les's accurate flying to ensure that the bombs fell on the aiming point. By then the noise of flak bursts could be heard and the Lancaster bucked from time to time in the turbulence. He was working furiously again. On a GH raid he didn't always have time to compute the course away from the target and once the load was dropped Les would have to fly a rough heading until the calculation could be completed. He felt the kite bound upwards as the load was released and seconds later wrote the new course on a chit, toggled his microphone to tell Les and stood up to pass it forward before having a look out.

As he turned and looked to starboard he was suddenly confronted by a great boiling gout of flame-centred oily smoke with what looked like exploding pyrotechnics falling away from it. Jack's voice came over the intercom laconically. "Fucking scarecrow," he said. [6]

A second later they had an even bigger shock when a small aircraft shot vertically past them at very close range. It seemed to pass between the fuselage and the tailplane and caused Geordie to emit a strangled shout of "What the Fook was that?" as it climbed above them at incredible speed and disappeared from sight. Les must have been pretty startled too, as he didn't bawl at Geordie for bad intercom procedure and Allen, who was still a great reader of aircraft intelligence bulletins, provided an explanation.[7]

"It was a Gerry rocket fighter," he said, "an Me 163. He couldn't have had time to line up on us after he broke cloud so he didn't fire!"

"Thank Christ for that!" said Les and the intercom went silent as they made a long shallow descent onto their outward track. The guns continued to harass them but after Homburg the flak seemed a good deal less concentrated.

They had been much more afraid of the Solingen flak than they had of the Homburg defences but it seemed a much less terrifying experience. It was not, however, restful and it was a slightly shaken crew that started the long descent towards the North Sea.

They managed a visual fix again coasting in and John could map read their final leg to base. The skipper had given them the OK to

---

[6] 'Scarecrows' were reputed to be projectiles sent up by the defences to simulate exploding bombers and intimidate crews but there is no evidence that any such thing existed; certainly post-war interrogation of flak crews produced a complete denial and no ordnance was ever recovered. What the crew probably saw was a real bomber blowing up.

[7] Apart from the rocket propelled Me 163 the Luftwaffe was also deploying even more sophisticated target defence weapons. They were already testing two anti-aircraft guided missiles, Wasserfall and Rheintochter.

smoke by now and Allen noticed that his own hand was a bit unsteady as he fumbled to light his pipe.

That evening in the George Allen realised that they were all getting a bit frayed. As usual they tended to talk shop and apart from discussing the Solingen raid, news of the previous night's attack on Bochum had just been released. Night fighters had got into the stream and twenty eight bombers had gone down. The general view was that daylights were now safer than night attacks but neither could be seen as in any way health cures.

They weren't in any sense cracking up, but after twenty operations the continued tension was getting to them. It had the effect of exaggerating their normal behaviour. Les and John, who had always grated on each other to some extent, bickered rather more. Harry and Jack became progressively more withdrawn for longer periods and Stan and Geordie became slightly sillier and in Geordie's case, even less coherent. He himself was prone to periods of introspection but he was also feeling decidedly more apprehensive. All of them were drinking a good deal more. They seemed to need the blurring effect of alcohol to take the unacceptable edge off reality.

They were on the battle order the next night with briefing called for three in the afternoon. The target turned out to be Koblenz and unusually it was going to be a night GH raid. They were less than pleased with this news. It was to be a smallish stream, only the GH equipped Lancasters were to take part, and the long straight and level approach of a GH bombing run would present night fighters with an easy target.

For Allen, cut off by a curtain in his little illuminated compartment, it was the usual long cold bind with the additional problem of directing the bombing run at the end. There was a good deal of flak on the final run and once he was able to look out at the receding target he could just make out the glow of fires on the ground. In the event it was a fairly uneventful trip and they had very little to report as they sipped their rum at interrogation in the early hours of the next morning.

It was a very tired group of young men that went to their beds and they slept into the late morning of the following day. After lunch they made their way to the flight office and, discovering that they were on the battle order for a daylight raid the following morning, decided against going out that evening. In the end they went off to their respective messes and after a couple of games of billiards and a quiet natter opted for an early supper and bed.

Pilots and navigators briefing was to be at five am, which meant an early call at about four, and if they were to be in any shape to face the day they needed some sleep.

Just after four Allen was shaken awake by the orderly corporal who silently proffered a clip-board. Bleary-eyed he signed the list, rolled out of bed, stuffed his feet into his flying boots and pulled on his great-coat, before making his way down to the ablution block for a perfunctory wash and shave. The others were similarly occupied when he left, fumbling to find their clothes without waking up the other crew in the hut. He dressed hastily on his return and then made his way down to breakfast. Coming in from the darkness he was dazzled by the lights and his stomach heaved queasily at the smell of frying that permeated the mess hall. The others seemed equally punch-drunk and there had been virtually no conversation so far. Being dragged out of bed in the small hours does not encourage idle chatter and they were tired before they started.

Once he had eaten he made his way to the doorway where he was greeted by Jack with news of the fuel and bomb loads. "twelve hundred gallons" he said "and ten thousand-pounders and a cookie. It looks like the Ruhr again". Allen winced and headed for the briefing room where he was greeted by an equally haggard looking Les. What they saw on the wall map put his heart into his boots. The ribbon on the map showed an outward course ending at Homburg. They were going back to the hottest target that they had ever encountered.

As he was busying himself inking in his courses the rest of the crew came in and the briefing continued. They were given the usual details of fuel and bomb loads (not that anybody needed telling), bombing heights, expected opposition and the rendezvous areas with their followers and their fighter escort. The meteorological officer predicted relatively clear skies over East Anglia. There would however, be layer cloud, with generous gaps between the layers, up to fifteen thousand feet en-route and over the target. He also expected a moderate tail wind.

The station intelligence officer finished the briefing with another harangue about the importance of the target. His, "You may encounter some fairly heavy flak", generated loud groans and raspberries. "Do it right this time and we won't have to go back again!" resulted in yells of ribald laughter and several offers to take him for the ride.

The Hough crew were not amused. Their last visit to Homburg had shaken them and, logically or not, it had become a jinx target as far as they were concerned; they would have preferred a trip to Berlin.

As soon as briefing was over they were into the furious activity of drawing kit, rations and generally preparing for the raid. The crew bus dumped them at the dispersal at about seven-thirty and were relieved to find that they were flying Charlie again.

Still a bit subdued they climbed aboard and started running through their various check lists. While this was going on Allen had settled down at his bench, pinned his first charts into place and made himself as comfortable as possible. Eventually Les signed the Form 700, accepting the aircraft, the intercom came alive and shortly afterwards the engines were started. Once the various generators were running electronics were warmed up, turrets were rotated and guns were elevated and depressed.

As Charlie came to life so did the crew. Voices on the intercom became lighter, they seemed to shake off their depression and settle into the collar. The engine noise rose to a crescendo as the magnetos were checked and then settled back to a fast idle to prevent them oiling up. Then came the slow wind from the dispersal button to the runway threshold. With two squadrons to despatch from one runway the crews were usually in their aircraft for at least an hour before they got airborne. Twenty overloaded Lancasters, lurching clumsily along the narrow perimeter track, throttles gunned to overcome the inertia of over thirty tons and brakes overheated by the effort of stopping them rolling when the machine in front stopped, could not easily be hurried.

Eventually it was their turn and as he got the green light Les rolled out onto the centre-line, smoothly opened the throttles and drove them squarely down the middle of the runway. Allen heard the wheels thump up and the familiar patter between Les and Jack as flaps were retracted and climbing power demanded. Then Les's voice on the intercom "OK nav, take-off at 0825". He gave him his first heading as they climbed for their initial rendezvous point at ten thousand feet over Aldeburgh. They climbed laboriously for height and then started a slow orbit until the gunners announced that their slaves, their followers, were approaching from astern. Soon the two Lancasters fell into position a hundred yards or so behind and much the same distance to each side and Allen gave Les his second heading as they commenced a long slow climb over the North Sea and France. As they flew steadily eastwards they began to penetrate layers of cloud until at about eighteen thousand feet they broke clear of the tops and could see other vics of Lancasters around them. The gunners started to report fighters but they turned out to be RAF Mustangs flying close escort virtually in the stream. They couldn't see their top cover but contrails high above them suggested that they were there.

It was here that things started to depart from plan. Comparing GEE fixes with the readings from his air position indicator suggested a very high ground speed. The forecast moderate tail wind was obviously well adrift and was still growing in strength. He asked Les to cut the revs a bit but at that height and all-up weight there was a limit to how much they could slow down without falling out of the sky. Then Les's voice on the intercom. "Met seems to have fucked up. I think that increasing tail wind marked the edge of a front, nav. There's a bloody great bank of cloud ahead going way above our height. The only thing we can do is go through it!"

Allen of course was glued to the GEE and could see nothing of this but he heard the gunners report that their followers had sheered off to a safe distance and heard Les call for more revs again to give him a better margin of control. Soon the onset of turbulence indicated that they were climbing through the clouds and he could hear ice being slung from the props and rattling against the sides of the fuselage. First Stan and then Geordie reported the proximity of other aircraft as they broke into odd patches of clear sky but soon these ceased and they flew on in intercom silence. As they progressed further into the gloom his plot showed that they were travelling at a phenomenal speed over the ground. Their 185 mile-an- hour cruise was giving them well over three hundred over the ground despite the fact that they were still climbing gently. Charlie was a remarkably good aircraft and Les, conscious of the fact that there was not much in front of them was trying to keep well clear of anything following them in the stream.

They still appeared to be bang on track however and when he switched the GH on the first marker came up almost immediately. He toggled his mike switch. "Ten minutes to go," he said. Les acknowledged and John stopped his task of pushing out window and went through the business of arming the bombs. Behind him Harry continued windowing and the gunners peered into the murk.

"I've heard of blind bombing," said Les, a few minutes later, "but this is fucking ridiculous".

He spoke too soon. Suddenly they penetrated the edge of the cloud. It was as if they had flown over the edge of a table top and in the sunlit air ahead of them they could see the curve of the Rhine and the target lying a few miles ahead. They were absolutely alone in a clear sky. Charlie's performance had carried them right to the front of the stream and there wasn't another machine in sight. John came up on the intercom. "Target dead ahead, lots of light flak coming up but it's well below us."

By now Allen had pressed the bomb release and started the clock running and was giving minor alterations of course to maintain the final bombing heading. Stan came up on the intercom.

"Our two followers have broken cloud behind skip. They're closing on us now".

Then Geordie from the mid-upper: "Mustangs above and behind us, skip. The fookin' escort are back!"

Les had lowered the nose and was making his usual shallow dive towards the target. As lead aircraft, with no window out in front of them to fox the radar, and clear skies giving the optical predictors an unobstructed view, he knew they were dangerously vulnerable. Their best bet was to get through the target as quickly as possible. With bomb doors wide open and everything fused even a minor hit would be enough to detonate the lot. Then the clock wound round to zero and Charlie gave an upward surge as the load was released.

Stan was just saying that their followers had dropped on cue when, in that brief instant, within seconds of bombing, all hell broke loose. There was a crash and a jolt that shook the whole airframe and the starboard inner engine exploded into flame and fragments. Allen gave a hasty glance over his shoulder and was shocked to see burning fuel spouting up into the slipstream and smoke filling the fuselage. Jack was on his feet now struggling to feather the prop, direct fuel away from the burning engine and trigger the Graviner fire extinguishers.

Allen collected his wits, grabbed a slip of paper with the course out of the target written on it and stood up to pass it forward. As he turned and pulled himself to his feet he saw that the perspex panels of the cockpit facing him were pierced by fragments of flak and the disintegrating engine, and discoloured by oil and fire. The fuselage skin was holed in several places, acrid smoke was still pouring in and the noise of the slipstream howling through the wreckage was deafening. Les banked Charlie starboard into the dead engine and steepened the descent to maintain airspeed.

Despite all his skill Jack could neither extinguish the engine fire nor feather the propeller. The Merlin engine must have been hit by a shell bursting close below it because the rear cowling had been blown upwards and it was reduced to a mass of burning scrap. Les by now had the throttles on the other three engines through the gates, pushing the noise level to the point where you could feel the vibration but it was little use. The drag from the wreckage was horrendous and they were losing height rapidly. Worse still, their airspeed was dramatically reduced and in turning west into the fierce wind they were making very little speed over the ground.

Les came up on the intercom, his voice raised over the racket but still calm. "Get your parachutes on fellers. I'll try and make it back over France but we're gonna have to jump".

The flak was still coming up, and losing height and in slowing down they were beginning to become an easy target. Then the inevitable happened and they were hit again. The starboard outer burst into flames and Jack's voice came flatly over the intercom. "It's no good skip, the alloy's started to burn and the main spar can't last much longer". Then there was another voice, not much more than a grunt, but Les obviously recognised it and replied. "Are you alright Stan?" Stan's voice came back from the rear turret hesitatingly, "I think me arm's hurt!"

Allen instinctively looked back down the fuselage and saw with a shock that there was a six foot hole in the starboard side of the fuselage, just forward of the rear door and the remote reading compass had been shot out of its mounting and disappeared through it. Then he heard the order "OK fellers, that's it, abandon aircraft!" and looking forward again saw that John had instantly jettisoned the forward hatch and rolled through it. In a momentary thought he was rather impressed by his decisiveness. He had always thought John a bit hesitant but when it came down to it he'd acted immediately. It was, however, a very fleeting thought and he promptly dived back under his bench in search of his parachute pack. He got up, snapped the big dog-lead clips open and secured it to his harness.

By now the slipstream roaring through the many holes had sucked the smoke out of the fuselage and when he pulled himself forward, plugged his intercom and oxygen jacks into spare points and folded back the Flight Engineer's seat, he saw Jack bending forward and clipping his skipper's parachute pack to his chest. It wasn't easy because Les was fighting desperately to retain some sort of control; column hard forward to maintain airspeed and rudder and ailerons hard over to overcome the dead engines and keep the starboard wing up. Then, in what seemed like ages but must have been seconds, he clipped on his own 'chute, patted Les on the shoulder, turned, ducked under the instrument panel and dived out through the forward hatch. In this weird slowing down of time he was able to reflect on Jack's courage and decency in looking after his skipper like that. He also had the chance to notice one of the escorting Mustangs sitting out just beyond the port wing, presumably protecting them from any possible fighter attack while they baled out. He even had time to think that this was a pretty brave thing to do, given that flak was bursting all around and there seemed every possibility that Charlie might blow up at any moment.

Then, Jack had gone and it was his turn. He leaned over, gently punched Les on the shoulder, received a nod of acknowledgement and saw his eyes crinkle above his oxygen mask in a tired grin. He turned then and slid feet first under the instrument panel with his boot soles planted awkwardly astride the open nose hatch. He looked back again, waved his hand, hesitated for a second and lowered a tentative foot through the hole. With that last glance he saw Les Hough, that kindly, raucous, irreverent, competent, sometimes irascible and very Australian skipper, sitting there stubbornly keeping a burning wreck airborne while his crew bailed out. Like the good Aussie he was, he stuck by his mates to the end.

20. Staying Alive

The exit was sudden and violent. As Allen gingerly lowered his booted foot it was grabbed and snatched backwards by the slipstream, pitching him out of the hatch in a clumsy forward roll. His fall was briefly checked with a neck-wrenching jerk and he realised that he had forgotten to unplug his oxygen and intercom leads. He grabbed frantically at the fastener on his mask but before his hand reached it the weight of his body and the slipstream proved too much. His helmet ripped off, taking a fair bit of skin with it, and he fell clear. Dazed by the jolt he found himself sprawling on his back looking upwards at the rapidly receding Charlie and in the relative quiet was suddenly aware of the nearby detonations of heavy flak around him.

He fell for a thousand feet or so in an effort to get away from the bursting shells and then reached across his body, grabbed the D-ring on the chest pack and pulled as hard as he could. The ring and wire came away in his hand and to his relief and surprise, the grubby, oil stained, sawdust covered article that he had excavated from under his bench functioned in the advertised manner. A bundle of fabric and rigging lines erupted from the pack, streamed past his face and a second later the parachute opened and his fall was abruptly arrested.

Looking up, as he drifted slowly down, he could see Charlie still closely followed by another Lancaster, although by now the escorting Mustang seemed to have sheered off. As he watched, the nose of the crippled aircraft pitched down about thirty degrees and as the bunt continued the main spar of the blazing wing failed and seemed to fold over the top of the fuselage before separating. The still burning remains rolled until the intact wing was underneath and then fell very fast, blazing like a comet, in a great arc down-wind until they exploded in a field below.

It was bitterly cold, his head and hands were freezing, his eyes were streaming tears of pain, and these and blood from superficial wounds were congealing on his face. Descending almost imperceptibly, he was however being blown rapidly eastwards and towards the line of the Rhine. The raid was nearly over now. The last of the attacking aircraft were wheeling away westwards and the defensive flak was petering out. He saw that his parachute canopy had been holed in several places and realised with a brief shock that some of it must have burst fairly close to him. Soon he was drifting down in complete silence. He could see two other parachutes spread out over about a mile and a half but apart from that the sky was empty. He felt very alone. After the first brief elation at getting out of the aircraft and deploying his parachute came the realisation that all the other crews were on their way back to England and that he was falling very slowly into a landscape filled with hostile people.

The descent seemed to take a very long time and at first he hardly seemed to be losing height at all. After a while he realised that he had blown back across the river and was going to fall into the heavily bombed city of Duisburg. As he got lower he could make out the lines of streets and see individual houses and it was then that he realised that he was being shot at with small arms. At first he didn't know what was causing the constant sibilant noises that hissed past him because the strength of the wind stopped the sound of shots from carrying, but as the ground became closer he could see the soldiers on the ground and the muzzle flashes from their weapons. He was struck by the notion that there seemed to be a lot of them and they couldn't continue to miss for ever. He had to do something, although precisely what continued to elude him. Then he realised that he was still clinging convulsively to the D-ring of his parachute. Clutching at straws, he suddenly released it and slumped in his harness as if he'd been hit. Given that several score of Volkssturm (Home-Guard) soldiers had been shooting at him for some minutes and had consistently missed it was unlikely that they could see well enough to notice the dropping of a D-ring but he was at least doing something.

As he came down still further he noticed that most of the houses in Duisburg appeared to be roofless and at the last moment, as the face of the town clock flashed past his dangling form, he realised that he was moving very fast indeed as apart from the speed of his descent the wind was still blowing at something like gale force. Then he was among the chimneys and his heels slammed into one of the few relatively intact roofs. Suddenly he was up to his waist in shattered pantiles, his canopy streaming across the roof, completely winded by the impact and conscious of the fact that bullets fired by troops in the garden were still continuing to ricochet off the tiles and the brickwork. He knew that the law of averages meant that they couldn't continue to miss and so he banged the release box on his harness to rid himself of the 'chute and struggled convulsively to break through the laths and tiles and seek the shelter of the rooms below.

The shattered structure around him disintegrated and he fell some twelve or fourteen feet through the plaster and onto the floor beneath him. He lay there, stunned and numbed by the accumulative impacts and was vaguely aware of the heavy clump of boots coming up the stairs below him. The door burst open with a crash, the room filled with men and he was hauled to his feet. He was aware that they were demanding his issue revolver but he wasn't carrying it. He had never fancied his chances of shooting his way out of Germany and had never bothered to lumber the thing around. Once they discovered he was unarmed they piled into him, everyone yelling at once and lashing out with fists and feet. As it happened the room was too crowded to allow anyone to get much of a swing at him and so he was dragged to the door and, still unable to stand, he was literally kicked down a long single flight of stairs that led to a street door below. He bumped and slid down on his back as far as the door and was then booted down a flight of stone steps from which he rolled into the middle of an angry crowd on the pavement outside.

As soon as he hit the street they were on to him all shouting and kicking and all trying to land a blow. It was rather like being down in the middle of a rugby scrum and like a scrum safety lay in curling up while the rest got in each other's way. A few kicks and punches went home but suddenly he heard a shot and in the subsequent relative quiet the sound of a voice shouting. He opened his eyes and looked up and saw a man in Luftwaffe uniform wrenching his assailants off and beating them back with the barrel of a formidable looking automatic pistol. As soon as the crowd parted he was yanked to his feet and half dragged, half carried to a motor-cycle combination parked by the kerb. He was pushed into the sidecar and his rescuer kicked the engine into life and pulled away from the still threatening crowd. In his haste to get clear he drove the machine into a narrow cul-de-sac and a dazed Allen remembers being surprised when he slipped the thing into reverse and backed out. He had never seen a motor cycle with a reverse gear before.

They drove through the streets of a city much of which had been bombed into rubble. Most of the buildings were roofless and the many people seemed to be dwelling in the cellars and the few habitable rooms left in the ruins of their homes. After a while they left the devastated built-up area and entered a semi-rural landscape of shabby fields, sooty grass and allotments. It was here that they drove into a road where there were no pedestrians about and the driver, who appeared to be a Luftwaffe feldwebel (sergeant) stopped. He had been driving the combination with one hand and in the other held a pistol which was pointed in Allen's general direction. Once the bike stopped Allen could not help wondering whether he was about to be summarily shot but the Feldwebel began to speak to him in halting but understandable English.

Surprised he said the first thing that came into his head. "It was lucky for me that you happened to come along!" At that the Feldwebel shook his head. "It wasn't luck" he said "I was sent by my battery commander with orders to capture you. I had been following your parachute ever since we saw it open after you baled out. You were lucky that I found you, had it been one of the others you would have been kaput!" Allen thought that "the others" meant the SS or the Gestapo but he later realised that his captor had the Wehrmacht or the Volkssturm in mind. The Luftwaffe still played it more or less by the rules but by that stage in the war neither the army nor the home guard retained much in the way of scruples and many civilians were, understandably enough, minded to form impromptu lynch mobs. The Feldwebel went on to say that he was taking him to the local police station to be held. After that he would be taken on for interrogation. He warned him to do his best to keep his head down for the next few days if he wanted to reach a the relative safety of a prisoner of war camp. "The RAF," he said "are not popular in the Ruhr area." At this point he re-started the bike and they drove on through the bright windy morning.

As the initial shock wore off a bit Allen's wounds were beginning to pain him. He was also more than a little confused. First he encountered large numbers of people who were earnestly if ineptly trying to kill him and now this completely unexpected kindness.

The combination was driven through a network quiet roads that skirted Duisburg before turning in to a walled garden and stopping in front of a good sized detached house.

Like just about every other building that he had seen it was shabby and fairly battered. Windows had been broken and boarded up, there was evidence of splinter damage to the walls and some of the roof tiles were broken. The paintwork was in bad shape and the drive and garden were neglected. It looked like an Edwardian mansion rather than a police station and indeed it probably was one, but it had been pressed into service when the central area was devastated by air raids.

The Feldwebel dismounted and gestured to Allen to get out of the sidecar. This was easier said than done. Although his flying boots had protected his shins the impact with the roof had badly lacerated his legs and they had stiffened badly. However he wasn't going to argue and he levered himself up and hobbled to the door. He was ushered inside, his guard uttered a brief word of farewell and showed him straight into what appeared to be a temporary billet. It was a largish room with windows obscured with plywood shutters and containing half a dozen crude double tiered bunks. His escort closed the door, and as he stood there listening to the murmur of voices in the hallway behind him he was greeted by a friendly Canadian voice. Seated on one of the bunks was a dishevelled young man in RCAF uniform with an Air Gunner's brevet on his tunic. Inevitably they exchanged stories. The gunner, who introduced himself as Bob Robinson, had baled out the day before. He had suffered rather less damage on landing but had experienced even closer shaves in the face of sustained small arms fire as he descended. He was still wearing his mae west life jacket for the sake of the little extra warmth that it gave him and was able to show a bullet hole that had gone up through the collar. He had another matching hole in the heel of his boot and had been fairly shaken by the experience.

The two talked for a while and Allen looked about him. It was obviously a temporary billet rather than a jail and it looked as if their captors were not too certain what to do with them. Recent heavy raids on Duisburg had probably disrupted the usual system for dealing with newly captured aircrew. The place didn't look so very different from the house in St John's Wood where he had stayed during his aircrew selection, or the hastily converted small hotel in Babbacombe that had been his billet at ITW. There was probably a degree of irony in that, did he but have the energy to consider it. The house had obviously been stripped when it was pressed into military service. The rooms were floored with bare boards, unshaded light bulbs were suspended from the sockets and blackout shutters combined the functions of keeping the draught out from the gaps left by shattered panes of glass and preventing the windows emitting light. There was one incongruous touch. Against the wall by the foot of the bunks stood a well tended upright piano.

After a while the door opened again and an elderly soldier in Wehrmacht uniform entered the room. To their surprise he wasn't carrying a weapon and far from seeming threatening he smiled at them rather shyly. He cut a remarkably unmilitary figure. He was short, balding and rather stout and looked more like a caricature stage Jewish tailor than a member of the *herrenvolk*. He may have looked unmilitary but the Great War medal ribbons on his tunic showed that he had been a real soldier and had certainly seen action. He gave the shutters a cursory check and said something to them in German as he left. They didn't understand the words but the tone was clearly sympathetic. Like the Feldwebel before him he clearly saw them as fellow soldiers in misfortune rather than *luftgangsters* or *terrorfliegers*. The afternoon dragged on punctuated by the usual shouting of Wehrmacht or Volkssturm NCOs outside and the warbling note of air raid sirens warning of further attacks. Once or twice they heard the noise of flak batteries in action but there was no sound of bombing nearby and they assumed them to be either nuisance raids or false alarms.

After a while the little soldier re-appeared and spoke to them again but as he spoke no English and they, at that stage, spoke no German, communication was difficult. By now neither of them had eaten much since the pre-operational meal immediately before they were shot down and as a result they were both ravenous. They were surprised and very grateful when the old boy produced a couple of apples from his pocket and pressed them into their hands. He turned to go and then stopped and spoke to them urgently. The word *essen* was repeated with a warning shake of the head.

"You mean we're going to Essen?" said Allen, but at this point the guard vanished through the door and came back with another slightly younger soldier, also wearing Great War decorations on his tunic. The new entrant was obviously a friend of his and he listened briefly before speaking to them in heavily accented but intelligible English. "My friend said that if anyone comes you must not tell them that he gave you something to eat. Without orders it is forbidden to give food to prisoners." They thanked him for his kindness and promised to be discreet. The ice thus broken they chatted together amicably, with the younger of the two soldiers translating for his mate. They were both reservists and, judging from their apparent friendship, had probably been together for some while. It turned out that the tubby little man was indeed a tailor and had run his own business in one of the Hanseatic ports.

The siren sounded again and they heard a clatter of booted feet outside as what turned out to be the Volksturm duty watch abandoned the place. After that the younger reservist went out to answer the telephone. When he returned he summoned his mate and turned to the two airmen. "Tommy comes" he said.[8] "We must go to the

[8] The Germans still referred to British and Commonwealth forces collectively as 'Tommy'. In this case "Tommy comes" meant an RAF raid.

bunker and you are to stay here. It won't be very safe but safer than out there!" At that he left, locking the door behind him.

Despite the raid and the bitter cold they slept and were awakened the next morning when their guards returned. After a while they were given a mug of ersatz coffee and a hunk of black bread and had not long eaten it when they heard the sound of boots and voices in the hallway and a pale and battered-looking Stan was pushed into the room. Allen tried to talk to him but he was barely coherent. All that he could say was that he had been suspended above the ground, as his parachute had been caught up in some overhead cables. Jack had fallen into the street and he had seen him mobbed by a crowd but he didn't know what happened after that.

They had little further opportunity to talk as, shortly after Stan's arrival, a dozen or so young soldiers turned up to collect them. The NCO in charge supervised while they were frisked and anything of value was taken away and pocketed by one or other of the escort. It was not a gentle process and as well as appearing fairly uncouth the soldiers seemed a singularly unimpressive crew. They were shabbily dressed, wore what looked rather like crude unpolished British army boots rather than field boots, and the bottoms of their long greatcoats were unhemmed and hung raggedly between knee and ankle. They were pretty poor physical specimens and it was clear that the barrel had been scraped pretty hard to produce this lot. The NCO ordered Stan and Allen outside, although for some reason Bob Robinson, the Canadian Gunner, was left in the locked billet. Once through the door their escort formed two files and they were pushed in between them. The NCO spoke again, this time in broken English. So far as they could understand they were, he said, "going to be shown what they had just done." Whether this was a matter of policy, a local decision or simply the whim of a particular officer they never discovered but it turned out to be a nightmarish ordeal.

They were led out through the gates and marched down the centre of the road until they reached a heavily bombed built-up area. There was very little wheeled traffic, little more than bicycles and the odd horse drawn cart but there were plenty of people about in the crowded streets and many of them were, not surprisingly, extremely hostile. They were spat at, sworn at, kicked, punched and a variety of missiles were thrown at them. Their guards didn't seem to care much what happened to their prisoners, indeed if anything, they seemed stirred to matching the crowd's hostility. Eventually they marched their battered captives away from the mob and down a deserted side-street which proved to be a cul-de-sac closed at the end by the blank wall of a factory. The little column halted and Allen and Stan were unceremoniously shoved up against the wall some ten feet or so from their escort, who were now shuffled into a single line. The NCO gave an order and his squad noisily cocked their rifles and machine pistols and aimed them at the pair of them.

Stan was visibly distressed. As Allen later discovered, his escape from the aircraft had been terrifying and this further ordeal was just too much for any boy of his age to cope with. Tears were streaming down his face and he was shaking violently. His had been an experience that would already have been too much for almost anyone to cope with, as the second salvo to hit the aircraft had smashed into the structure of the turret, jamming the traverse mechanism and damaging his right arm. It had also cut the hydraulic power and intercom systems leaving him out of communication with the crew. The last instruction that he had heard was to prepare to bale out. After that he was alone, isolated in his turret with burning petrol spewing back past him and his parachute on the wrong side of the turret door. He had managed to hand crank the turret far enough round to force the doors back and exit into the fuselage. Once into the wrecked rear fuselage he had found his parachute pack, clipped it on and jumped through the rear door just before the main spar had folded. His experience in simply getting out of the aircraft would have been enough to put most of us into hospital for a prolonged stay. Nor had it ended there. He had then descended through a barrage of ground fire, been swept into overhead wires by a howling gale and hung there helplessly while a mob appeared to lynch one of his closest friends.

Allen too was convinced that they were about to be shot out of hand but for him the experience seemed unreal, unbelievable, like a waking nightmare and like a nightmare he couldn't quite believe that it was happening. Then the reality broke through. He wasn't going to wake up, it was happening, and what is more he couldn't do a thing to stop it. Although sick with fear he tried to appear calm and, looking at his young mate he spoke urgently

"Don't show 'em you're afraid, Stan," he said. Afterwards he wondered quite why he had uttered anything so apparently irrelevant. He was frightened stiff himself and, with the benefit of hindsight, God alone knows what difference it would have made had he showed it.

Suddenly they heard a shrill voice raised in anger and a plump elderly woman appeared from one of the flanking houses, pushed her way between them and the impromptu firing squad and started to berate the soldiers. They couldn't understand what she said but the word propaganda was repeated several times along with what sounded remarkably like some fairly powerful abuse. In the end the squad uncocked their weapons, re-formed their double column and the pair were marched back to the relative safety of the temporary police station. Whether the soldiers ever intended to shoot them they never knew. One suspects that had it been their firm intention they would not have let one old lady stop them. It is however possible that without her intervention a cruel bluff might have got out of hand and developed into a reality but if their intention had merely been to terrify their prisoners they succeeded admirably. The word is much misused in our decade, but they had in a very real sense been traumatised by their series of narrow escapes from death. It was to have long lasting effects on both of them.

On their return the NCO handed them over to the little ex-tailor and his friend who once more appeared to be in charge of the post. Once the squad had departed they greeted them amiably enough and ushered the badly shaken pair back into the billet to rejoin the Canadian gunner. The whole incident couldn't have taken much more than a couple of hours, because shortly after their return they were given the mid-day ration of cabbage soup, but it had seemed like a very long time indeed.

The day wore on. They heard the sound of most of the troops leaving the building and then the door of the room opened and the two reservists entered once more. The younger one went out shortly afterwards, presumably to man the desk, but to their surprise his tubby friend slid a stool to the piano, opened the cover and proceeded to play to them. He started with an impromptu medley of classical music and it was soon evident that he was a very accomplished musician. He tried to speak to them but this was defeated by their lack of a shared language. Then, as if struck by a bright idea, he began to play English soldiers songs of the Great War. He played Tipperary, Take Me Back to Dear Old Blighty, Madamoiselle from Armentieres and even Two German Officers. After a while his mate re-entered and after a few more choruses the pianist smiled at them and asked a question. It was translated for them as "Do you know this one?" and he played the first few bars of Lili Marlene. They all said "Yes, it's Lili Marlene", but to their surprise he shook his head and said "neine, Marie Marlene", which probably spoke volumes about a cultured man's lack of interest in German popular music.

The sound of heavily shod feet outside spurred their two guards to leave the room and shortly afterwards the younger one came back with the news that an escort had arrived to take them to the Luftwaffe interrogation centre at Oberursel near Frankfurt-on-Main.

Packing didn't take long, all they had was the clothes they stood up in, and in seconds they were standing outside while an NCO signed for three RAF prisoners of war to be delivered to Oberursel. By now the early November darkness had fallen and they were flanked by four guards and marched through cold, blacked out, deserted streets until they arrived at the railway station. The scene looked like a Frith painting reworked by Hieronimus Bosch. It was a big place, a mainline station for a good sized industrial city, and hundreds of people were milling around in the dim blue light of the few shaded lights that were permitted. There were people from all over the collapsing Third Reich : German civilians, refugees from the east, forced labourers from all over occupied Europe, and troops from dozens of German and satellite powers. There were Hungarians, Rumanians,

Cossacks, Belgium, Dutch and Scandinavian SS volunteers, as well as Spaniards from Franco's Blue Division and Italians from the forces of Mussolini's rump fascist state.

Their escort led them to the back of the station and stood with them in the shadows cast by the rear wall and some cast iron pillars. They tried to be as unobtrusive as possible and happily for them, in the darkness their RAF blue was almost unidentifiable. In the Nazi Germany of late 1944 half the population seemed to be wearing a uniform of some kind and nobody gave most of them a second glance. Allen, noticing the way the metal crowns of his flight sergeant's badges glinted in any stray rays of light, took them off and slipped them into his pocket. The fabric stripes and flying badge he left in place. It might be important to be wearing an identifiable uniform before he arrived for interrogation and in the dim light chevrons were not very obvious.

Trains were few and far between. Faced with overwhelming Allied air power nothing travelled by day on German roads or railways. As a result they were faced with a very long wait and after a couple of hours the inevitable happened. Someone was jostled, said something to one of the party, and then took a close enough look to notice that they were captured airmen. Those nearby reacted almost immediately, a buzz of conversation ran through those around them and in a few seconds they were at the centre of a shouting, jostling, hostile crowd. Their guards were not initially very disturbed. They didn't much care what shape their prisoners were in when they delivered them. They would however be in trouble if they failed to deliver them at all. Dead prisoners cannot yield information and the struggling German air defence system needed all the help it could get. After a while it began to look as if they might get out of hand and at this point one of the escorts decided to do something. He said something loudly, the crowd quietened a bit and then a train came in and in the general struggle to board it everyone seemed to rather lose interest. Eventually they boarded the decrepit train and were seated on wooden seats in a sort of four-seater partitioned compartment separated by a central aisle from a similar space. There was just enough room for the three of them and their escort in the two adjoining sections.

Allen found himself sitting next to the unteroffizier (corporal) in charge. It was he who had been responsible for saying whatever it was that had earlier calmed the crowd. Later on it became apparent that he spoke some English and Allen tentatively asked him what he had said. "I told them that you were from a bomber" was the reply. Allen's expression obviously revealed that he didn't understand and the Unteroffizier explained. "They don't mind the bombers so much" he said, "you can shelter from them, but the *jabos*, the fighter-bombers, they come down on you suddenly and if they miss on the first pass they try again. They are bastards, swine, they shoot without mercy, indiscriminately at anything that moves"!

It soon became apparent that most Germans were absolutely terrified of the roving fighter-bombers and they loathed the men that flew them with a fierce hatred. Under the circumstances it was hard to blame them. It would have been tactless and extremely unwise to remind the poor devils that it was the Luftwaffe that had first used the tactics on the roads of Belgium, France and Eastern Europe. It is impossible to take prisoners from the cockpit of an aircraft and air war is a bloody and barbarous business.

The crowded train jolted on through the night with frequent starts, stops and halts at stations. It was a miserably uncomfortable journey and nobody spoke very much. Then, as it started to get light, they pulled into a camouflaged siding and stopped. It wasn't until dusk that they re-started their journey and they arrived at the Frankfurt railway station at about mid evening. It had taken two cold and dangerous and days to cover a distance of not much more than a hundred miles.

From the station at Frankfurt they were marched nine or ten miles through the city and its suburbs and out into the countryside. They were bone weary by now and were not sorry to be halted by a gate in a high barbed wire fence behind which they could see a collection of wooden huts. This was the Oberursel camp, named after the nearby town. The gate was opened and they were led into a low building where, without any further ceremony Allen was jostled down a corridor and shoved into a windowless wooden cubicle. From now on he was to be in the custody of the Luftwaffe.

The guard showed him how to move a lever that dropped a signal arm in the corridor if he needed the lavatory then the door was slammed behind him. He had noticed a bare light bulb in the ceiling but it appeared not to work and so he explored his cell by touch. It seemed to be about five feet square, certainly there was insufficient room to lie at full length, and contained nothing more than a low ledge which was presumably intended to serve as a bed. He curled up uncomfortably on the narrow platform. At first he felt freezing cold but after a while it seemed to grow warmer and he fell into an exhausted sleep. He woke with a jolt when he rolled off onto the floor some time later. By now he was sweating freely and as he looked slightly upwards at the skirting, he realised that he could see the faint glow of electric elements through gaps in wooden louvres. It was reassuring to know that he wasn't blind which had crossed his mind when he first woke.

He had no idea how long he was isolated. As he received no meals he couldn't measure the time by judging the intervals and he had no idea whether it was night or day. The heating seemed to be turned on and off randomly so that he was either unbearably hot or unbearably cold and he continued to be confined in total darkness. All that he had discovered about the regime was that merely signalling that one needed the lavatory was a waste of time. It was necessary to shout and hammer on the door before a guard could be summoned and then submit to the indignity of being watched until returned to the cell.

Paradoxically enough, once he had time to reflect he found the techniques that were being used to disorient him curiously reassuring. A few shot-down airmen who had passed through Oberursel had escaped and made it back to Britain. They had been carefully debriefed, their accounts had been analysed and a training programme devised. As a result, most members of aircrew had a very clear idea of what might happen to them once they fell into the hands of the Luftwaffe intelligence organisation, and so far it was exactly as predicted.

If the pattern was continued he knew that the next few days would be unpleasant, and he didn't relish that, but he knew that after that he would be despatched to a prison camp where he would be among friends. After his recent experiences that was a remarkably comforting thought to hang on to. His confidence was shaken a bit at this point when he was taken to an ablution block and instructed to undress and take a shower. Even in 1944 sufficient information about the extermination camps had leaked out for him to know that it wasn't always water that you encountered in a shower. To his relief it was only lukewarm water that sprayed from the pipes above and he soaped himself gratefully before drying off and dressing to return to his cell.

The next stage he knew would be the arrival of someone masquerading as a Swiss Red Cross official who would require him to complete a form which would demand answers to a number of compromising questions. Sure enough, eventually he heard the sounds of footsteps, and bolts being drawn further along the corridor and eventually his door was opened and a uniformed man with a Red Cross arm band stood in the lighted opening. He introduced himself as an official of the Protecting Power and duly produced a form bearing a number of questions which he started to work his way down. To start with Allen was asked for his name, rank and number and the the address of his next of kin. He cheerfully gave the first three and then jibbed. He wasn't required to do that he said, name rank and number only. The official protested. It would speed up the business of informing his family. In any case he would be allowed to send a postcard soon. He was sure that Allen would want to write one and the Germans could merely read the address on that. He conceded the point and gave his home address but at that he stuck. Squadron, base, aircraft type, none of these he said, were questions that he could be expected to answer. What's more, as an official of the Red Cross his questioner should know that. He also complained for good measure that he had nothing to eat or drink since his arrival and the light bulb in his cell didn't work. The official rather grumpily tucked the largely uncompleted form into a folder, promised to pass on his complaints and backed out. The door was slammed and bolted and Allen was returned to the darkness.

An hour or so later the door opened again and this time he was summoned outside. He was expecting this. The next part of the process was usually an interrogation at the hands of a senior officer, but he wasn't expecting to be confronted by the form of Parkinson, the New Zealand Wop/AG from his first Hampden crew. It was pure coincidence. One was off for interrogation and the other was merely going to the lavatory but they were facing each other at a range of about two feet.

"Bloody Hell!" said Allen, "it's Parky!"

"Bugger me!" said Parkinson, "it's Clifford!" and at that they were marched off in opposite directions, never to meet again.

Sure enough he was ushered into an office where a Luftwaffe major was seated behind a desk. He was invited to sit down and offered a cigarette. He took one, accepted a light and at the first puff it was obvious that although the packet and the paper had been made to look like a familiar American brand the tobacco was the usual vile ersatz stuff that the Germans were smoking.

The major was a polished looking character who appeared to be in his middle thirties and spoke impeccable public school English. He opened the initial exchange by announcing that he had attended Reading university. To be precise he called it "Reeding" but made it clear that he understood the conventional pronunciation because he said "I know that you people call it Redding". He then made it very clear that he knew England well and spoke very knowledgeably about London pubs, Betty's Bar in York, the Trip to Jerusalem in Nottingham and innumerable theatres.

Then he abruptly changed tack.

"Have you been here before?"

"You mean to Germany?"

"No, Frankfurt. You were shot down over Duisburg. Had you been there before? What were you bombing?"

"You know what I was bombing."

"Women and children, that's what you were bombing."

The questions became more pressing.

"Where were you based? What was your squadron? Tell me about GEE? What about H2S?"

Allen stonewalled, alternating between "I was based in England", "You know I can't talk about that" and "I don't know about that".

The major followed the line predicted in every security briefing that Allen had ever heard when he went on to say: "You call yourself a navigator? You haven't the faintest idea where you came from? You haven't the faintest idea where you were going to and you have heard of neither GEE or H2S? The only conclusion that I can draw is that you are a spy!"

"With respect," Allen countered, "I bailed out of a burning aircraft in broad daylight over a strongly defended target. I was dressed in RAF uniform, complete with rank and flying badges and I landed in the middle of a city, bloody nearly getting lynched in the process. It was hardly the way to make a secret arrival in Germany!"

The major was losing and knew it, but he pressed on with an attempt at intimidation.

"Spies have done stranger things that. You make a very unconvincing navigator and in any case your attitude leaves me no alternative. The matter is now out of my hands. We will pass you over to the Sicherheitspolizei, the Field Security Police or the Gestapo. They will not stand for your nonsense. In the meantime no more cigarettes for you, it's back to your cell".

With that he called a guard and Allen was bundled unceremoniously back to his darkened hutch. He was a bit shaken by the threats but clung on to the fact that, so far at least, the process had been exactly what he had expected. They were trying to scare him into giving operational information to prove his bona fides. They had also done that to the escapers that had passed on this knowledge, and they had all survived to tell of it. Once alone again he took some comfort from the fact that he had held his ground and his interrogator had not really pressed him very hard. Even his anger had not been all that convincing. Probably the promise to send him on to the hard men was indeed a bluff and with a bit of luck the worst bit was over.

He sat there in the dark for another three or four days. Every so often the door opened and a bowl of cabbage soup, or ersatz coffee and a hunk of black bread, was shoved in but whether these were served at regular or irregular intervals it was impossible to tell. Then the door opened again, he was ordered out and ushered into another office containing another Luftwaffe major.

If the first interview had started sweet this one started sour. His interrogator was a fat, overbearing man who tried to intimidate him from the start.

"We're passing you on to some people who will make short work of your nonsense but in the meantime tell us about H2S!"

Allen said he didn't know anything about it. The Major then opened a steel cupboard which was full of H2S consoles, all obviously salvaged from crashed aircraft, but Allen stoutly denied all knowledge. The Major then asked about GEE and repeated the trick with another steel cupboard. Allen continued to stonewall and the Major became progressively more irate.

"How did you find your way to the target?" he asked and Allen replied that he had navigated his way using dead reckoning. This produced another outburst of threats.

"What were the yellow stripes painted on the tail of your aircraft for?" Allen claimed that they were squadron markings. He hadn't been shown a cupboard full of GH sets and presumed that the Luftwaffe weren't onto this new device yet. The Major pressed him but eventually gave up and was probably more than half convinced that they were squadron markings. His next card was a good deal stronger.

"Your squadron was 218," he said, and with that pushed an open pink file jacket across the table. Allen was visibly taken aback and the Major pressed home his advantage.

"It's not difficult," he said. "Your Lancaster was shot down into a field near Duisburg. It's still lying there. The letters HAC are stencilled on the side and HA denotes 218 Squadron. We know all about you, you know." He flipped through the pages as he spoke, naming the commanding officer, the navigation, bombing and gunnery leaders and a great mass of detail about the squadron. Much of this was lost on Allen who, by that stage in the war, took little interest in anything that didn't immediately affect him. Little did he care about the gunnery and navigation leaders. Then the Major got something wrong. He told him that they were based at Downham Market, a place they had abandoned in March 1944. Allen began to realise that although the enemy had painstakingly collected a great deal of trivial detail they didn't appear to know anything about GH and they were months out of date with the RAF order of battle.

Then the major changed pace with an apparent dismissal.

"Right, off you go," he said. "We will deal with you elsewhere," but as Allen rose to go he added: "While you are here, tell me about Village Inn."

Allen sat down again.

"What village inn?" he said, with quite genuine bewilderment. "I know hundreds of village inns".

At this the Major became positively incandescent with rage.

"I am sick and tired of your arrogance!" he screamed. "I will not tolerate it and neither will my comrades of the security services! You call yourself a navigator and you haven't heard of Village Inn?"

"I haven't heard of Village Inn," Allen repeated and indeed he hadn't. Its existence was a very closely kept secret and it was very far from general knowledge in Bomber Command.[9] After a good deal of loud hectoring the Major seemed to calm down. He was once again

[9] 'Village Inn' was the codename of a new gun-laying radar being fitted to the rear turrets of Bomber Command Lancasters and Halifaxes. It combined a pair of 50-calibre machine guns with a scanning and direction system that would automatically open fire on any target approaching from behind. It would have been lethal to Luftwaffe night-fighters, which needed to close to within visual range before they could engage their targets. The only problem was that it could not discriminate between friendly and hostile targets and so could not be used operationally in 'blind mode' until all RAF 'heavies' were fitted with forward-facing infra-red searchlights to identify themselves. Although Charlie had been fitted with these lights Allen knew nothing of their purpose. He had been told to switch them on en-route to the target and had done as directed, but that was as far as his curiosity extended.

becoming fairly convinced that Allen was telling the truth and this time he was correct. Having failed on this tack he seemed to give up and the interview came to a close. Allen was dismissed and returned to his cell and once more he formed the conclusion that his interrogators were more than a little half-hearted about the process. As intelligence officers they must have had a pretty fair inkling of the likely outcome of the war.

Shortly after this session Allen was allowed to complete a preprinted postcard to his parents informing them that he was unwounded and a prisoner of war. Then he stayed alone in the darkness for what he thought was probably another day until, as abruptly as he had been locked up, the door opened and he was hurried outside. There waiting, was an escort of half a dozen Luftwaffe soldiers as well as Stan and about twenty other aircrew, mainly from Britain or the Commonwealth but with a few Americans among them. Without ceremony the gates were opened and they were marched out, along a road which passed through a landscape of low wooded hills and eventually into the city of Frankfurt.

They were footsore when they reached the railway station and after a long and this time uneventful wait, dusk fell and they boarded a shabby old local train. Although they only travelled about twenty miles there were endless stops and starts. The journey took much of the night until at last they were decanted onto the station platform in the town of Wetzlar. Outside the station they boarded a tram, one end of which was occupied by ordinary German civilian passengers. These, like all of the other inhabitants of the place, took very little notice of them. Soon, speeded by the familiar sound of its bell, the tram car started off and carried them up the hill and on to the edge of the pine woods fringing the city. They saw that they were approaching a floodlit, barbed-wire fenced compound, flanked by wooden machine gun towers. It was exactly like those they had seen in a dozen war films; they were about to enter their first prison camp.

21. Kriegie

The tram stopped opposite the camp gates where they were ordered off and, to their mild surprise, were required to form five ranks in parade order. A Luftwaffe feldwebel called the escort to attention, the gates swung open and they were marched into the compound where they were punctiliously handed over to the Senior Allied Officer, an American Air Force lieutenant-colonel.

They stood there and, as the strengthening daylight began to dim the arc lights, the Colonel briefed them. Despite the presence of a number of guards it was a frank no-bullshit address and they warmed to him immediately. Wetzlar was a small holding camp he told them. Their stay would be a brief one, perhaps a week or so, and once large enough drafts could be assembled they would be posted on to larger camps elsewhere. He told them to keep their spirits up, not to "let the bastards grind you down!" and to remember that "every building there was wired for more than just the lights". He also drew their attention to the distant rumble of artillery. "That's the sound of freedom" he said "So don't do anything stupid"!

It was good advice. The western Allies were only about sixty miles away but the Rhine and the front line lay between them and neither the military nor the civilian population of the area were likely to show much mercy to escaping allied prisoners. The war seemed all but over and it made a great deal more sense to let the liberators come to them.

The Colonel did not waste time. Once he said what he had to, they were dismissed with the welcome words "now go over to the mess hall and get something to eat. You could probably use it." The mess turned out to be staffed mainly by British army NCOs and, thanks to the availability of Red Cross parcels, the food was good and plentiful. Bully stew, with tinned vegetables, followed by bread and jam and two generous mugs of tea. It was the best meal Allen had seen since he was shot down some ten days before.

Once they had eaten they were led over to a shower block where they stripped, their clothes were searched and they were subjected to their first experience of de-lousing. A German sanitary corporal passed along the line with a long stick and a bucket of what looked like lime wash which was applied liberally to armpits and crotches. The stuff smarted fiercely and the discomfort was only eased when they were allowed to enter the showers and sluice it off in lukewarm water. After that they were taken to the camp office where they were searched, photographed and fingerprinted before being allocated to their billets in groups of four.

The accommodation wasn't too bad; three tiered wooden bunks in huts heated by wood burning stoves, and the food seemed wonderful after their recent privation. Every prisoner received a Red Cross parcel every week and these were taken into a central store to be allocated by the permanent staff. The camp dealt with all ranks and all Allied nationalities and, despite the fact that it only held about a hundred prisoners at any time, had a permanent staff of much the same size also made up of allied prisoners. The guards manned the gates and the perimeter machine-gun towers but within the camp the show was largely in the hands of the POW staff. Apart from morning and evening *appell*, or roll-call, conducted by a couple of bored corporals they saw little of their captors.

On the first day they were issued with a cardboard suitcase containing a spoon, an earthenware bowl glazed on the inside, a canvas holdall which held a razor, shaving brush and soap, toothbrush and toothpaste, a spare set of underwear, a spare shirt, a pair of collarless winceyette pyjamas and a towel. To this lot was added a US Army greatcoat, a sweater, some woollen socks and a scarf.

Because Wetzlar was the only all-ranks reception camp it was very much in the eye of the protecting power and as a result it was given the best possible treatment. After a few days of this, Allen decided that life in a POW camp could be reasonably comfortable. He was well fed, reasonably warm, reasonably clean and among friends. The war couldn't last much longer and in a fit of euphoria he decided that he might survive it after all.

Each day he walked around the compound and chatted to the polyglot collection of allied aircrew that were mewed up within it. He looked through the wire, across the road and over the Leica camera works that lay between them and the town below. Knowing what he knew about bombing accuracy he wondered what might happen if allied air forces had a go at such a target but took comfort in the fact that the location of the camp was well known.

The burghers were remarkably lacking in hostility and on Sundays, in a country where most eligible young men were away with the armed forces, the local girls would ride the tram up to the camp and conduct shouted conversations with the boys behind the wire.

It was too good to last and predictably enough, it didn't. A week later Allen, together with Stan Lee and Bob Robinson, joined a draft of some forty other Allied prisoners, who were told that they had been posted to Stalag Luft 7 at Bankau in Silesia. He didn't know with any exactitude where Bankau was but he understood it to be east of Breslau and Breslau itself was a hell of a long way east. Each pair of them was given a Red Cross parcel to serve as rations for the journey. Then, in the darkness of a late November afternoon, the draft, now burdened with their newly acquired kit, were escorted through the camp gates and on to a tram which carried them down to the town. Once there they were marched a few hundred yards until they boarded a cattle truck which was held at a siding just outside Wetzlar railway station. It obviously wasn't going to be luxury travel. Apart from straw strewn on the planking the truck was empty and the nearest thing to a lavatory was a small hole cut in one corner of the floor. The truck was windowless and apart from an oblique view of the ground given by the ventilation louvres they could see nothing.

After a long wait in the siding a series of jolts suggested that they were being coupled to a train and with a series of further jolts they slowly rumbled into motion. Their progress was a matter of fits, starts and interminable waiting. Every day they were halted in a siding somewhere and a gammal of esatz coffee was shoved through the door and several times they appeared to have been shunted onto another train. They could hear a good deal of air activity, air raid sirens, the sound of guns and sometimes the noise of aero engines, and knew enough to be seriously worried at the prospect of the train being strafed or bombed while they were trapped behind locked doors.

During the journey the cold made it difficult to sleep and so they passed the time as best they could in talking among themselves. It was only now that Stan spoke of his last few minutes in the aircraft and his eventual bale out. He said that his German captors had told him that the bodies of three of the crew had been found in the wreckage. While he was still caught up in the overhead wires that had snagged his parachute he had seen Jack roughed up by the mob and then driven away.

He didn't know why Geordie and Harry hadn't baled out. While he was searching for his parachute after escaping from his turret he had seen them apparently "doing something" in the rear fuselage but didn't know what it was. Allen changed the subject then. Stan was still badly shocked and obviously found it very distressing to discuss the fate of his mates.[10]

---

[10] Allen never discovered why Geordie and Harry failed to jump. They certainly had a clear exit and plenty of time to escape. Les had simply stayed too long trying to ensure that his crew got out. He may have been struck by the wing folding across the cockpit or have been pinned down by G-forces. Ease of exit in an emergency was not high on the list of priorities in the design of the Lancaster and escape from the pilot's seat was particularly difficult. It was only after the war that they discovered that Jack had not survived either. A couple of Wehrmacht soldiers had freed him from the crowd and handed him over to two members of the SS named Opretza and Schoeinsten. He was driven away in a motorcycle sidecar with a third man sitting behind him. They took him to a minor road, led him into a field and shot him. Someone from a nearby farm heard the shots and, finding that Jack was still alive, ran back to the farm for help. By the time they returned he was dead. John survived to be a POW at Stalag Luft 1 at Barth on the Baltic coast until his release at the end of the war; John and Allen never met up with him again.

After four freezing days and nights the doors were slid back and they were ordered out at a little wayside halt set among pine woods. They had arrived at what served as the Bankau railway station, a wooden building and a siding set in the middle of nowhere. There was a certain amount of desultory yelling as they were formed up, before being marched along a tree lined road that terminated in front of another wire fenced compound.

The gates swung open and as they were escorted to the Headquarters building groups of prisoners shouted to them, asking after old friends and seeking for news from that private air force world in which they had all once lived. Once inside they were again made to undress before being searched, de-loused and showered. After that they were divided up into mess-groups of four, allocated to huts and each issued with a three legged wooden stool and a big multi-ply paper sack to serve as a mattress cover. Finally they were taken to the joiner's shop where their sacks were filled with wood shavings and they were given eight short planks to serve as bed boards on which to rest them. Eventually they were directed to their huts where they were immediately greeted by groups of men eager for news of the world beyond the wire.

Bankau proved to be a brand new camp still smelling of the unseasoned lumber of which it was largely constructed. With a few exceptions the inmates were NCOs from the RAF and Dominion air forces. It was a big compound with hutted accommodation for nearly two thousand men. There were sixteen or twenty men to a room and as each room was twenty five to thirty feet square they were not unduly crowded. Three tiered wooden bunks left a fair amount of circulation space, there was a good sized wooden table, and a cast iron wood-burning stove kept the room tolerably warm when it was lit.

By now it was late November and Allen settled down to learn the survival skills needed by a prisoner of war. He met a few friends and acquaintances from squadron and training days and it was pleasant to catch up with them but, as one fresh from the outside world he was constantly quizzed by men who had been "in the bag" for months and sometimes years. Some of them, taken prisoner in the early years of the war, simply couldn't believe that it was nearly over and that the Allies were firmly on top. He also started to acquire a smattering of German and an entirely different argot which was superimposed on RAF slang. Prisoners were known as "kriegies" short for *Kriegsgefangener*, the German word for prisoner of war. Guards were known as goons and these too were divided into two types: the wire goons, the uniformed Luftwaffe soldiers who manned the machine gun towers and the ferrets, the English speaking security troops who roamed about inside the compounds.

He learned how to make a "stufa", a little multi-fuel, fan-assisted cooker, out of re-cycled sections of milk tins, a pie dish, cardboard, scraps of wood and string. He also learned how to make brew on one of these cookers using almost anything combustible as fuel.

His days were fairly busy. In a society in which most of the necessities of life have to be improvised, keeping fed, clean and warm took up an enormous amount of time. The construction of a stufa without any proper tools was the work of several days for a novice and every other task was proportionately difficult. Clothes were washed in cold water without the aid of soap, mending was done with re-cycled thread and improvised scissors and needles, and boots were re-soled and heeled with wood.

There was never enough fuel and hence stoves were only lit for a short part of the time and exercise was the only reliable way of keeping reasonably warm during most of the day. Various ball games were played and an endless stream of kriegies walked around the perimeter of the camp.

Ten yards or so inside the main fence was a single strand of wire which it was forbidden to cross without permission. Transgressors could and would, be shot. Walkers couldn't cross the line and if a ball went over games players would shout to the guard in the nearest tower for leave to retrieve it. If there was an air raid they were required to stay inside their huts and anyone that ventured outside would be shot without further warning. It isn't clear why this rule was enforced. Even if they had something important to say it would have been impossible to signal the Fortresses flying twenty five thousand feet above them. The rule was enforced however. Sometimes air alerts would last for a very long time and one unfortunate prisoner simply forgot what was happening and went outside for a walk. A perimeter guard shot him dead when he was less than a foot from his hut door.

Walks around the perimeter were important to the RAF prisoners as almost all of them were pretty badly battered when they arrived in Bankau. An aircraft which has been raked with flak or night-fighter cannon and machine gun fire was not a healthy place to be. Even if they were not hurt in the attack that brought them down not many men escaped from an aircraft without sustaining some sort of injuries and fast parachute landings and hostile crowds added to these. For the majority of new prisoners walks around the compound were the first stage of a return to some kind of normal mobility

The other major source of entertainment was conversation. They talked of old friends, they speculated about the end of the war and they shared survival stories. For instance it was widely believed that escaping from the top hatch of the De Havilland Mosquito was all but impossible. You could clear the cockpit but as you blew back the high tail fin would hit you every time and you would be killed by the impact. One Mosquito pilot who Allen met on the circuit had read in "TEE EM", the service information journal, that it was possible to survive by crawling on to the wing root first. The cockpit was in flames, the bottom hatch unreachable and so he tried it. He survived to tell Allen the tale but God alone knows how he did it. There was the Typhoon pilot who had attacked a train with rockets and was following up with cannon fire when the locomotive boiler blew up. The next thing that he knew he was regaining consciousness hanging upside down in his straps after the aircraft had crashed inverted in a nearby field. Happily nobody from the train came looking for him or he would have been shot out of hand. Ground attack pilots were not popular in Germany at that time. Fighter bombers were ruthlessly shooting up everything that moved and baling out anywhere near the target was not recommended. Survival for those few shot down fighter pilots who did manage to bale out was largely a matter of luck.

Prisoners also had some access to more conventional sources of entertainment. The Red Cross supplied paper-backed books which were fairly widely available. A prisoner would be given a book from the camp library which he would be expected to swap informally once he had read it. There was also a concert party a theatrical group and film shows were presented from time to time.

Food was a constant preoccupation. As the Reich collapsed so did the distribution networks and the supply of Red Cross parcels began to decline dramatically. The kriegies were being thrown back on a version of the usual Wehrmacht ration scales. Ersatz coffee or tea in the mornings, with an eighth of an Afrika Korps loaf of Rye bread (a piece about four inches square by three quarters of an inch thick) and a few grammes of ersatz margarine to spread on it. There would be soup and potatoes for lunch and then nothing until coffee and bread again the next morning. Until Christmas they were still getting about one parcel between twelve at irregular intervals and some hoarded food still survived, after that they were to go hungry. They also relied upon Red Cross parcels for cigarettes and these and chocolate were the unofficial currency of the camps.

The senior allied NCO, the Man of Confidence, nominally in charge of the prisoners maintained a fairly low profile. There was also an NCO who spoke perfect German and was responsible for the translation of news bulletins and announcements. He undoubtedly appeared to have a good deal of influence with the Commandant and his staff but he was mistrusted by the majority of the prisoners who were uncertain as to exactly where his loyalties lay.

They rapidly learned to treat German news bulletins with a good deal of scepticism but, as they enjoyed daily access to the BBC overseas service, they were able to keep fairly well up to date with the progress of the war. Canary, as the secret radio was called, was hidden in the camp and very few of the kriegies knew even vaguely where it was. The BBC news was taken down verbatim and a small group of prisoners would carry a copy of the summary and circulate round the camp. As they entered each hut a lookout would keep watch and the news of the day would be read aloud. A high degree of security had been necessary as the ferrets spoke fluent colloquial English and were always wandering freely around the compound. It is probable that by that point in the war they may not have been too zealous in hunting out sources of information but nobody was prepared to take a chance on that. Superficially they were friendly enough. Most of them were working class Germans that had worked for long periods in the United States. One of them, known as Tex, had lived in Texas and been unlucky enough to return to Germany on holiday in the Summer of 1939. Caught by the call-up, he was immediately drafted into the Luftwaffe and had wound up in the security service. How much enthusiasm he felt for National Socialism was anybody's guess but prudence suggested that he still needed to be treated with deep suspicion.

By and large their relationship with the Germans was fairly tenuous. They were basically only required to parade for morning and evening appell. This was a formal affair supervised by the Commandant in person and in general it was over in about twenty minutes because neither side wanted to be out in the cold any longer than they had to. Every ten days or so however, they would be kept outside while the ferrets mounted a search of the huts and every couple of weeks the word would go out among the kriegies to dress warmly for appell. On these days, instead of cooperating and allowing themselves to be counted in fives, the prisoners kept shifting position and made accurate counting almost impossible. This pantomime would be continued for an hour or so and then, honour for the time being satisfied, things would return to the usual wary tolerance.

By early December 1944 Allen was conscious of a kind of normality. He knew what to expect each day, was reasonably adequately fed, and the bruises and gashes gained in his descent and roughing up by the crowd were nearly healed. What was beginning to bother him was the emergence of an increasingly painful skin complaint. He was developing large red lumps on his face and body which cracked and formed raw lesions, some of which were beginning to become infected. At first he put them down to the lice which had infested the truck in which they were transported but even after he was able to thoroughly clean himself they continued to spread. At first they were merely uncomfortable and disfiguring, later they were to become a more serious problem.

As Christmas drew nearer the camp buzzed with activity. Each hut organised a party and great ingenuity went into making it as memorable as possible. To simplify the issue of rations the Germans made the kriegies organise themselves into informal groups of four and each little group tried to contribute to the celebrations. Allen's made a cake by cooking a mixture of soaked rye bread crumbs held back from their rations, with margarine, sugar and dried fruit from the remnants of their Red Cross parcels. Tinned prunes from the same source were stoned, the syrup mixed with water and hoarded sugar, and the mash fermented. The resultant brew then passed through a home made still and a passable brandy was produced. They also discovered that the prune-stones, if cracked, contained edible nuts which could be added to the cake-mix instead of almonds.

A slight pall was cast over the preparations by the loudly trumpeted initial success of the German offensive in the Ardennes but at the beginning it was dismissed as yet more propaganda bullshit. By the time their own sources told them that there really had been a German offensive the BBC news made it clear that the whole thing had turned into a bloody fiasco for the attackers.

On Christmas Eve the kriegies organised a grand variety show to which the Commandant and his staff were invited. The star turn was a surprisingly talented female impersonator (What we would now call a drag act!), who dressed in a convincing looking evening gown constructed from white towels and sang romantic songs of the period.

There was also a good deal of fairly clumsy burlesque but the organisers seemed to have gone to some lengths to avoid upsetting the Germans. At the finale all of this went out of the window as a series of placards was carried on stage commencing with one which said "It won't be long now"! The Commandant and his companions stormed out in a huff and general confusion reigned.

After Christmas things deteriorated radically so far as Allen was concerned. First of all the cigarettes finally ran out and secondly his rash became so bad that he was forced to report sick. He avoided consulting the RAMC Captain the camp contained. He had been confined ever since 1940, seemed to have lost all interest in anything and appeared to have more or less given up. Instead he saw the German camp doctor who was a Luftwaffe medical corps feldwebel. His diagnosis was swift and confident. "Your condition is the result of extreme stress" he said. "Apart from keeping the lesions clean there is no effective treatment but it will eventually go away. It will probably return for the rest of your life, mainly in the winter and mainly when you are under stress but it will not recur on your face again".[11]

Next he suffered the indignity of having his head shaved in order to dress the sores on his scalp. He didn't feel too sorry for himself. When he looked at his fellow inmates most of them were in much worse shape. One of them, a Mancunian called Bob Hope, looked like Wells' Invisible Man as he was entirely swathed in paper bandages. By then they had run out of cigarettes and it was Bob's custom to leave his bed, stand alongside people queuing to see the MO and scrounge partly smoked fags. He then returned to the ward with his tin of what he called dimps, rolled up the tobacco in the ultra thin pages of a Red Cross Bible and shared them with his mates.

The next thing the doctor did was to admit him to the camp hospital where he found himself in the "skin room", a small ward containing a dozen or so kriegies suffering from the same condition.

By mid January it was possible to hear the sound of artillery fire, the Russians were obviously drawing closer and rumours of an evacuation were buzzing throughout the camp.

On 17th January rumours became reality when the Commandant ordered the entire camp to pack up and be prepared to move at once.

---

[11] As it happened this Luftwaffe NCO doctor proved a better diagnostician than Britain's leading skin specialist. Back in England a year later, Allen was sent to see him and the distinguished consultant put the problem down to living in unsanitary conditions. He said that tar ointment and rigorous cleanliness was the only effective palliative. Over Fifty five years later it is clear that the Feldwebel's predictions were absolutely correct.

It was obviously serious, civilian refugees could be seen streaming westward on the road below the camp and armoured vehicles and horse-drawn army transport were moving in the opposite direction. All Hell was let loose in the compound but after numerous false alarms things calmed down again. Much the same thing happened the following day but in the small hours of the 19th the camp was roused and the patients told to get up, dress and pack their kit. At about five in the morning a straggling column of about eighteen hundred prisoners and their escorts formed up and after an unexplained wait of ninety minutes or so, moved off westward preceded by a field kitchen and the camp records carried in a cart. They were told that they were heading for the west bank of the river Oder where it was intended to establish another defensive front.

They were to be marched for fifty minutes and rested for ten and the guards told them that any stragglers would be shot. It was dark and bitterly cold with heavy driving snow accumulating on the road in front of them. The prisoners plodded onward, carrying their packs or dragging their possessions on improvised sledges. Allen's group were at the head of the column and so they were breaking ground, continually marching through deep snow. After three weeks in hospital he was in poor condition and before long he was aching from his sodden feet to his hips.

At first they were walking through heavily wooded terrain but after a couple of hours they reached the little town of Kreuxburg. They couldn't see much of the place in the dark but couldn't miss the fact that the verges were covered with civilian refugees, resting in what shelter could be gained from the lee of the houses. They did not halt but continued on into more open cultivated country. The narrow dirt road road wound on across the frozen landscape and from time to time columns of troops passed them going eastwards. The width of the road already restricted their column to not more than three abreast and guns or armoured vehicles going the other way would force them into the deep ditches that flanked it. As it grew light they could see their column stretching out of sight in both directions and again became aware of the sound of artillery in the distance.

Despite the lowering snow clouds there was constant air activity. High above they saw the vapour trails of US Fortresses. Below the cloud they it was mainly Russian Stormovik ground attack bombers or low flying fighters which were obviously also supporting ground troops. They were afraid that they might be mistaken for Wehrmacht formations and strafed but the Fortress escorts stayed high and the Red Air Force, fully occupied in attacking immediate tactical targets, left them alone.

They marched slowly on through a countryside containing the odd small town, no villages but punctuated by the occasional isolated farmhouse. These farmsteads appeared to be made up of a rectangle of crude stone buildings which presented to the outside a blank wall pierced by what seemed to be loopholes. The inside walls were windowed and faced into a big farmyard, about half the size of a football pitch, with a midden in one corner. They were to examine these houses rather more closely fairly soon.

There were of course no latrines available and so men were reduced to squatting by the roadside. Before long exhausted stragglers began to fall out of the column as well and were seen simply lying in the fields. So far as Allen could see, the threat of shooting proved an empty one and they were merely left where they lay. By now their elderly guards were in as bad a state as they were and as they were heading westwards and away from the Russians they probably had no desire to further alienate their prisoners. They might be needing a bit of goodwill in the fairly near future.

They marched all through that day and well into the next night. By now they were all exhausted, staggering asleep on their feet with the elderly guards in equally bad shape. It was about eighteen hours later that Allen's group were herded into one of the farm compounds. They found that the structure appeared to be made up of housing for several families as well as a range of stables and cowsheds. There was no electricity or piped water and the sanitary facilities consisted of access to the midden. They made themselves as comfortable as possible in barns and outbuildings but had no drinking water and nothing to eat but the few items of food that some of them had hoarded. It was here that Allen made the mistake of taking his boots off. They had long ceased to be water-tight and as a consequence were sodden. Body heat had served to prevent them from freezing but once removed they froze solid. It took a difficult half an hour with an improvised fire the next morning before they could be sufficiently thawed to be pulled on again.

It was some time before five o'clock the following morning that they were roused and once more the ever more scattered column moved on. Already the ranks of both guards and prisoners had been significantly thinned but the threat to shoot stragglers continued to seem an empty one. They were merely left by the roadside to catch up as best they could or take their chances with the advancing Russians.

By now they were sharing the road with more and more civilian refugees. Some of these travelled in great high sided wains loaded with all their possessions, some on flat farm carts, some pulled hand carts or pushed perambulators and some carried all they had on their backs. As it grew light they could see that the great stream of slow moving traffic stretched in both directions as far as they could see. By now, debilitated by the constant pain of his sores Allen was keeping moving largely on will power. His feet were frozen and covered with bleeding blisters and he was so thirsty that he was eating any clean looking snow that he could see. Moving in a haze of exhaustion the most irrelevant things registered. He noticed, for some reason, the fact that the fields seemed to be largely planted with turnips and that hay, instead of being stored in thatched ricks, seemed to be merely piled in the corners of fields. It was medieval subsistence farming in a landscape that might have been drawn by Breughel.

Somewhere towards the middle of the day Allen's party were herded into another farm compound and rested for a while. Some soup was made and those that had the makings brewed tea on fires fed with the wood from doors and fences. Some time around mid evening they were driven out of their shelter and again marched throughout the freezing night. They could hear the thudding of guns in the distance and realised that the Red Army was close on their heels. They even spared a passing thought for the Wehrmacht soldiers who shoved them off the road from time to time travelling the opposite way. These poor devils were almost certainly making a one way journey as they knew that the Oder bridges were due to be blown as soon as the last of the refugees had crossed.

The next three or four days blurred into one another. Many more collapsed by the roadside and the guards had long since ceased to make any attempt to keep track of their numbers. Each night the survivors were herded yet again into a farm compound to rest as best they could. Sometimes the cooks made some sort of soup with hot water and root vegetables foraged from the fields; on one occasion they were fed what looked and probably tasted like dog biscuits.

They crossed the Oder on a fine steel bridge after marching for must have been about ninety miles in all. As they crossed, Wehrmacht engineers were blowing gaps in the ice on the river below them while assault pioneer troops were preparing the bridge spans for demolition. About half an hour after their passage they heard the charges detonate. Germany east of the Oder had been effectively abandoned.

It was still snowing and still dreadfully cold. They still had a little black bread and were usually able to brew something to drink but their food intake was nothing like enough to replace the energy they were burning. They were all becoming progressively more exhausted as they marched on, spending their nights unheated farm buildings and always roused again long before it became light

A days march beyond the Oder a thaw had set in and they were forced to abandon their sledges and discard what they could no longer carry wrapped in the blanket slung across their shoulders. The dirt roads were ankle deep in mud and ploughing through that impeded them horribly. The civilian refugees were also in a pitiful state and the deep ditches that flanked the roads were filled with abandoned tables, chairs, sewing machines and other household goods as well as people forced to relieve themselves wherever they could.

On the third or fourth day after the crossing they approached a high-sided cart parked by the road and standing by it the RAMC officer who had been nominally in charge of the camp hospital. He lunged across the road, said "I want you" and plucked a prisoner out of the column. When he spotted Allen he repeated the performance and told both of them to climb up on the cart. They wondered quite what they were in for but he kept repeating the action and they soon realised that he was selecting those prisoners that had left the wards to join the march. When about thirty of them were packed into the vehicle it was led off and after a short journey, turned in through the gates of what had once been an imposing red brick building.

The place looked like a big work-house infirmary and both the wrought iron gates and formal gardens suggested that it had been kept up in some style. By now it was almost roofless and most of the windows had gone but it was still being used as a casualty clearing station for the wounded being sent back from the front line. The staff were kind but overwhelmed. They were frantically busy patching up the injured, sending as many as possible back into action and trying to evacuate the rest. They gave the kriegies a space to lie down on the floor of one of the corridors and contrived to feed them from time to time with the inevitable coffee, black bread and soup. That was the best they could manage and under the circumstances it wasn't a bad best.

On the evening of their second day in the hospital, which they discovered was in a place called Schweidnitz, they were loaded onto another cart and driven slowly to Breslau railway station where they were loaded into a couple of compartments at the end of a railway carriage. After another three nights in transit and three days spent hiding in camouflaged sidings the train eventually stopped at a halt. There they were turned out of the carriage and again loaded onto a horse drawn wagon which carried them a mile or so through the inevitable pine woods to yet another POW cage. They had arrived at Stalag Luft 3 at Sagan. The gates were opened, they were ushered into the compound and simply told to find themselves somewhere to sleep.

Sagan was like the Marie Celeste. Apart from a small cadre of Wehrmacht soldiers who for some reason appeared to be billeted there the whole camp was completely deserted. The thirty of them split up and started to forage. At first they could barely believe their eyes because the huts looked almost as if the previous inmates were merely in hiding. They were neat, tidy and well furnished with easy chairs and household articles that had obviously taken a very long time to make. Some of the earlier occupants were obviously determined to sit out the war in as much comfort as possible.

They had evidently been well supplied because the first hut that Allen entered gave him the shock of his life. It was the Kriegie equivalent of Ali Baba's cave because in the middle of the floor was a three foot high stack of American cigarette cartons that would have covered the area of a snooker table and it had merely been abandoned. Such was the shortage of decent tobacco in Germany that here was a supply of currency that would keep him fed until the end of the war if only he could carry enough. He glanced outside and saw one of the Wehrmacht detachment striding across the compound. He was a big, sturdy, fine looking young man. He didn't look a bit like the elderly crocks that usually guarded the camps and more importantly he was still carrying his full equipment. Part of this kit was a good-sized Bergen rucksack and when Allen saw it he reached a speedy decision. He stuffed a carton of 200 cigarettes into the front of his tunic, ran out of the hut and shouted to the soldier.

The big man stopped, looked round and politely greeted the scabby, shaven-headed, scruffy apparition who had hailed him. Allen, in fractured German, asked him if he was willing to sell his Bergen. "How much" enquired the Landser and to the reply "two hundred cigarettes" came back with a one word question "American?" When Allen said that they were, his face lit up, he uttered a cheery "Ja" and, peeling off the rucksack he stuffed the contents into his pockets and handed it over in return for the carton of Lucky Strikes. The soldier went on his way happily and Allen returned to the hut where he crammed the Bergen with as many cartons as it could possibly contain before going out to seek the rest of his group. To this day he wonders why the Germans had left such a Klondyke untouched and, with the benefit of hindsight, more importantly why the amiable private didn't simply take the cigarettes?

They only spent one night at Sagan and apart from issuing a ration of black bread and cabbage soup the guards didn't trouble them. The next afternoon they were taken back to the station and this time a two night train journey took them to Luckenwalde, just south of Berlin.

Gathering their scanty kit they marched, or rather staggered, the two miles from the station and found themselves confronted by a vast shabby looking complex of compounds, surrounded by the usual barbed-wire and machine-gun towers but somehow down-at-heel, with sagging roofs to the big old huts and a general air of decrepitude. This was Stalag 3a, and later they were not surprised to find that it dated from the First World War. The gates of one of the lagers were opened and the thirty invalids were herded through them.

22. Home Run from Luckenwalde

Stalag 3a, Luckenwalde, as well as being remarkably shabby, looked enormous. The compound into which the little group had been escorted was only one of several, each of which seemed to contain prisoners from different allied nations.

This time, added to the process of search, de-lousing and documentation, their clothing was taken away and baked in an oven to kill the lice breeding in the seams of the fabric. They waited, naked and shivering and when their clothes were returned not only had the material turned brown but they were too hot to wear for some time. Eventually they were allocated to billets and Allen found himself in a large hut filled with closely set four-tiered bunks and containing several groups of khaki-clad army prisoners. They seemed oddly well turned out in a rather old-fashioned style. They were meticulously clean shaven, their uniforms were immaculate, some wore peaked dress caps and a few sported pre-war style skirted tunics, buttoned up to the neck. They seemed friendly enough, however, and as he dumped his scanty kit on an empty top bunk some of them gathered round him asking the usual questions. What was the latest news of the war? Where had he come from? How and when was he captured? The lesions on his face had cleared a bit but his hair was still cropped, he was heavily bearded and after the "cold march" from Bankau he looked starved and exhausted. They seemed very sympathetic and one of them fetched him a mug of ersatz coffee. In turn he asked them how long they had been 'in the bag' and was not surprised when they said that most of them had been captured at St Valery in 1940.

They were all Irish, there were about a hundred and eighty of them in the billet and they had all been regular soldiers. This little group treated him with a curious kind of deference. He attributed this to the fact that they were professional soldiers and as a flight sergeant he would have been equivalent to a staff sergeant, pretty heavy metal in their currency. He also wore an RAF Navigator's brevet and it was clear already that his new friends were not overly bright and were impressed by his status as a highly skilled technician. To his surprise they didn't seem at all elated when he told them that Germany was on the verge of collapse, but he put that down to the fact that many long term prisoners still couldn't envisage an end to their captivity. He was grateful for their kindness, however, and before he strolled outside for a breath of air gave them each a packet of cigarettes.

As he got up to go he saw an overalled guard, a ferret, gazing through the door. Once outside, the guard accosted Allen and like most ferrets he spoke fluent idiomatic English.

"What did you give those guys your fags for?" he said, evidently puzzled.

"Well, they're my comrades and they took the trouble to find me a cup of coffee," replied Allen, in mild surprise. "Why do you ask, do you want one?"

The German nodded but also laughed sardonically.

"They were my comrades as well," he said. "Haven't you heard of the Free Irish Corps?"

Allen looked blank, he had no idea what the man was talking about and then suddenly the penny dropped.

"You mean those buggers were fighting on *your* side," he said. "Well what's changed? Why are they locked up in here? Have they changed their minds?"

The ferret drew on his cigarette gratefully, thought for a second and glanced round. "You know very well what's changed," he said quietly. "We all know who's going to win now, don't we?" There was a pause then he asked "Do you still have a high opinion of them? Would you still give them your cigarettes?"

"No I bloody wouldn't!" said Allen, but then went on. "The Irish are different you know. Most of them come from a neutral state and only joined up before the war as an alternative to being on the dole. They've no great love for England. In 1940 they probably thought we'd had it and they may as well look for another employer."

The ferret nodded understandingly and moved off. When Allen went back into the hut he exploded with, "You bastards didn't tell me!

No wonder you're not very excited at the prospect of getting out. I wouldn't give a lot for your chances!" At this his companions had the grace to look abashed and he climbed up to his bunk, lay down and went to sleep in an uneasy silence.

To his surprise, the next morning the soldiers continued to treat him politely, if rather sheepishly, and as the next few days passed it was quite clear that they were fairly apprehensive about the impending end of the war. [12]

It might have been nearing its end but there was plenty of war left to go round and they were reminded of the fact a couple of nights later. Allen was woken by a crackle of multiple cannon fire and the roar of aero engines, as strafing Soviet fighters attacked the camp. They had come in hugging the ground and luckily for the kriegies they were forced to pull up to avoid the trees that surrounded the laager. Some of the guard towers were hit but the only casualty in Allen's hut was the badly winded man who had rolled out of the bottom bunk on Allen's tier. As he heard the sound of the Stormoviks approaching Allen, who was fully dressed and still wearing his ruined flying boots, rolled off his top bunk and landed squarely on top of the unfortunate soldier who was sprawled seven feet below him.

A few days later, at about mid-day on Thursday 8th of February, they heard a racket outside the billet and ran outside to see a column of ragged kriegies entering their compound. It was the survivors of the march from Bankau arriving. They disappeared into the headquarters block for de-lousing and documentation but an hour or so later the first of them began straggling out. A guard directed them across the compound and they carried their scanty belongings into some empty huts opposite to where Allen was quartered. Wasting no time, he grabbed his kit and ambled across to join them, followed by those of the Bankau sick that had not been obliged to go back to

---

[12] As it happened nothing was done to the handful of Irishmen who turned their coats. With unusual common sense the United Kingdom government seem to have shared Allen's spontaneous judgement and after the war ended they were simply sent home.

hospital. He soon found a few familiar faces and slinging his gear on a vacant bunk, settled down among them.

For the next two and a half months Allen faced the twin enemies of hunger and boredom. Food was critically short and they were living on meagre rations of ersatz coffee, black bread and potato soup. The guards were desperate for a smoke of any kind and many of them were not above smuggling in food, which was bartered for the cigarettes or chocolate that some of the prisoners had hoarded from Red Cross parcels. Apart from the one that he had shared on the train from Wetzlar, Allen, shot down late in the war, had never received a parcel, but the rucksack full of cigarettes he had liberated from Sagan was valuable currency. Lucky Strikes and Camels were the most desirable brands, so he tended to trade with those and smoke the others.

The hunger faced by the English, French and American prisoners was trivial compared with that suffered by the Russians. They received virtually no food and as a consequence died in their hundreds. At one stage, unable to dig graves in the frozen ground, the German guards caused the bodies to be stacked like logs and merely covered the pile with a tarpaulin. Hungry as they were, the British and American prisoners would sometimes throw scraps of food across the wire into the adjoining Russian compound but there was never enough to offer any real relief.

For the Anglo-Americans the problem of boredom was nearly as bad as that of hunger. No books had come out of Bankau because nobody had the energy to carry an ounce of unnecessary weight. As a result all the prisoners had to do was talk and play improvised card and board games. Hunger, deprivation and close confinement made everyone irritable and people were constantly squabbling. The little syndicates of four to whom the rations were issued were constantly changing in a kind of frustration induced Brownian motion. One man, who had been a newspaper cartoonist, used to draw and post daily a series of three frame cartoons. In them "The Man With The Knife" was always faced with another kriegie with a mildly irritating habit. Possibly the annoying one talked in his sleep or chewed his nails but the third frame inevitably involved the knife being plunged into him. It sounds horrible in retrospect, but it typifies the way in which minor niggles could become intolerable to overstretched nerves.

Bored prisoners would do the most ludicrous things for the sake of a change and one morning Allen found himself being addressed by an American Fortress gunner wearing a Red Cross orderly's brassard. He had used this flimsy disguise to wander between the various national compounds and kidded Allen into trying the same trick to gain access to the French hospital. He said that the doctors were good and they could probably do something for his skin complaint. In the event they couldn't and Allen had a devil of a job in talking his way past the guards and back into his own laager. To his surprise the American turned up again a few days later and asked if the British had any weapons. He offered to find Allen a revolver and was quite surprised when his offer was declined. He thought that self-defence might be important before the end, but neither Allen nor any of the others fancied trying to take on the Wehrmacht and the Waffen SS armed with a few pistols.

February shaded into March and the weather began to improve a bit. Apart from a daily walk around the compound to ensure that their legs continued to work, few prisoners had the energy to exercise but they did begin to sit outside in the early spring sunlight. Allen was doing so, sitting with back propped against a hut when another kriegie came and sat beside him. "You're a navigator, I hear," he said. "Is that right?"

The question was legitimate enough. Brevet, stripes and most of the tunic buttons were long gone, lost in the aftermath of being baked nearly to destruction while being de-loused. Allen admitted that he was a navigator and the questioner introduced himself as Bill Dunbar, one time stationmaster at Buckie in the west of Scotland, one time soldier in the Argyle and Sutherland Highlanders and most recently a sergeant in the Glider Pilot regiment who had been captured at Arnhem.

Bill's first question threw him a little. "Do you like poetry?" he said and Allen noticed that he spoke in the precisely accented English of the northwest coast of Scotland. Allen admitted that he did "as much as the next man" and the next question seemed a little more practical.

"If we got out of here could you find your way to the nearest point on the Elbe?"

"I can find anywhere you like within bloody reason!"

He seemed satisfied with the reply, then reverting to poetry he began to quote large chunks of The Rubayat of Omar Khayam. He loved Fitzgerald and had learned the vast poem almost in its entirety. He rapidly infected Allen with his enthusiasm and soon, happy to have found something which both engaged his mind and pleasantly passed the time, under Bill's tutelage, he began to learn the work himself. Eventually he found his way into the same messing group and they became good friends from then onwards.

It soon became clear that Bill didn't share his cheerful assumption that the Russians would merely turn them loose when they overran the camp. He thought that anything might happen in the subsequent confusion.

"Ye ken that bloody politics will come into it," he said. "Those buggers will hang onto us as a bargaining counter as long as it suits them."

Allen didn't really share his view. The jokey line "Joe for King" reflected a genuine and widely shared popular respect for the Russians, but he couldn't see any harm in a contingency plan.

"You don't want to try now do you?" he said, glancing up at the watchtowers? Bill shook his head.

"No. Those bastards will still shoot you and forbye the woods are crawling with Wehrmacht and SS troops. The fucking Hitler Jugend division are there and they don't give a shit what they do. I dinna know what they got up to on the Eastern Front but from what I've heard of them they won't get much shrift from the Russians. If we get mixed up with them the best we'll get is a bullet in the back of the neck."

Allen, who had never been a proper foot soldier, had developed a shrewd regard for his new mate's expertise.

"So what do we do then?" he asked.

Bill drew deep on a shared cigarette and paused thoughtfully before replying.

"We wait until the Russians overrun the camp. There's bound to be the usual confusion for a day or so and we use that to get ready. Cut a few holes in the wire ye ken? As soon as the camp radio tells us that they've joined up with the Yanks we give it a few days to settle down and then we head west. We'll have to watch out for stragglers but the bulk of the SS will either be in the bag or dead. In any case they'll have better things to worry about than a couple of kriegies on the run".

By mid-March the continental spring had properly begun. The weather began to grow a lot warmer and it was positively pleasant to sit outside. Canary, the camp radio, kept them abreast of events and they knew that the German armies were being sandwiched into an ever smaller pocket between the advancing allies. They could hear the sounds of gunfire coming from the east and if the wind was right they could also hear the artillery from west of the Elbe. Air activity was intense, with USAAF Fortresses and Mustangs at high altitude and Soviet Stormoviks, Lags and Yaks mixing it with FW190s down at 500 feet and below.

More and more prisoners were being piled into the camp and a large new American contingent was reduced to living in big tents that had been furnished with bales of straw for beds.

Bill Dunbar and his fellow glider pilots urged the kriegies to begin digging slit trenches. When the fighting got nearer they were going to need better protection than the half inch planking of the huts. There was a certain resistance on the part of the RAF but a couple of strafing aircraft and some near misses from bombs or shells were enough to turn them all into believers. Suddenly the compound was filled with men trying to dig slit trenches with nothing more effective than spoons or bed boards as digging tools. As soon as they started the goons in the towers started to take an interest and the ferrets came running. They thought that they were watching a mass escape attempt and things became ugly for a few minutes. The kriegies explained that they were trying to take precautions against being caught in the middle of a battle and the goons calmed down a bit. A compromise was reached, digging stopped for that day to give the Germans a chance to consult, but it started again the next morning and nothing more was said. After a while the holes sunk into the sandy soil started to collapse but at least the prisoners had some means of taking cover.

The pocket was squeezed smaller and smaller and on the night of 20th April the prisoners were woken up by the sound of trucks pulling away from the complex. By then the Germans were reduced to using horse-drawn transport for everything, even hauling artillery, and so the trucks must have been using fuel hoarded for use in the last resort. When they came out of their huts that morning they realised that most of the Germans had gone. Rumour had it that some of them were banged up in their own cooler but if it was so, Allen saw no first-hand evidence.

The kriegies immediately cut a number of escape holes in the wire and then proceeded to raid the stores and headquarters buildings. Allen broke into the camp office and stole his own records. He was quite flattered when he saw that he was recorded as having been "*deutschfiendlich*" – unfriendly to the Reich.

"I wasn't truculent," he said afterwards, "they misread me. I was simply shit-scared and trying to hide it."

Allen, Bill and a number of mates wasted very little time on this. Their next step was to go down to the nearest village in search of something to eat. The villagers had all locked themselves into their houses and they found nothing but a couple of ornamental beer steins in a deserted bar. As they came back however they crossed a farmyard with a few tatty looking hens scratching around in it. They could see the farmer and his family looking out at them but they wouldn't move from behind their doors. Unable to buy or scrounge food they started to chase the chickens and in the end collared one by the simple expedient of throwing a battle-dress jacket over it. They then returned to camp with their prize and had to ask around for someone who knew how to kill it. One of the kriegies told them and the hen was rather clumsily despatched, gutted and dismembered, and an old iron kettle that someone had found was used to stew it.

That evening the sound of fighting was all around and at about half past ten a twin-engined fighter circled the camp threateningly. The kriegies dived for what cover was available and the machine, an Me110, dived towards them under full throttle. A blaze of muzzle flashes and streams of tracer showed that they were being fired on, but after one pass the Messerschmitt went away. Happily the rounds all went into an empty hut or buried themselves in the soft sand of the compound. Artillery, mortars and small arms fire went on all around them and nobody slept much that night but in the early light, at about six in the morning, a column of Russian armoured vehicles was seen coming up the road to the camp. They saw that the tanks and armoured cars were being ridden on by infantrymen and in turn being followed by more truckloads of troops.

One of the armoured vehicles rammed open the camp gates, heedless of the soldiers clinging on to it, who were knocked off by the trailing barbed wire, and came to a halt in the middle of the parade ground. There was a brief pause and a Russian colonel climbed out of the top hatch and stood on the top of the hull. The senior British Officer, an RAF wing commander, came forward with a Russian-speaking Polish pilot in tow. The Colonel, through this interpreter, offered them arms and invited them to take part in the liberation of Berlin.

The Wingco responded very loudly in English saying that his men were airmen, not trained soldiers, and in any case were not fit enough. The Colonel's response to the translation was volcanic and with no further ado his vehicle swept out of the compound. Within half an hour the sick and ragged starvelings from the Russian compound had been issued with weapons and were stumbling westward, but the gates of the Anglo-American lager were propped back into position and Russian sentrics occupied the watchtowers.

It was now, as the Red Army flooded past the camp, that the circus came to town. Self-propelled guns, tanks and armoured vehicles of all types thundered by at high speed; soldiers of both sexes drove past in trucks, some of which, for lack of fuel, were being drawn by horses; more soldiers armed with lances, PPSH sub machine guns, swords and machine pistols swarmed past mounted on stunted ponies. Most of the riders seemed to be Asiatic Russians, dressed in quilted tunics despite the heat, and the resemblance to the hordes of Genghis Khan was intensified by the exhausted cattle they were driving before them. There appeared to be no supply train; they were all simply living off the country.

After a while another colonel appeared on the scene, presumably from the local headquarters, and asked them if there was anything they needed. The SBO asked for food, that the camp water supply be maintained all the time and for a couple of decent radio receivers. The response was almost immediate. Half a dozen cows were driven into the camp and despatched with a machine pistol. A call for butchers produced several from among the prisoners and the carcasses were promptly dressed ready for cooking. Shortly after this bread was sent up from the town bakery in Luckenwalde and the mains pressure was turned up. Finally a high-sided cart full of requisitioned radios appeared. Unfortunately these had been loaded by throwing them into the vehicle and neither valves nor bakelite cases had stood up to the treatment very well. Happily there were enough radio operators in camp to salvage the necessary parts to make a couple serviceable and the news could be listened to openly once again.

When they woke up the following morning the sounds of fighting had moved away a little but there was macabre evidence that it had not been far away in the night. The bodies of German casualties had been stacked in piles outside the wire, just as the dead Russians had earlier that year.

Conditions were better now. They had food and water in sufficiency and artillery shells and strafing aircraft were no longer passing over the camp. Over the next few days the Americans sent trucks to collect the Anglo-American prisoners but the local commanders refused to release them without permission from Moscow and they were turned back empty. Although a general exodus was forbidden, prisoners were tacitly allowed to forage for food in the neighbouring villages as long as they stayed away from Luckenwalde itself.

On 28th May the American and Russian forces met up at Torgau on the Elbe and a week later, satisfied that most armed Germans would have been mopped up, Bill decided that it was time to go. By now it was generally understood that the Russians planned to eventually evacuate them via Odessa, nearly a thousand miles away on the Black Sea coast.

"If we wait for those buggers," he said, "we'll wait for a damned long time. This is where we grab our bonnets and go."

Allen, who was rather less optimistic about the Russians than he had been, nodded.

"Okay," he said. " When?"

"Now," said Bill. "Put what ye need in your greatcoat pockets and we're off!"

Ten minutes later, at about mid morning on 5th May, they walked over to a nearby hole in the wire. While the guards were occupied watching a desultory game of football they slipped through the hole, turned left and walked off until they picked up the approach road to the camp. They were nearly into Juterbog when Allen heard the sound of a motorbike coming from behind them. It slowed to a walking pace and from the corner of his eye he saw that it was ridden by a Russian soldier armed with a machine pistol. The rider drew alongside and, pointing the gun at them, made it very clear that they must go back. He followed, shepherding them at walking pace. When they reached the gate he yelled at a sentry to open up and, after a spate of angry shouting, literally kicked their arses back into the compound.

Allen was shaken and a bit chastened, but he followed Bill who was silently walking back along the line of the wire. His manner was purposeful but he continued to say nothing until Allen asked him where they were going.

"Back to that bloody hole," Bill said. "This time we turn right and try to mingle with the orderlies and civilians that are wandering about out there."

Without further discussion they did just that and this time walked away from the camp and down onto a local road. It was an uncomfortable feeling. The roadside was dotted with wrecked vehicles and here and there the bodies of German soldiers were scattered around distended and decaying in the spring sunshine.

They plodded along for a while, sweating in the hot sun, until about five miles down the road they came to the site of a village that had been completely flattened. They walked along the road which had been bulldozed through the waist-high rubble until they saw the ruins of a drinking fountain at a crossroad in the centre. They drank thirstily and were sitting down resting for a few moments when they saw a truck approaching.

As it drew near they recognised it as a big American M32 "six by six" and the bold white star on the bonnet and the black sergeant that was driving was enough to confirm that it belonged to the US army. They stood up, intending to flag it down, but it stopped anyway and the driver leaned down to speak to them.

"Hi! Do you guys know the road to Magdeburg?" he said. God knows how he expected anyone to understand English that far into eastern Germany, but as it happened he had got lucky. Allen pointed back the way he'd come and answered. "You're going directly away from it. Magdeburg is about sixty miles west of here. You're on the East bank of the Elbe bloody miles inside Russian territory!"

The Sergeant uttered a loud and heartfelt "shee-it!" and started to turn the truck round.

"Hey, hold on chum," they shouted, and both of them climbed up into the cab. "We're British, escaped prisoners. Give us a ride and we'll find the way back for you."

God knows how the truck had reached that point. It was part of an ordnance supply echelon and was loaded with ammunition. The big sergeant had crossed a major river and wandered sixty miles east on minor roads without noticing any Russians.

"Believe me chum, the woods are full of 'em!" said Allen. "They've kept us behind the wire since late April and if you're going to see home this side of 1949 we need to keep moving west."

The Sergeant, who appeared to have a well-developed talent for self-parody, rolled his eyes expressively and manoeuvred his mount until it was pointing the right way.

They drove west along relatively quiet minor roads until they hit a junction with a major highway. Allen glanced at the sun and pointed. "Just keep heading west," he said. This road was busy with civilian traffic, mainly heavily-burdened pedestrians and cyclists, but still the odd cart and a few motorcycle-mounted Russians. There were no other motor vehicles in sight. There were, however, plenty of signs of hard fighting, unburied German dead and thick fence posts with a red star nailed to the top which marked the site of groups of Red Army graves.

The Sergeant weaved his way slowly through the traffic, sounding the horn from time to time until it thinned a bit and ahead of them they saw the red and white knife rest and pole that indicated a check-point. The pole was lowered and a handful of Russian soldiers with slung rifles were lounging around it. They didn't look particularly alert. Bill glanced at Allen.

"We bounce the bastards," he said, and Allen nodded and turned to the driver.

"Put your foot down really hard, sarge," he said. "If we stop here we're all behind barbed wire".

The sergeant didn't need telling twice and shifting down a gear he accelerated fiercely. They hit the pole at about fifty miles an hour and the massive girder bumper and the bull bars reduced it to fragments while the knife rest flattened several of the guards. Allen saw the others running forward, frantically unslinging their rifles but by the time they got off the first hasty rounds the truck was a hundred yards down the road and still gaining speed. Obviously their was no communication between the posts because they repeated the trick a few miles further on, although this time the barrier was actually open.

They pounded on for about an hour and a half until they found themselves entering a little town. Allen knew that they couldn't be far from the Elbe here and told their driver to slow right down while he searched for the approach road to the bridge. Unfortunately their man mistook an instruction and turned right into a narrow residential road just before the end of the built up area. To their horror they were driving down a cul-de-sac of fine but rather knocked-about middle-class houses and right at the end they could see the finest house of the lot with a Soviet sentry standing outside. It was clearly the local military headquarters.

There was nothing for it but to turn round at the end. The sentry was a young, moon-faced fellow armed with a stubby PPSH submachine gun which had a circular drum magazine mounted below the barrel. It looked horribly business-like and they felt about as conspicuous as three whores at a wedding. The Sergeant was struggling to reverse the direction of a very large vehicle in a very small space. It involved making what seemed like about a thirty eight point turn and the sentry seemed ever more curious. Allen and Bill chattered aimlessly and strove to avoid making eye contact.

"Don't look at him," they said to their driver, "just turn the bloody thing round!"

Then, to his horror, Allen noticed that their last reverse had knocked over an ornamental sapling in front of the gate. The sentry stepped forward and, as their hearts sank, he carefully lay his gun on the ground and with a look of extreme disapproval at their carelessness, tried to push the damaged sapling back to the vertical again. Sweating furiously, they slowly drew away and, with a cheerful wave to the sentry, turned westwards on the main road again.

Minutes after this they breasted a low hill, the road widened and they could see the Elbe in front of them. Soon they found themselves running down what seemed to be the bridge approach. Unfortunately, they now faced two entirely new problems. First and most importantly, the bridge did not appear to be there. Second and by far the least of their troubles, there appeared to be a minor Russo-American difference of opinion going on. Mortars were being pooped off in a desultory manner and the odd small arms burst was adding to the niggling. In the absence of an alternative they kept going and were cheered as they ran on down the slope to see that the bridge had been replaced by a pontoon structure. It was a flimsy looking affair, a line of barges traversed by two metal channels in which truck wheels could run, but it did at least cross the Elbe, which seemed about as wide as the Thames at Westminster at this point.

There were no Americans on this side of the river but the throng of Russians who were half-heartedly guarding the east end of the bridge did not seem very alert.

"Don't bloody well stop," said Allen, "just keep going. After our antics in the last few hours they'll lock us up and throw away the fucking key!"

The Sergeant may have been a lousy navigator but he was a terrific driver. He hammered his toe down on the accelerator, shifted down through the gears and put the truck wheels squarely into the channels at about fifty miles an hour. The pontoons bucked and swayed, river water fountained skywards and the six-by-six crossed the Elbe raising a bow wave like a destroyer. They went up the bank without even slowing and didn't stop until they drew up in front of the chain link fencing round what looked like a small estate of workers housing and some temporary office buildings. They later discovered that it was part of a complex that formed the nearby Junkers aircraft plant and was being used as a temporary camp by the US Army.

Both Allen and Bill were still shaking. They had never been so scared in all their lives as on that last wild ride across the river. They climbed down thankfully, however, and bade the sergeant an admiring farewell before he drove off in search of his outfit.

Nobody seemed to take much notice of the two ragged apparitions and so they found their way to the regulating office (the orderly room in British parlance). The sergeant seated at the front desk looked up to be confronted by what looked like a couple of particularly scruffy refugees. He didn't turn a hair. "Hi guys," he said quietly.

Allen replied "We're RAF prisoners" and at that the Sergeant's eyes gleamed and his voice went up a couple of decibels.

"Spitfire pilots?" he said. They didn't argue. The Spitfire was the only British type that most Americans had heard of and it was much simpler to go along with it. He was however, a man of action and he proved that with his next question. "Come in, what can I do for you guys?"

Allen reflected for a second before saying, "Well... you could get us home".

The Sergeant was a master of the cool response because he came straight back with, "Well... we can't do that today because the last plane's gone, but we can find you some something to eat, something to smoke and then find you a shower, some clean clothes and a comfortable bed. How does all that sound?"

It sounded too good to be true, but he kept his promises to the letter, if not in that order. He wasted no more time but handed the office over to someone else and appointed himself their sponsor. First he took them down to the clothing store where they were issued with a complete new kit from clothes to a toothbrush. Then they went along to the showers where they wallowed in soap and steaming hot water before having their first shave in months. Allen discovered that the worst of the sores had disappeared from his body and the first mirror that he had seen since Bankau revealed that his face was completely healed.

As they emerged from the shower block clean, sprucely dressed and with Allen's beard replaced by a neat moustache, their guide was waiting for them. He took them down to the mess hall where they were sumptuously fed before leading them through to the PX where Bill was given a several packs of Camels and Allen was presented with a new pipe and a pouch of "Prince Albert", which had been his favourite pipe tobacco when he was in Canada. Finally he took them to a comfortable billet with clean sheets on the beds and with a final "Take it easy fellas" left them to their own devices. From start to finish of the process they had been asked few questions and didn't have to sign a thing.

The fact that they had 'made it' began to sink in. They wandered out into the warm evening sunlight and sat chatting to the curious GIs, all of whom seemed as friendly as the sergeant. They discovered that the little town was called Schonebeck and in the end they were to spend a week there, during which time more and more allied prisoners trickled in. There was an almost carnival atmosphere to the town. Even the German civilians seemed relieved that the war was nearly over and that they were in the hands of the Americans and not the Russians. There were pretty girls on the streets dressed in civilian frocks and apparently perfectly willing to talk to their invaders. If there were any no-fraternisation orders in force they were completely ignored in that part of the world.

The war in Europe ended, VE day was on 8th May and on the 12th Bill and Allen, accompanied by a truckload of companions were flown to an airfield just outside Brussels.

Compared with the treatment that the Americans had given them, theirs was a grudging reception. They were met by army transport officers and Bill was promptly hustled off to an army reception centre pending return to his unit. Allen was not to lay eyes on him again until some time after the war. None of the returning prisoners were allowed out of camp that night because nobody could be bothered to lay on transport into town. The following day things improved radically when the RAF contingent were divided into groups of about thirty and loaded into Dakotas. These were obviously supply dropping aircraft because the big cargo doors had been removed and there was a gaping aperture in the fuselage. The passengers sat on narrow benches that ran along the length of the cargo compartment and clung onto netting fixed to the stringers if they needed support. It was cold, noisy and very draughty but they were going home and Allen was contented.

They flew at fairly low altitude and Allen clung on to the netting and looked out of the door opening. They had crossed the Channel and were over Kent when he made his way forward and asked the crew if he could stand there for a while. It was a good deal quieter there and he was able to ask where they were going. When he was told Wing in Buckinghamshire, he was quite pleased and told them that he had done his second ANS there. After a while he went back to his vantage point and continued looking out of the door. Suddenly the engine note changed, the machine banked and they started descending steeply. He could see the edge of a substantial built-up area and runways ahead of them. They were making a curving descent without any attempt at a circuit and seconds later the wheels thumped onto the tarmac and they were taxiing rapidly towards the apron.

One of the engines coughed and stopped and Allen pulled himself forward to the cockpit again.

"What's going on?" he asked. "This isn't Wing."

Once they had rolled to a stop the pilot pulled off his helmet, turned and said, "No, it's Northolt, we were a bit short of fuel," then, rather apologetically, by way of explanation, "I thought we had done three trips today but it was four."

For the first time since he became a kriegie Allen lost his temper. He didn't know what the pilot's rank was and he didn't care.

"You silly bastard!" he said. "We've gone through all that and you nearly bloody killed us on the way home!" [13]

The pilot maintained a diplomatic silence and the flight engineer sitting in the co-pilot's seat continued to say nothing.

Allen went back, still fuming, and presently a bowser drove up to refuel them and they took off, landing at Wing shortly afterwards.

The place was unrecognisable. The hangars behind the apron were decorated with bunting and they were met by buses crewed by WAAF drivers, all of whom were wearing civilian summer dresses. All of the women who met them that day were similarly dressed and whether it was a policy directive or whether it was their own idea the returning prisoners found it particularly touching gesture.

They were first driven to one of the bunting-hung hangars which was set out with tables laid with starched white cloths and polished cutlery. One of the young women hosted each pair of ex-prisoners and they sat down to good meal. Once they had eaten sufficient they were told that, when they were ready, they would be fitted out with new RAF uniforms.

In another hangar they were faced by an assembly line along which they moved and collected a complete new kit. Alterations were

---

[13] It is some sort of a defence, although not a good one, to say that the crew had flown for more than ten hours that day and must have been fairly tired.

made and badges, brevets and medal-ribbons were sewn on their best blue tunics while they waited. When they emerged they were once more transformed into officers and NCOs of the Royal Air Force.

After they were kitted out they were taken by car to a pay office, where they all drew a substantial advance. With fifty quid in his pocket Allen felt like a lord, but it didn't end there. He was offered the use of a telephone and, recollecting that a neighbour who was a commercial traveller had one of these rare items, he rang him up. He identified himself and then his first question was to ask if his father was still alive. Once he knew that everyone at home was well he asked that a message be passed that he was back in England and would be home soon.

The next day he drew his railway warrant and nearly eight hours later stepped off the train at Darlington station. Having spent most of his days outdoors since the warmer weather came he looked tanned and fit. In reality he was down to a weight of under a hundred pounds and in indifferent shape, but he wanted to walk home from there. Shouldering his kit he went out into the afternoon sunlight and half an hour later he knocked on the front door of his home.

The long odyssey had ended. The great adventure, that became a test of endurance and then a nightmare, was over.

It would be over a year before he became a civilian again but he was alive and home, and that for the moment was enough.

~ END ~

The only surviving picture of the crew of C-Charlie.

John Baron (bomb aimer) ~ Harry Burnside (w/op) ~ Les Hough (pilot)

Allen (nav) ~ Geordie Lawson (m/u gunner) ~ Stan Lee (rear gunner)

Flying Officer Leslie Markham Hough RAAF ~ pilot and skipper of C-Charlie, who went down with his aircraft in 1944.

Stan Lee ~ rear gunner of C-Charlie.

John Baron ~ bomb aimer of C-Charlie.

Allen with fellow warriors of the LNER Home Guard.

Passing Out at Babbacombe, September 1942.

Navigators in training, RAF Mount Hope, Ontario, March 1943.

Outside the billet at 5 Air Navigation School, Mount Hope, Hamilton, Ontario after the thaw, 1943.

With other cadets at Mount Hope, March 1943.

Learning to use the sextant, Mount Hope, June 1943.

Made it! New brevet and NCO's stripes prominently on view. Margaret's garden, Hamilton, Ontario, July 1943.

Outdoor life ANZAC-style. A picnic on one of the islands. British Colombia, October 1943.

All the ANZACs, Patricia Bay, November 1943.

'B' Squadron Navigators, RAF Sidney, Patricia Bay, Sept 1943.

Christmas 1943. Margaret's family entertain Allen and Norman Birkett. Norman was killed in March 1944.

Allen, newly promoted to Flight Sergeant, April 1944.

On leave in Darlington with Rita, spring 1944.

Gaunt but free – Allen in 1945.

Back home with Rita, summer 1945.

60 years on. Allen in the navigator's compartment aboard preserved Lancaster NX611 at East Kirby, Lincolnshire Aviation Heritage Centre. Fred and Harold Panton, the founders of the centre, maintain Lancaster NX611 as a memorial to their brother Chris, who was killed on the Nuremberg raid on his 30th and final operation. Alan was particularly grateful for the opportunity they gave him to board the aircraft, his last exit having been from the front hatch 22,000 feet over Homberg.